MARRIAGE AND FAMILY RESEARCH SERIES

FAMILY RELATIONSHIPS AND THE CHURCH

A sociological, historical, and theological study
of family structures, roles, and relationships

Planned and edited by
OSCAR E. FEUCHT

Developed by the Family Life Committee
The Board of Parish Education
The Lutheran Church—Missouri Synod

CONCORDIA PUBLISHING HOUSE ● SAINT LOUIS, MISSOURI

Acknowledgements

We thank the following publishers for permitting us to quote from their materials:

America Press, New York: Joseph Gallagher, trans. and ed., *The Documents of Vatican II*.

Appleton-Century-Crofts, New York: Paul H. Landis, *Making the Most of Marriage*, 4th ed., 1970.

Association Press, New York: Ray W. Fairchild and John Charles Wynn, *Families in the Church: A Protestant Survey*.

Barnes & Noble, Inc., New York: G. G. Coulton, ed., *Social Life in Britain from the Conquest to the Reformation*.

Crowell, Thomas Y., Company, New York: Ruth Shonle Cavan, *The American Family*.

Doubleday & Company, Inc., New York: Gibson Winter, *Love and Conflict: New Patterns in Family Life*.

Dutton, E. P., & Company, Inc., New York: Henry Daniel-Rops, *Cathedral and Crusade*, Vol. 1.

Fides Publishers, Inc., Notre Dame, Ind.: John L. Thomas, S. J., *Looking Toward Marriage*.

Fortress Press, Philadelphia: Harold C. Letts, ed., *Life in Community*.

Ginn and Company, Boston: M. C. Elmore, *The Sociology of the Family*, copyright 1945, by Ginn and Company.

Harper & Row, Publishers, New York: Ruth Nanda Anshen, ed., *The Family: Its Function and Destiny*.

Herder and Herder, New York: Pierre Grelot, *Man and Wife in Scripture*.

Irwin, Richard D., Inc., Homewood, Ill.: Donald A. White, *Medieval History: A Source Book*.

Lippincott, J. B., Company, Philadelphia: J. Richard Udry, *The Social Context of Marriage*.

Luther-Verlag, Witten, Germany: Helmut Begemann, *Strukturwandel der Familie*.

Lutheran World Federation, Geneva, Switzerland: Vols. IV, V, and VI of *Lutheran World*.

Macmillan Company, New York: Talcott Parsons and Robert F. Bales, *Family, Socialization and Interaction Process*, copyright 1955.

National Council on Family Relations, Minneapolis: Vol. XVII of *Journal of Marriage and the Family*.

Paulist/Newman Press, New York: *Casti Connubii*, Pope Pius XI's encyclical letter of 1930. Copyright 1941, The Missionary Society of St. Paul the Apostle.

Random House, New York: Jay Williams, *Life in the Middle Ages*.

Ronald Press Company, New York: Clifford Kirkpatrick, *The Family: As Process and Institution*, 2nd ed., copyright © 1963.

Stanford University Press, Stanford, Calif.: William C. Bark, *Origins of the Medieval World*.

The United Presbyterian Church in the United States of America, Philadelphia: John Charles Wynn, "The American Family — Surviving Through Change," Vol. 23, No. 5, *Presbyterian Life*.

Yale University Press, New Haven, Conn.: Horace Bushnell, *Christian Nurture*.

Marriage and Family Research Series

Concordia Publishing House, St. Louis, Missouri
Concordia Publishing House Ltd., London, E. C. 1
© 1970 Concordia Publishing House
Library of Congress Catalog Card No. 72-148039
ISBN 0-570-03214-8

MANUFACTURED IN THE UNITED STATES OF AMERICA

Contents

Contributors   5

Preface   7

1. Contemporary Concerns and Key Issues   11
   David S. Schuller

2. God's Pattern for the Family in the Old Testament   25
   Walter Wegner

3. Family Relationships in the New Testament   57
   Herbert T. Mayer

4. Christianity and the Family A.D. 100-1400   76
   Carl A. Volz

5. Family Ethos in the Light of the Reformation   99
   Edward H. Schroeder

6. Family Relations in North America   119
   Herbert T. Mayer

7. The American Family in the Midst
   of Socioeconomic-Technological Change   137
   Ross P. Scherer

8. Family Relations and the Behavioral Sciences   159
   Paul G. Hansen

9. The Churches' Response to Changing Family Structures   187
   David S. Schuller

10. The Family Under God   217
    Oscar E. Feucht

Indexes   233

The Contributors

DAVID S. SCHULLER, PH. D., Professor of Practical Theology at Concordia Seminary, St. Louis, 1956–1964; now Associate Director of The American Association of Theological Schools, Dayton, Ohio.

WALTER WEGNER, PH. D., Academic Dean and Professor of Old Testament, Concordia Seminary, St. Louis, Mo.

HERBERT T. MAYER, M. A., S. T. M., Professor of New Testament and Chairman of Department of Historical Theology, Concordia Seminary, St. Louis, Mo.

CARL A. VOLZ, S. T. M., PH. D., Registrar and Professor of History, Concordia Seminary, St. Louis, Mo.

EDWARD H. SCHROEDER, TH. D., Chairman of Department of Theology of Valparaiso University, Valparaiso, Ind.

ROSS P. SCHERER, M. A., PH. D., Chairman of Department of Sociology, Loyola University, Chicago, Ill.

PAUL G. HANSEN, M. A., Pastor, St. John's Lutheran Church, Denver, Colorado; part-time Instructor in Sociology at the University of Denver.

OSCAR E. FEUCHT, D. D., St. Louis, Mo., Secretary of Adult Education, Director of Family Life Education, The Lutheran Church – Missouri Synod, 1946 to 1969; Chairman of the Editorial Committee of the Research Project.

Preface

The stability and effective function of the family is essential for society. This is clear from history, since both religion and culture are largely relayed from generation to generation by families. In the past as well as in the present the moral and spiritual images which children develop come largely from the values lived in the home. Respect for law and order in the state is closely tied to the respect of children for their elders. Emotions, attitudes, and beliefs rooted in the family give coherence to our whole way of life. They supply the social cement which holds not only families but whole communities together. If families do not function effectively in nurturing wholesome emotions, attitudes, and beliefs, it is questionable whether our civilization can survive.

Some basic concerns regarding the family need to be faced. Can the small, conjugal family in isolation from the larger extended family survive the rapid changes of our current culture? An ever larger percent of women are adding a second vocation to their vocation as wife, mother, and homemaker. Since the industrial revolution the absence of the father from the family has lessened his influence, especially in the nurture of his children. The family today is more mother-centered and the home more child-centered than in any past age. Urban living in suburbia as well as the ghetto has made more children prone to delinquency. Part of our problem may lie in the small, isolated family of today which lacks the support of the extended family. These are only a few of the concerns that are related to family structures, roles, and relationships.

Studies and analyses by the psychological and sociological sciences have emphasized that many functions formerly claimed mainly by the family have been taken over by schools, hospitals, and community agencies. Yet the family must still give the child his self-identity, his sense of security, and his value system. No outside agency can adequately provide the affection and those aspects of nurture which every child needs. Moral and spiritual values can be effectively transmitted and exemplified only as the family is vitally involved in the development of the whole person through every stage from infancy to adulthood. It is the family that must help the child get self-esteem, a sense of "belonging," a feeling of being loved and cherished. This demands the kind of personal attention which comes only in the day-to-day helpful relationships with the whole person by someone who deeply cares for that person.

The problem of good relationships is a religious, a moral, and a social one. The decline of the family is coincident with the decline of sound morality and religion in the life of man. It is exactly these that the church through the centuries has cultivated and upheld. Sometimes its emphasis on authority and responsibility outweighed its emphasis on forgiveness, love, and mutual service. With a new openness and freedom in interpersonal and male-female relationships, there has come a renewed need for moral and spiritual norms. The marriage relationship plays a crucially important role. In American society the mother role is more acutely needed than in most societies; yet it is more difficult and precarious due to her multi-role function in today's economy. Almost the same can be said of the father role.

Three interacting factors relate to the family in modern society: (1) the historical-cultural factor, (2) the sociological-psychological-technological factor, and (3) the ethical-theological factor.

The historical-cultural factor emphasizes that we are never divorced from our environment, folkways, and accepted patterns. Even when Christians are in danger of maintaining a sealed-off existence in their own house of faith, their house stands in a world to which they have a mission. It is in the world that they make a living and have their social existence. There they are influenced by the moral patterns of society. There they are to communicate the Gospel by what they are and by what they say. We are always part of our environment.

The sociological-psychological-technological factor emphasizes the new household gadgets, the new mobility, and the mass communications media. Yet these are only parts of a much larger category of factors in the social-scientific, citizen-government, employee-corporation configuration. Fortunately the behavioral sciences have made significant contributions toward healing our dissensions, giving us a better understanding of the importance of interpersonal relationships.

The ethical-theological factor emphasizes our value systems. It gives us our operational objectives, our place as persons in the universe, and the basic guidelines for the relationships of man to woman, of parent to child, of family to family. The bases for these relationships are found in the creation design of man and woman and come to their deepest expression in our religious faith. For Christians this means being subject to one another in reverence for Christ (Eph. 5:21). Religion gives us our bearings in life, a respect for God's authority, and a working philosophy of faith, love, and service. All individuals face the question: Should our norms and goals be determined by sociology or theology?

The most important of these interacting factors is the ethical-theological factor, because this identifies the "religion" the family lives by. From the Christian point of view the basic structures are derived from the creation design of man and woman (Genesis 1 and 2). Christianity supplies the precepts, examples, and motives.

To help us identify the various aspects of family relationships, six key issues are set forth in Chapter 1. The findings of this extended review are summarized in Chapter 10. A look at the table of contents will show that this survey includes all three factors: the ethical-Biblical, the sociological-psychological-technical, and the historical-cultural. The study begins with the creation narratives and continues through significant epochs of history down to the present age. This approach involves many disciplines. Above all, this study is a quest for the basic principles of family living fundamental for all societies and for all times. The aim is to supply a total perspective and supply Biblical-Christian bearings for a ministry to families in our age.

Our generation is a product of the past and present. We are heirs to many traditions. We are not only biological beings; we have a psyche, which constitutes the inner spring of action. We have a spiritual background and a religious inheritance. Christians are committed to the Holy Scriptures and find in the Gospel the integrating factor. Their working philosophy is faith in Christ—a faith that is always working in love. (Gal. 5:6; Eph. 2:10; Phil. 2:13; Heb. 13:21)

This book is the third volume in this research series. *Engagement and Marriage* (1959) examined the essence of marriage and the place and reasons for engagement, ancient and modern. *Sex and the Church* (1961) explored questions related to sexuality and the teachings of the church through the centuries. These studies developed out of a request from churches for a reexamination of marriage, divorce, and remarriage. The parent church body authorized the exploration. The Board of Parish Education accepted the assignment. The Committee on Scholarly Research provided the funds. The board's Family Life Committee planned studies that would embrace mate selection, engagement and marriage, divorce and remarriage, family authority and responsibility, sex attitudes, and birth control. In the meantime many additional areas of concern in the family field have appeared which deserve reexamination and research.

We are indebted to many persons who assisted at various stages and in various ways: to the Family Life Committee, which constructed the research design; to Paul G. Hansen for the sociological survey (see footnote 66 in Chapter 8 for a description); to those persons who made preliminary explorations in limited historical and theological areas (see pages xi and xii of *Sex and the Church* for subject areas and writers). We especially thank the review committee that gave helpful critique to an earlier draft of this volume: Dr. Richard R. Caemmerer Sr., Dr. Carl S. Meyer, Dr. Erich H. Heintzen, Dr. Fred Kramer, Rev. Victor A. Constien, Dr. Wm. H. Lazareth, and Dr. George H. Muedeking. We are grateful to Dr. David R. Mace for his encouragement to continue this kind of research; to Dr. John L. Thomas, S.J., for evaluating sections regarding Roman Catholic contributions; to Dr. Robert Bertram for insights into Martin Luther's thinking on "divine orderings"; to Dr. Carl F. Reuss for evaluating sections dealing with the behavioral sciences; and to Dr. Rudolph F. Norden of Concordia Publishing House for editorial assistance.

The purpose of this book is to help families identify, clarify, and evaluate the many contributions to family structures, roles, and relationships and use them constructively. We hope it will help marriage and family counselors, social scientists, and particularly pastors, educators, youth leaders, and social workers as they assist families, congregations, and communities.

This book is more than a symposium. It is a comprehensive survey. It sees family structures and the roles of individual members in the light of the Gospel's forgiving and freeing grace of God.

The Editor

CHAPTER 1

Contemporary Concerns and Key Issues

DAVID S. SCHULLER

"It was the best of times and the worst of times." With these words Charles Dickens opened his classic *A Tale of Two Cities*. The phrase is peculiarly appropriate for describing the condition of family life today. The general welfare of the family, the role of women, the position of children, a positive attitude toward sex, and the easing of the workload through timesaving appliances have all indicated advances, particularly for the families on the North American continent. Increased pressures upon the small nuclear family,[1] the absence of the father from the home, new tensions for mothers who attempt to embody the traditional roles of both father and mother within themselves, and the increase in the number of marriage failures are symptomatic of the "worst times" which have come upon families.

Close to the heart of many of these changes lies the question of family structures and relationships. We are dealing with change in roles. Traditional patterns which are relatively unchanging in simpler, agricultural societies have shifted with tremendous speed in the last two decades in the United States. Such shifts, however, are not uniform. The extent to which a change of roles among the members of the family takes place is largely dependent on the area in which the family lives, its socioeconomic background, its religious affiliations, and its ethnic background. Patterns of authority could be placed on a continuum from the completely patriarchal family in which the father is still the undisputed head, through the democratic type of family in which the children are encouraged to take part in family policy decisions, to the extreme of the female-dominated family of a modern matriarchy. In other cases the concept of authority is foreign to the thinking of a family. The family members are concerned with tasks to be performed and with responsibilities. Upon examination, however, we discover this is but the other side of the same coin. Authority, structure, roles, responsibility, and relationships are the major concepts in which our fundamental question usually is clothed.

Let us begin by detailing some of the major factors which have made the question of family structure and authority a significant problem today.

The Effects of Cultural Change

If an institution is to remain viable, it must continue to meet the changing needs of society. Thus over a period of several millennia and across every segment of our planet the institution of marriage and its expression in forms of family life have varied considerably. In the early days of the United States the motives which drove one to marry were virtually the same as the needs to exist.[2] The family conferred status, provided personal and social companionship, established a division of labor, and brought children and the warmth and solidarity of an extended kinship. This is to say that in a pioneer culture success in marriage was measured primarily on the level of individual and group survival. This emphasis has changed significantly. In an earlier day a girl was almost forced to marry if she was to survive. Today she has many options before her, only one of which is marriage and a family.

While a family still provides the factors noted above, it is no longer imperative that one achieve them solely through a family circle. A woman, for example, can enter the world of business and achieve status, friendship, economic independence, and a considerable degree of personal fulfillment. Marriage is no longer necessary for personal survival. This shift has arisen from an industrial economy in which many functions once performed exclusively by the family have been transferred to other agencies. In fact, it has progressed to the point that American business and industry could not operate if women were pulled out of the labor force.

Changes in Family Functions

It is relatively easy to catalog the most significant changes in family functions which have occurred in the past 50 years. In doing so we must make sure that the change is truly significant in relating to the basic meaning of a family. A compilation of statistics may describe only surface changes or causes of change. Which are truly significant? We classify these family functions in two major categories: (1) Those affecting the internal structure of the family, and (2) those affecting its social relations and marking changes in the material as well as in the nonmaterial culture. In the latter category, therefore, one would examine the new status of children and women, the rural-urban shift, the change from a producing to a consuming unit, birth control, mobility, and the decline of religious authority.[3]

Typically, sociologists have defined seven areas in which a family performs its tasks: the economic, educational, religious, recreational, protective, biological, and the affectional. In the first five areas the modern family performs fewer functions than did a family of a century ago. The major economic, educational, and protective tasks have been transferred to other agencies. Commercial concerns, public or private schools, and private and governmental agencies have begun to specialize and to perform the services once centered in the family. The last two functions, dealing with love, sex, and the procreation and rearing of children, still center in the home.

There is a complex relationship between family functions and the structure of a family. These functions cannot be thought of simply as causal—that they "caused" a shift in family authority. All the factors involved combine into a relationship of mutual influence. What initiated the change is not our major concern. We must be interested in the fact that external changes in the culture, family functions, and the pattern of authority have been interacting.

Increasing Urbanization

The relatively simple homogeneous life of rural America has been giving place to a more complex, diverse, and heterogeneous pattern of family life in densely populated, urban America. The change implies much more than a greater concentration of people in a confined area, for the increase brings with it changes in attitudes, values, and behavior. The artificial environment exerts an influence. Work is separated from the family residence. Money becomes more significant as a means of exchange. Entertainment is something offered for sale to the one who has been confined to one place in the industrial machine. People with differing sets of family and religious values both exert and are subject to a greater influence, not only because of sheer numbers and proximity but chiefly through the influence of newspaper, magazine, radio, and television. The patterns of the family are directly influenced by office and factory, by community and its organizations, by church and labor union, by theater and drive-in eating places, and by the mass media.

The Absence of the Father

Related to and arising from the more fundamental factors already noted is a more specific problem: the increased absence of the father from the home and its immediate community. A great deal has been said about the new and increasing leisure arising from the shortened work week. Much of this new "free time," however, is a fiction. Virtually all men spend a greater period of time in travel between home and place of work than in an earlier day when work centered on a farm or in a home craft. Most men spend from 10 to 20 percent of their working lives traveling back and forth to the job.[4] Further, many men who have been granted shorter hours invest some of them in holding down a second job. Those who are "moonlighting" average about 12 hours per week on the second job. When DeGrazia considers all the demands made on the modern man, he indicates that the actual difference in free time between the worker in the 1850s and the 1960s comes down to a difference of a few hours.[5] Longer free weekends for most men do modify this situation.

While men's traditional roles in marriage have changed less than women's, there has been a significant change in their function as a result of their increased absence from home. They remain the financial mainstay of the family, but they have withdrawn from much of the child-rearing processes. They can no longer train their sons naturally as they work together on the farm; they are not available for almost 10 hours a day as disciplinarians. Frequently they are so fatigued at the end of a workday that they want little to do with this task in the home. Women, then, are forced to fill this vacuum.

Working Wives

The first half of the 20th century has experienced a major change in our society's attitude toward working wives and in the number of women employed. At the beginning of the century the folkways held that a woman's place was in the home. A husband demonstrated his competence and respectability by providing economically for his wife and family. Except among the lowest-class families, as long as a man was physically able, he was considered the chief and (until his children reached maturity) the sole breadwinner. In this period wives tended to work only in emergency situations — when a husband was ill or disabled, or when he deserted. As recently as 1890, then, we discover that only 4.6 percent of all married women were employed outside the home.

By the 1960s this pattern had changed. Women now worked without adversely affecting the family's status and position in the community. Their employment no longer cast aspersions on the quality of the husband's job or his successfulness in it. Perhaps the most significant change was in the reason for their employment. Just two generations before, women had worked to meet the most primitive needs of a family. Now they work primarily to provide for the extras and to meet a higher cost of living that exceeds even an adequate single salary. The change began with the men who returned from military service and continued their education under the GI bill. While their husbands studied, wives sacrificed and went to work in order to support the family during this period of schooling. It was usually a mutual decision. The richer rewards for the entire family which increased education would bring made the temporary hardships worthwhile. But the situation in the 1960s and 1970s is much more than a wartime phenomenon.

The expanding, prosperous economy that followed the war further strengthened this pattern. Workers were needed. Women who worked for lower salaries than men provided a ready supply of help which could be utilized when needed. The result of their work was an increased supply of consumer products. Families desired all the appliances, services, and new gadgets that a resourceful, imaginative technology was supplying. In order to buy them, the families needed increased income. The part-time extra jobs of the mother seemed to provide the ideal solution.

The number of women in the working force continued to climb. In the 10-year period from 1948 to 1958, for example, the number of mothers in the labor force increased by 80 percent and the proportion by almost 50 percent. Of the total labor force approximately one-third — 32 percent — was female. By 1960 over 27 percent of all married women were in full- or part-time work outside the home, and by 1966 over half of married women of the age of 25 and older were in the U.S. labor force.[6] The most significant features from the viewpoint of our problem is the fact that the number of working married women (living with their husbands) was higher than the total number of single, widowed, and divorced women employed. An earlier pattern, in which a girl worked only from the time she completed her formal education until she married, has undergone a major revolution in a single generation.

In the early 1960s approximately half of the working wives — about 7.5 million — had children under the age of 18. For the most part these youngsters were already in school; slightly under 3 million mothers with children under the age of 6 were employed. The numbers are not large, but when spelled out in terms of individual lives, this absence of the mother from the home is exerting an influence on our society.

Adoption of Democratic Family Patterns

The ancient patriarchal pattern of family control with absolute authority vested in the father is passing away in widening sectors of our culture. Until very recently the father was the sole member of the family who could hold property, make contracts, be sued, vote, and hold office. Under common law arising in Britain, women were deprived of most legal rights when they married; by law their husbands administered in all legal and civil affairs for them. The disenfranchisement was an indication of the widely held doctrine of the basic inferiority of women.

However, a significant change has taken place in our society's evaluation of women. In the last 75 years the number of women with a college education has risen phenomenally. There are almost as many women college graduates as there are men graduates. Women have been freed increasingly from complete economic dependence on a husband. They can vote and hold office. In many cases they manage the entire household and spend the greater part of the family income. In contrast to the former pattern wherein the husband had a legal right to discipline his wife, the wife may now sue for divorce in virtually every state.[7]

A new democratic family pattern becomes apparent when we focus on the changed status of children. In simple outline the older family pattern centered on the adults; the contemporary pattern revolves about the children. Visitors from other cultures are usually dismayed by this seeming dominance of the American child. One of the axioms for child-rearing in middle- and upper-class families of today is that a child is to be treated as a person at his own age-sex level. Instead of training him to remain quiet and in the background when adults are present, the contemporary child is conditioned to consider himself an individual of worth. In extreme cases the child appears selfish and overly aggressive, dominating a group of adults. Usually he appears confident of acceptance and assured of his place in an adult society.

This new accent on equality and democracy in the modern American family is a natural outgrowth of the smaller nuclear family. The extended family which characterized a simple agricultural people has been replaced by a closely knit unit of husband, wife, and their own children. The three- and four-generation family with an assortment of unmarried aunts is now a rarity. As a result, a peculiarly intense emotional relationship develops among the members of the new small family. Deeper sentiments and affections are likely to develop as this smaller number of people interacts frequently in intimate and reciprocal services. It appears that psychologically many parents tend to identify very closely with their children. Their youngsters become almost an extension of themselves. Thus, to discipline a child or to deny him is much like disciplining or denying oneself.

The result is a family where the male is no longer the chief and sole authority. Both wife and children have an arsenal of devices by which they can manipulate him even in situations where he remains the nominal head. In many cases the family makes decisions by formal or informal majority votes. The will of the father is no longer law. Even the youngest child enjoys an elevated position in the family group today. Discipline is shared by both parents. In general, coordination and cooperation become the new watchwords.

Family Roles and the Churches

When all is said and done, many are not sure that all of these changes in the family unit spell advances. In 1929, when some of these changes were becoming recognizable, a great sociologist of the last generation, C. E. Cooley, suggested that while the traditional pattern of subordination might be distasteful to some, nevertheless it was a factor in holding families together:

> For, after all, no social organization can be expected to subsist
> without some regular system of government. We say that the mod-

ern family is a democracy; and this sounds very well; but anarchy is sometimes a more correct description. . . . So long as members are one in mind and feeling there is an unconscious harmony which has nothing to do with authority; but with even slight divergence comes the need of definite control.[8]

Conventional lines of authority in the patriarchal family have broken down. As a result each member's rights and duties can no longer be easily defined. The move toward sex equality has brought an increasing tendency to share both authority and responsibility. The division of labor varies not only from one subculture to another or from one family to another, but even within a single family. But it must also be said that disorganization sets in and conflicts arise when members of the family are not clear about their own roles and their relationship and responsibility to one another.

The major question for the Christian is whether these changes are ethically and religiously neutral — purely cultural patterns which are equally good and thus are to be evaluated in terms of their effectiveness — or whether there is a pattern of roles between husband and wife, parents and children which God has given. One of our chief goals in this volume will be to answer this question.

Some theologians give an unequivocal answer: Man is to be the head of the household, for this is the law of God. The concept that husband and wife can exercise equal authority is absurd and contrary to both reason and revelation. Christians immersed in our present secular culture are urged to "recapture the full Catholic vision of the unchangeable roles of men, women, and children in the Divine Plan for marriage." [9] The apostle Paul is cited as providing the Scriptural basis for this divine plan:

But I want you to understand that the head of every man is Christ, the head of the woman is her husband. . . . For a man ought not to cover his head, since he is the image and glory of God; but woman is the glory of man. (For man was not made from woman, but woman from man. Neither was man created for woman, but woman for man.) 1 Cor. 11:3-9

In fairness to this group it must be said that they do not advocate a return to a pattern of authority in which the father is the despotic, dictatorial head of his household and the wife an uneducated, submissive, colorless individual who serves as the husband's personal slave. They are concerned, however, lest women who fight for freedom within marriage slowly corrupt it into license, confuse identity with equality, and in the process lose the distinctiveness of the physical and spiritual qualities which man and woman possess.

Other theologians feel that this authoritarian view oversimplifies the picture. They criticize the acceptance of certain cultural assumptions as being uniquely Christian. Also beginning with Saint Paul, they remind us of the first sentence which introduces the famous passage describing the relationship of husbands and wives:

> *Be subject to one another out of reverence for Christ.* Wives, be subject to your husbands, as to the Lord. For the husband is the head of the wife as Christ is the head of the church, His body, and is Himself its Savior. As the church is subject to Christ, so let wives also be subject in everything to their husbands. (Eph. 5:21-24)

They suggest that we are dealing with a relationship that is primarily theological, and not sociological. We are concerned with an interrelationship which God wills. It is a divine arrangement. The basic command is for one to be subject to the other. While every human society, including the family, needs a pattern of order and authority, the Christian man or woman is not to ask the primary question concerning authority.

The basic structure to which these Christians point is the "headship" *(kephale)* structure — the awareness that there is a head, the one with whom the power begins. This, they assert, is built into the whole theological universe. Man is the head of the woman; Christ is the Head of the man; God is the Head of Christ (cf. 1 Cor. 11:3). This view rejects the concept that male and female roles are interchangeable. Rather, a man and a woman are placed into an order of creation where positions cannot be reversed. In a brilliant exposition of this view, Peter Brunner proposes that this relationship can be defined by the two prepositional phrases "from" and "for the sake of." He suggests in these phrases that theologically woman comes "from" man and is there "for his sake." He asserts that "each in its created existence differs from the other for all time. Their positions cannot be interchanged." This is true also of the procreative roles of man and woman. (1 Cor. 11:11) [10]

This basic *kephale* structure has been affected by the fall into sin and by mankind's redemption through Jesus Christ. Through sin the original association hardened into a subjugation which had almost oppressive power. Christ, however, redeems man and woman to reenter the relationship God had initially planned. The headship of man is not cancelled out, but is transferred into a new dimension through agape. This is apparent in Ephesians 5, where the relationship between man and woman is compared to that between Christ and His church. The relationship is absolutely not interchangeable. Head and body remain in a constant relationship. But the "Head" (Christ) is the One who gives Himself for the "body" (church). Analogically, the husband is the head who is to love his wife as Christ loves His church.

The Key Issues

In addressing ourselves to the broad field of family structures, roles, and relationships we have attempted to subsume the multitude of immediate and related questions under a number of key issues:

1. *What are the chief family structures and patterns in changing American society today, and how do they compare with those of other cultures?* We have noted that we are living in a period in which the patterns are changing because of many cultural pressures. We shall provide a perspective by sketching the chief family-relationship patterns from the earliest Old Testament period to the present. This should aid us in keeping our formulations from being unduly parochial. It is natural that most people judge the rest of society by the patterns they learned as children and which they are still using with perhaps some modifications. Our analysis will include both historical and sociological views.

In addition, we shall attempt to shape an answer which is not bound to a Western or, even more narrowly, to the American scene. Realistically, we presuppose that the majority of our readers will be Americans. But the basic question of family structures and patterns is being asked across the world in this generation. In the Far East, where Western family styles are being adopted by the younger generation, long-honored patterns of family authority are being shattered. In Africa and in sections of the Near East similar disruptions and chaos are being experienced. We shall survey the most significant readjustments.

2. *What does the Old Testament teach or imply regarding family-life patterns with particular reference to husband-wife and*

parent-child relationships? One of the most challenging tasks confronting us is that of distinguishing between Scriptural material that is descriptive of what happened under varying sociological conditions and that which is prescriptive, namely, its more precise theological teaching that has meaning for all time. Our concern is to find the plan which God set forth with regard to the man-woman relationship, particularly the husband's relation to his wife and her relation to him. We are concerned also with the broader patterns of family government, with the parents' relations and obligations to their children, with parental guidance and nurture, and also of course with the filial relation of children to their parents. Do these teachings give us basic patterns, even for families in our modern culture?

3. *What does the New Testament teach or imply regarding these family relationships, and how are we to interpret the passages dealing with the submission of the woman* (hypotassein)? Since the New Testament contributes its own Gospel-oriented "way of life," which deeply affects all relationships, what does it teach about Christian husband-wife and parent-child relationships and family patterns? Is the Old Testament family structure altered? What difference does being "in Christ" make in family living?

Particularly pertinent to our quest are the meaning, scope, and implication of those passages which speak of "headship of the husband" and the "submission of woman."

The concept of "subjection" or "submission" is at the heart of our investigation. Many would contend that Scripture presents a pattern in which every woman is subjected to man by her creaturely existence, whether or not she marries and in marriage is subject to a particular man. Is this concept related to God's fundamental plan at creation, or is this a result of the Fall? Thus, is the dominance of man perhaps a result of sin? Is the idea simply a reflection of the culture of the New Testament period and not binding today? In what way is the husband's rule not to be arbitrary? Should the word "obey" be retained in the Christian marriage ceremony? If so, how is it to be defined?

4. *Is a single, universally normative family structure and operational pattern ordained by God, or are family patterns and forms usually established by culture?* This is a basic question. From the viewpoint of the will of God, is there one ideal, normative pattern

which every family is to follow? If so, what is it? Is the role of man and woman set for every society and culture? Does the order of creation set a pattern that is basic to family patterns and relationships, Christian and non-Christian? Or must a qualified answer be given, namely, that God has provided a basic order in which a particular society will be able to work out a variety of forms of family administration?

5. *In what sense and in which spheres does the Bible teach the equal personhood of man and woman and of husband and wife?* Many churches have been slightly fearful of the term "equality" as a concept to describe the basic relationship of a man and woman. We shall ask in what sense the word "equality" can be used in a Christian context. How does it relate to the concept as used politically and socially in Western culture? In which sphere does the Bible speak of the equality of men and women? In which areas are there restrictions? Is there a priority or monopoly of the man taught in Scriptures or advocated in the later teaching of the church?

6. *To what extent is Christ's relationship to His church as Servant, Savior, and Head to be the pattern for Christian family structure and interaction?* A Biblical theology of the family must focus on the interpersonal relationships of men and women, husbands and wives, parents and children in the light of man's creation; on the distortions which came with the fall into sin; and most importantly on the effects of Christ's redemptive work and the work of the Holy Spirit in the believer's life. The Gospel is the central and life-changing power in the Christian's life. How is it to effect family structures and patterns? What difference does acceptance of Christ as Head, Savior, and Servant make in family attitudes and relationships? How does it affect various authority patterns? How does the uniquely Christian ethos modify husband-wife and parent-child relationships?

7. *How are order, responsibility, and authority related to love, nurture, and service in the Christian family?* Does the New Testament set up a new order or structure for the family? Are creation orders set aside, and is a new social structure given by Christ for family living? Or are the old orders given a new and deeper meaning? How is the Christian ethos related to responsibility, roles, and parental authority? What new elements does the New Testament contribute? How does the Gospel alter family relationships, child training, and interpersonal services?

8. *How should the Christian family of today regard the many modifications that are taking place in our changing culture?* There were changes in family patterns in past cultures. This occurred in most epochs of history within many tribes, nations, and peoples, also in the life of God's people in the Old Testament. Family roles and divisions of labor have undergone great modifications. We are experiencing more changes in family-life patterns in our age than in any comparable period of history. Many terms are employed to describe the modifications and types of family patterns in different parts of the world. What terms of today best describe the Christian family pattern and relationship? What changes in family patterns are taking place in the non-Western world? How is the Christian to evaluate them? Honest answers to such questions have been hampered frequently by an emotional appeal to a particular concept as the only one which could effectively describe what God wills for the Christian family. We shall attempt to reach beneath these various formulations objectively in order to aid the reader in taking a Christian stance.

9. *On the basis of Biblical theology, what position should the church take in regard to woman's role outside the home?* A theology of family patterns and relationships will have implications beyond the immediate realm of the family. For example, does the Biblical concept of the "subordination" of women deny them the possibility of running for public office and holding positions which would place them in positions of "ruling" over men? Obviously social structures. will demand different forms of answers in various centuries. What are the specific implications for the late 20th century and the 21st century?

Our quest is related also to woman's role in structures of the church. The family is seen as the primary and most fundamental segment of any social order. However, of necessity it relates to the other organizational structures in a society. How do these interrelate? At what point should the church speak a prophetic word of judgment on certain forms and relationships of today?

10. *What are the theological and educational implications of this study for the church today?* So often the organized church seems to be reacting to its surrounding culture. The world appears to initiate action; the church reacts. In what sense should the church take the initiative in developing a family ethos? To lead people more effectively, the church must have a clear picture of family

operational patterns today and guide its people toward Biblical thinking and a Christian family practice. Only then can the church formulate policies and programs of education which will have the ring of authenticity.

NOTES – CHAPTER 1

1. The universally human biological family consists of parents and their children. It is variously called the *nuclear,* the natural, the immediate, the primary, and the restricted family as distinguished from the extended family which includes other relatives and may include the clan or tribe. Often (but not always) *nuclear* is used by sociologists in opposition to the term *patriarchal,* which describes a family in which the father is supreme in the family or clan in both domestic and religious functions; the legal dependence of the wife (or wives) and children; and the reckoning of descent and inheritance in the male line. See *A Dictionary of the Social Sciences,* edited by Julius Gould and William L. Kolb, compiled under the auspices of the United Nations Educational, Scientific, and Cultural Organization. (New York: The Free Press [Macmillan Co.], 1964), pp. 257 – 60; 485 – 86.

2. John Sirjamaki, *American Family in the 20th Century* (Harvard, 1953), pp. 77 – 78.

3. Ray E. Baber, *Marriage and the Family* (New York: McGraw-Hill, 1939), p. 597.

4. Sebastian DeGrazia, *Of Time, Work and Leisure,* Twentieth Century Fund (Garden City, N. Y.: Doubleday, 1962), p. 73.

5. Ibid., p. 86.

6. Forest A. Bogan and Edward J. O'Boyle, "Work Experience of the Population," *Monthly Labor Review* (January 1968), p. 36.

7. See also Burgess, Locke, and Thomes, *The Family from Institution to Companionship* (New York: American Book Co., 1963), pp. 444 – 60.

8. C. E. Cooley, *Social Organization* (New York: Charles Scribner's Sons, 1929), p. 369.

9. Alphonse H. Clemens, *Marriage and the Family* (Englewood Cliffs, N. J.: Prentice-Hall, 1957), p. 75.

10. Peter Brunner, "The Ministry and the Ministry of Women," *Lutheran World,* VI (December 1959), 247 – 74.

CHAPTER 2

God's Pattern for the Family in the Old Testament

WALTER WEGNER

The authors of the Old Testament Scriptures were neither anthropologists nor sociologists. They were above all else theologians. Their concern with marriage and family forms was always subordinate to recording and interpreting the events of salvation history in such a way as to call men ever and again to worship God. Nevertheless their writings contain innumerable direct and indirect references to family structures, roles, and relationships. Like all other aspects of man's existence, family life is seen and interpreted in the light of Israel's covenant relationship with Yahweh. Our purpose is to ascertain what the Old Testament Scriptures report and to determine what these same Scriptures have to say to 20th-century man.

GOD'S PATTERN ACCORDING TO GENESIS 1 AND 2

God's pattern for marriage and the family finds expression already in the creation account of Genesis 1 and 2. Here, as nowhere else in the Old Testament, we find the basic concepts which were to be the model for every Israelite marriage. The first couple serves as "a human prototype, created in the beginning by God, which remains a perpetual model and example." [1] This pattern was to be actualized not only by the people of God, later known as Israelites, but by the human race.

Of fundamental importance is the concept that the marital union of man and woman is a creation and institution of God. Like all else that God created, marriage is a good gift of the Creator for the well-being of mankind. "Male and female He created them" (Gen. 1:27) asserts the divine origin of human sexuality. "Be fruitful and multiply" (Gen. 1:28) blesses and empowers human propagation. "Behold, it was very good" (Gen. 1:31) pronounces divine approbation on marriage.

In the account of the creation of Eve, Gen. 2:18-25, particularly the words, "It is not good that the man should be alone; I will make him a helper fit for him" (Gen. 2:18), the Creator establishes the companionship which is of the essence of marriage. Unlike any other created being, she is of his very own kind, far superior to any animal, since in the entire animal world "there was not found a helper fit for him" (Gen. 2:20). In Gen. 3:20 the first woman is named Eve and is called "the mother of all living." With Adam she is the progenitor of the whole human race.

The creation of woman from one of the man's ribs may be understood as pointing to the divinely established affinity between husband and wife. This is also Adam's perception, which prompts him to say: "This at last is bone of my bones and flesh of my flesh; she shall be called Woman, because she was taken out of Man" (Gen. 2:23). The creation of woman out of part of the structure of man is also the basis for the religious explanation of the implanted impulse which brings man and woman together in marital sexual union. In accord with the Creator's will and by His own doing, the two who *were* originally "one flesh" *become* "one flesh" again in marriage. In this relationship, created and blessed by God, there is no room for shame. The account reads: "The man and his wife were both naked, and were not ashamed." (Gen. 2:25)

The Question of Relationships

Of special interest to our study of relationships between the first husband and wife is the creation account of Genesis 1 and 2 and what it infers. The opinions of interpreters are divided on the question of whether Genesis 1 and 2 ascribe to the husband an authoritative superiority over the wife. Gerhard von Rad, for example, states that in Gen. 2:18 "the wife receives quite an unromantic valuation that the Old Testament never forsakes." By designating the woman as a "helper" *(ezer)* this text, he holds, is speaking "only of an assistant." [2] Other interpreters hold that what is called the first creation account (Gen. 1:1 – 2:4a) establishes no superiority/inferiority relationship between man and wife but presents them as "partners." Ilse Bertinetti argues that since the term *ezer* is at times used to designate even God Himself (for example, Ps. 33:20; Ps. 70:6), "a minority of woman over against man scarcely allows itself to be derived from the word *ezer*." [3] Nevertheless Bertinetti admits that what is called "the second creation account"

(Gen. 2:4b-25) takes for granted a priority, albeit a limited priority, of the man." [4]

The Roman Catholic Biblical scholar Pierre Grelot, on the other hand, regards Genesis 2 as the older and more vivid account of man's creation and as giving support not only to the partnership of man and wife in "the same nature and equal dignity," but also supporting the monogamous form of marriage. [5]

The disagreement of interpreters in this matter is not surprising. The simple fact is that Genesis 1 and 2 provide no definitive answer to the question of whether or not, by the Creator's action or intention, the man was given a position of superiority over the woman. Nor is there any express statement in these chapters to the effect that the woman was assigned a role of subjugation, servility, or inferiority to her husband by the will of the Creator. Taken in isolation, chapter 1 does indeed provide a basis for the view that the members of the married couple stand in a *partnership* relationship. Both male and female are included in the term *adam* (Gen. 1:26 ff.). In this chapter there is not even a temporal priority ascribed to man, for the creation of male and female is here portrayed as simultaneous. Both are created "in the image of God," even as both alike are given dominion over the animal world. Similarly the divine blessing is placed equally upon the woman as upon the man, even as the divine commission to "be fruitful and multiply" is addressed to both without distinction.

On the other hand chapter 2 in point of time ascribes a priority to the man's creation (Gen. 2:7 and 2:18-23), although it makes no explicit statement regarding a priority of rank or authority. It designates the woman as a "helper" who was provided for the benefit of the man, since "it is not good that the man should be alone" (v. 18). Further, the man who is commanded by the Creator to exercise authority over the animals by naming them exercises a similar authority over the woman by his act of naming her (Gen. 2:23; 3:20). Nevertheless the chapter closes with a statement of the grown son leaving his father and mother, which again may be understood as implying an equality of authority between man and woman in their roles as father and mother (2:24). The words suggest a shared authority or partnership rather than a superiority of one parent over the other.

In view, then, of the inconclusiveness of the answer which these two chapters provide to the question of the relative authority of the man and the woman in marriage, we do well to refrain from insisting that these chapters (Genesis 1 and 2) provide a definitive answer.

Divine Institution of the Family

Helmut Begemann raises the question whether the first two chapters of Genesis — or any other statements of the Old Testament — portray a divine institution of the family. He admits that Gen. 1:26 ff. and 2:18 ff. are the Biblical basis for the divine origin of *marriage*. He asks whether there is in the Old Testament a similar establishment of the *family*. He asserts that "Lev. 18 is the Old Testament's testimony to the divine establishment of the family." [6] The chapter does not expressly say that God instituted the family, only that He meant to preserve it through the regulations there set down. Begemann points out that Leviticus 18 is a basic passage because it expresses "the Lordship of Yahweh" in the family in terms of Israel's faith in and relationship to Yahweh. Begemann maintains, "The institution of the family is not a result of the creative command, 'Be fruitful and multiply' (Gen. 1:28), even though it is related to it." He sees the Old Testament statements on marriage, on honoring parents, and on the prohibition of adultery as being closely related not only to the welfare and protection of the family but also to the welfare of the tribes and the nation.[7]

Nevertheless Begemann apparently overlooks significant terminology in Gen. 2:23-24 which does appear to give expression to the Old Testament understanding of the family as a divine institution rooted in the creative activity of God. Specifically does he seem to overlook the words "bone of my bones and flesh of my flesh" and "they become one flesh."

The Hebrew words for bone *(etzem)* and flesh *(basar)* are frequently used idiomatically to express family or blood relationships, either in combination (Gen. 29:14; Judges 9:2; 2 Sam. 5:1) or as parallels (1 Chron. 11:1; 2 Sam. 19:12-13). Examples of the separate usage of flesh *(basar)* in the sense of "family" are found in Gen. 37:27; Lev. 18:6; 25:49; Neh. 5:5; and Is. 58:7.[8] When therefore Gen. 2:23-24 employs terminology taken from the milieu of Israelite family life, we are justified in understanding the terms *etzem* and *basar* (in combination) and the term *basar* (alone) as references to the family. Adam's exclamation of recognition (v. 23) suggests that the woman is of his very own *family*; and the phrase "one flesh" (v. 24) encompasses not only the marital union of the man and the woman but also the *family* which results from that union.[9] In these key terms we find the confession of faith which acknowledges the family as such to be an ordinance of God established by His creative will and act and not merely a cultural phenomenon.

The Pattern of Monogamy

There remains the further question of what Genesis 1 and 2 contribute to the question of monogamy versus polygamy. If we are correct in viewing the union of Adam and Eve of Genesis 1 and 2 as the family as God wants it to be, then there can be no doubt about the fact that the marriage held up for the emulation of ancient Israel was a *monogamous* one. Our subsequent survey of the family in Old Testament history will make abundantly clear that marriage practice in ancient Israel did not always match God's plan of one man and one woman in marriage. We will see, too, that not only Genesis 1 and 2 but also other portions of the Old Testament similarly represent the monogamous pattern of the first couple in the Garden of Eden and constitute a call away from polygamy (specifically polygyny). For the Christian the interpretation given by Jesus in Matt. 19:3-9 is definitive.

FAMILY RELATIONSHIPS AFTER THE FALL
AND UNDER THE PATRIARCHS

While the basic marriage-family pattern is established in Genesis 1 and 2, a significant new influence is introduced in Genesis 3 with the apostasy or fall of man. All history is a commentary on this act. It is not surprising that this first sin against a command of God should express itself in that closest of all ties: marriage and family relationships. The whole question of family authority has for centuries revolved around the statement in Gen. 3:16. The RSV renders the words spoken by God to the woman after the fall:

> I will greatly multiply your pain in childbearing;
> in pain you shall bring forth children,
> yet your desire shall be for your husband,
> and he shall rule over you.

In the Hebrew text the third and fourth lines of this verse (as shown above) begin with a simple copulative *waw* (meaning "and").

Hebrew grammars and lexicons point out that the copulative conjunction *waw* is widely used to express nuances of meaning which in English rendering call for other conjunctions expressing not merely connection but contrast or concession or concomitant circumstances, depending on the requirements of the context. The RSV rendering demonstrates this very point by its translation of the first *waw* with "yet." The Jerusalem Bible (1966), to cite another example, does not translate the *waw* of the third line but renders the *waw* of the fourth line as an adversative conjunction: "Your yearning shall be for your husband, *yet* he will lord it over you." The "yet" shows contrast. The woman feels closely drawn to her husband but does not thereby improve her position with him. Despite her tender feeling toward him, he will still lord it over her.

The passage under discussion may legitimately be rendered also:

> I will greatly multiply your pain in childbearing;
> in pain you shall bring forth children,
> nevertheless your desire shall be for your husband,
> even though he rules (lords it) over you.

The first two lines state the consequences of sin for the woman: the pains of childbearing and the travail of childbirth. The next two lines go on to speak of the strong desire of the woman for marriage and children *even though*[10] marriage brings with it the pains of pregnancy and childbirth and the possibility of tyrannizing treatment at the hands of a husband. Both renditions given are valid possibilities. The exegete must decide therefore between either a prescriptive or a descriptive understanding of the last two lines of this passage.[11]

A *prescriptive* interpretation understands them as a divine decree ordaining a relationship in which a husband "rules over" his wife, although the precise nature of this "ruling" is not defined. A *descriptive* interpretation understands these lines as describing what happens in marriage as a result of sin. According to the latter interpretation, there is the added implication that a tyrannical domination of woman by man is contrary to the divine will. Thus in neither interpretation does this text assert that a domineering role was *assigned* to the husband as part of the original plan of creation. Wherever such a domineering relationship exists, it is to be traced to sinful human willfulness rather than to the divine will.

Nevertheless Old Testament history consistently reflects the subservient role of the wife and the corresponding headship of the husband in the family. In the immediately following chapters (Genesis 4 to 11), which some refer to as "primeval history," women play a very inconspicuous role. It is taken for granted that the men named in these chapters were married, but their wives are in most cases not even referred to. The exceptions are Adah and Zillah, the two wives of Lamech who stands out in the Biblical record as the first man to have more than one wife (Gen. 4:19). The only woman whose words are recorded in this portion of Genesis is Eve. Her statements at the birth of her sons Cain and Seth are preserved not so much to highlight *her role* as to call attention to the *significance* of the two sons (on whose names her statements are "wordplays"; see Gen. 4:1, 25). The impression is quite clear that the events of Genesis 4 − 11 have their setting in a cultural background which is seen primarily as a "man's world." And it must be admitted that this is not too different from the recording of world affairs today!

This impression does not change when we enter the era of the patriarchs. Family authority is definitely patriarchal, as opposed to matriarchal, in the technical sense that the status of the father is decidedly one of supremacy.

The Era of Israel's Patriarchs

The authority of a husband over his wife in this era was such as to make it possible for Abraham, in the interest of self-preservation, to instruct Sarah to pose as his sister rather than his wife and to allow her to be taken on two occasions into another man's harem.[12] A similar readiness to sacrifice his wife's honor to save his own life is manifested by Isaac, who also was ready to pass off his wife Rebekah as his sister.[13] Whatever factors are taken into account in interpreting the three "wife-sister" incidents, the fact remains that the husband in the patriarchal era is portrayed as a figure who wields definite authority over his wife. Moreover, the very Hebrew word for husband (*ba'al*) used in the patriarchal narratives is also the word which means "master" or "ruler." [14]

Greater Freedom for the Man

The subordinate role of the woman in the patriarchal era may be seen also in the social and legal restrictions placed on the woman and in the corresponding greater freedom of action for the man.

Here we must acknowledge a complete absence of codified Biblical law relating to this era. We are dealing with information gleaned from narratives rather than from legislation. The narratives reveal, for example, that it was apparently acceptable for a husband to have a plurality of marriage partners[15] whereas there is no record of a similar privilege accorded a woman. Also legal concubinage was a practice which favored the male.[16] Again, the practice of levirate marriage provided a man, at least temporarily, with another marital partner in addition to his wife.[17]

The authority of the husband and father over wife and children in certain narratives is expressed in ways which appear strange and harsh to modern readers. These incidents include the dismissal of Hagar, which involved Sarah (Gen. 16:6 ff.; 21:9 ff.), and Lot's offering of his daughters to the men of Sodom for sexual gratification.[18] Normal custom seems to have granted to the father the right to give (or withhold) his consent to and to arrange for marriages for both his sons and his daughters, especially for the latter.[19]

Israel's Nomadic Era

Our knowledge of the forms of Israelite family life during the Egyptian sojourn and exodus and the nomadic era in the wilderness is relatively limited, especially for the earlier portions of this period of Israelite history. We may assume that this was the time in which Israel's tribal structure developed and, within that structure and constitutive of it, the typical forms of Israelite family life. This is very likely also the period in which to locate the gradual determining of the family-clan-tribe terminology which was eventually given fixed expression and is reflected in passages like Joshua 7:14-18. In its societal structure Israel saw each individual as a member of a family.[20] Each family was united with other families to form a clan.[21] The clans in turn were united in larger groupings, each of which was called a tribe.[22] The entire nation was in effect a large "family of families." *The individual family was thus the basic unit of society and the father was the recognized head of this fundamental social unit.* These familial heads — or at least some of them — functioned also corporately as the authoritative group within the clan, where they were known as the "elders." [23] The entire structure of society around the "father's house" gave expression to the significant role of authority played by the Israelite father.[24]

MOSES AND ISRAEL'S LAW CODES

God's man for leading His people out of their Egyptian bondage
and giving them an entity as the people of God was Moses. During
the wilderness wanderings, as the Books of Exodus and Deuteronomy illustrate, Israel's codified covenant laws were given to the
people. They gave special attention to man's relation to God (three
commandments) and to his fellowman (seven commandments).
They were also Israel's authority and norm for husband-wife and
parent-child relationships. The basic commandments given at
Mount Sinai include the child-parent norm of honoring parents,
the husband-wife norm forbidding adultery, and between them the
code for respecting human life. Positively put, the latter calls for
loving the neighbor. These basic directives were interpreted and
elaborated in the entire Pentateuch and the worship (Ps. 78:2-8),
and in didactic literature (Proverbs, for example). Not only the
children's duty to parents but parents' duty to children is stated
in many places (Ex. 20:12; 21:15, 17; Lev. 20:9). Deut. 5:16 adds
a special promise to those who honor parents. Fidelity in the marriage relationship is explicitly commanded in warnings against
adultery and fornication (Ex. 20:14; 22:16; Lev. 20:10-14; Deut.
5:18; 22:13-30). Purity of the marriage stock is safeguarded by
many passages in the Pentateuch, the Prophets, Ezra and Nehemiah,
and the like (Ex. 34:15-16; Deut. 7:1-7). This was also the motive
for the forbidden degrees of marriage (Leviticus 18; Numbers 36).
The divorce decrees of Deut. 24:1-5 we shall discuss later in the
light of the prophetical teaching. It is largely to keep family lines
pure that the Old Testament gives such scrupulous attention to
family genealogies.[25]

Parental authority over children is explicitly taught. If an earlier
age seemed to concede to a father an authority over the life of a son
or daughter, the era of the kings and the prophets of Israel witnessed
a limiting of that authority. The Biblical authors express strong
disapproval of child sacrifice (2 Kings 16:3; 21:6; 23:10; Jer. 2:23;
7:31; Ezek. 16:20-21; 20:31; etc.). That children in the family were
to respect the authority of the mother as well as of the father was
an Israelite expectation based on the commandment of Ex. 20:12;
Deut. 5:16; 27:16. There are, to be sure, examples of children,
specifically sons, who at times dishonored their parents by disobedience or even revolt (Deut. 21:18-21). The paucity of stories
which reflect filial disobedience is remarkable, although it is ex-

plained less plausibly by the assumption that sons were consistently obedient than by the recognition of the fact that the Biblical documents are not intended to be a sociology of the family.

There is danger in a study of this nature to see only the negative side of family structures, roles, and relationships. That is partly because the aberrations recorded in Scripture, as in all reporting, are often more prominent than the normal relationships. Roland de Vaux in his scholarly work keeps pointing out, for instance, that the authority of the father was limited (Deuteronomy 21). Abraham took Hagar because Sarah up to that time was barren (Genesis 16). Pagan cultural patterns invaded the ethos of Israel. Polygamy and concubinage were practiced. Yet the most common form of marriage in Israel was monogamy. The Decalog includes man's wife among his "possessions" (Ex. 20:17), but she was by no means his slave. (Deut. 21:14) [26]

The Priestly and Educational Functions of the Family

Family relationships were strengthened and given a religious cast by two factors in Hebrew life: the instruction given by father and mother in the Israelite home, and the priestly functions of the family in the home. Examples of the latter are the annual Passover celebration, with its rehearsal of God's deliverance from Egyptian bondage (Ex. 12:21-27; 13:14), and postexilic festivals like Hanukkah, the 8-day Feast of Lights.

There were no synagogs until about 500 B. C.[27] Schools in the modern sense came much later.[28] Religious instruction was chiefly the task of the family. The cairns on the west side of the Jordan River were object lessons used by fathers in teaching their children (Joshua 4:1-7; Ps. 78:1-8). This instruction was however to be more than a rehearsal of religious history. It was to embrace a whole style of life. We can say it was "functionalized," since it was related to everyday events and activities (Deut. 4:9; 6:4-7; 11:18-21; 27:46). In short, it was to be nurture of persons, so that sons and daughters by situational, relational, and formal teaching in the family might grow up spiritually, mentally, socially, and physically.

The religious teaching within the Hebrew family is forcefully reflected in the Book of Proverbs. Such teaching in the Old Testament home was a major factor in cultivating family solidarity and good family relationships. This "religion in the home" aspect was closely related to keeping the covenant God made with Israel

(Deut. 7:6-11). The nurture of children was a basic concern of the Biblical writers insofar as they have a direct relationship to the *religious* history of Israel.

Throughout the Old Testament God is pictured as Father. As a corollary, the earthly father is given his goals as well as his methods in parent-child relationships. In the intertestamental period Sirach (23:1-4) appeals to God as "Lord, Father and Ruler of my Life." Helmut Begemann carries out this comparison in detail.[29] Thus the familial responsibilities for the nurture of children given by God demanded close parent-child relationships and take for granted the family structure and unity.

THE ERA OF THE JUDGES

As we have seen, the institution of the family overlaps the social structures of clan, tribe, and nation. This is apparent also in the centuries between the conquest of Canaan and the setting up of the monarchy. It is a period when the landless, stateless groups of seminomadic tribes (family clusters) are held together, not so much by any political organization but above all by a common faith in their covenant God.

In the conquest and during the period of the judges foreign, and sometimes pagan, elements chiefly from Canaanite civilization infiltrated into the families of the conquerors (Judges 1:21, 27-35; 2:23; 3:5-6; Joshua 9:3 ff.). In this period we meet the puzzling incident of Jephthah offering his daughter in sacrifice (Judges 11:30-40).[30] The patriarch is still very much in evidence. Women are regarded as legitimate spoils of war (Judges 5:30; 21:12) and generally cast in inferior, if not degrading, positions.

The inclusion in the Book of Judges of accounts of the practice of concubinage (or bondmaids) without explicit disapproval, and the many marriage-family-related episodes of Samson (Judges 16:1, for example), can be interpreted as approbation, but just as well a subtle way of expressing critical disapproval.[31] The reference to Gideon's "many wives" (Judges 8:29-30) is, in fact, the first mention of a polygamous *Israelite* marriage since the patriarchal era.[32] By presenting this incident within the context of evil consequences, the Book of Judges suggests the undesirability of such multiple marriages. Helmut Thielicke sees in the portrayal of bigamous marriages "an inclination [*Gefälle*] toward monogamy."[33]

Two chapters in Judges (4 and 5) are unique in portraying women in roles of aggressive leadership. The women are Deborah, "The prophetess," and Jael, wife of Heber the Kenite. Deborah is one of five women in the Old Testament to bear the title "prophetess." She was recognized also as a judge to whom the men of Israel turned for legal decisions (Judges 4:5). Deborah predicted that the deliverance from Canaanite oppression would be accomplished by the Lord through another woman identified as Jael, at whose hands the Canaanite general Sisera met his death. The roles played by these women are unusual, especially in matters of religious, legal, social, and military activity. We may see here "a reminder that women can exercise prophetic and creative leadership in God's plan." [34]

THE PERIOD OF THE KINGS

As Israel's governmental structure changed from rulership by judges to the leadership of kings, there is a growth of nationalism and militarism alongside the function of worship under a priestly order set up by God under Moses (Leviticus). Israel became a nation among the nations of the ancient Near East. There were advantages to closer contacts with other nations. But there were also disadvantages, as the pagan cultures of these nations influenced Israel's life, also its family life. There were many intrusions which were inconsistent with the life prescribed by God for His people. The Biblical record shows serious aberrations in the ethical and religious fields under Saul, David, and Solomon, as well as during the period of the divided kingdom. The attempt to fuse pagan practices with the traditional faith in Yahweh called forth the protests of the prophets from Elijah to Malachi.

The polygamy practiced chiefly by some of the kings is cited by Scripture as not pleasing to God. It forms a serious departure from the monogamic norm. What is not always apparent is the fact that polygamy was the practice especially of the kings of surrounding nations. The extent of this phenomenon is seen from the Biblical record, for instance, that 1,000 wives are attributed to Solomon in 1 Kings 11:3. Saul appears to have had one wife plus a concubine (1 Sam. 15:50; 2 Sam. 21:8). David had at least nine (and probably more) wives (1 Sam. 18:27; 25:42-43; 2 Sam. 2:2; 3:2-5; 5:13; 11:27; 1 Chron. 3:1-8; and 1 Chron. 14:3-7) as well as a harem of concubines numbering no less than 10 (2 Sam. 15:16; 20:3).

Rehoboam had a total of 18 wives and 60 concubines (2 Chron. 11:21), while King Abijah had a more moderately sized harem totaling 14 wives. (2 Chron. 13:21)

The multiple marriages of some of Israel's kings were very likely dictated by the contemporary standards in the royal courts of the ancient Near East. The number of a king's wives was a status symbol reflective of and made possible by the degree of his wealth. In addition, marriages of a king with daughters of foreign rulers were the means of cementing desirable political alliances between the respective countries. Such factors fostering multiple marriages would not exist for the average Israelite. For this reason Ludwig Köhler warns that the Biblical notices regarding polygamy at the royal courts must not lead to the unwarranted conclusion that "such polygamous marriages were the fashion" for the ordinary people.[35] Even kings were required by the legislation of Deut. 17:14-17 not to multiply wives for themselves,[36] and this, coupled with financial inability, would certainly also serve to discourage the average Israelite from "multiplying wives." There is reason, therefore, to agree with Fr. de Vaux's statement that "the most common form of marriage in Israel was monogamy." He adds, referring to the period here under discussion: "It is noteworthy that the Books of Samuel and Kings, which cover the entire period of the monarchy, do not record a single case of bigamy among commoners (except that of Samuel's father at the very beginning of the period)." [37]

The Role of Women

Elsie Thomas Culver has implied that the role of women in the period of Israel's monarchy is portrayed by the Biblical narrators with something less than sympathetic fairness. She asks whether in the perpetuation of "the worst rather than the best about women" the contemporary narrators were not simply making women the victims of a "bad press." She comments: "Soon it is not enough that women simply are nothing: our accounts begin to blame the wife or queen mother whenever there is a bad king." [38] This criticism overlooks the fact that in the Biblical record far more men are cast in undesirable roles than women. There is no statistical or factual basis for any allegation of antifeminism on the part of the Biblical writers. At the same time there is a realistic appraisal of the influence—for good as well as for evil—which women exert on men. If women like Jezebel in Israel (1 Kings 16:31 — 2 Kings 9:37) and Athaliah in Judah (1 Kings 11:1-20; 2 Chron. 22:2 — 23:21) are described by the Biblical authors as influences for evil, the same books portray in a most sympathetic way the activities of other women who exerted a positive influence for good on their husbands as well as on other men (1 Kings 17:8 ff.; 2 Kings 4:8 ff.; 2 Kings 5:1 ff.; 2 Kings 11:1-21; 2 Kings 22:14-20).[39]

Male Domination the Accepted Rule

Basically it is true that the Israelite world in the monarchic period was one in which male domination was the accepted rule. A woman was still regarded as being under the authority of a man: either her father (or his male heir if he himself were dead) or her husband. This is exemplified fully in the story of Saul's daughter Michal, who was *given* by her father to David (1 Sam. 18:27), later taken back and *given* by her father to Palti, or Paltiel (1 Sam. 25:44), subsequently, after Saul's death, demanded back by David, and then *taken* from Paltiel by her brother Ishbosheth and *given* again to David (2 Sam. 3:14-16). In none of these transactions did the woman herself have an opportunity to express her personal wishes in the matter of the choice of a husband. The initial transaction between Saul and David involved the Israelite practice of the bride-groom's giving of a "marriage present" (1 Sam. 18:25-27), called in Hebrew a *mohar,* to the bride's father. The term occurs in the Old Testament in Gen. 34:12 (where it apparently consists of a sum of money), also in Ex. 22:16 (where it is expressly said to consist of money and where the preceding verse contains the only undisputed occurrence of the related verb *mahar*), and in 1 Sam. 18:25, where the *mohar* takes the form of a service rendered to the father-in-law.[40] The future husband thereby acquires a right over the woman, but the woman herself is not bought and sold.[41]

THE VOICE OF THE PROPHETS

The role of the prophet in Old Testament history is always to call Israel to steadfast faith in the Lord of their salvation with ethical pronouncements and theological assertions. These included distinctive statements regarding marriage and family relationships. Their messages cover a period exceeding 500 years and overlap the monarchial and exilic periods of Israel's life. While "polygamy and concubinage were taken for granted in the narrative of the Hebrew

Bible," according to R. H. Kennett, "there is no passage in the canonical Prophets which so much as hints at the recognition of such practices, and there are several which apparently presuppose monogamy." [42]

Hosea's Witness for Monogamy. — Among the prophetic writings which "apparently presuppose monogamy" we may cite the Book of Hosea as an important illustrative example. Hosea is the first of the prophets to use the marriage relationship as a symbolic portrait of the covenant relationship between Yahweh and His bride, Israel. His prophecies must be read against the background of the syncretistic inroads which the fertility cult of Baalism had made on Israel's religious life and practice. [43] The tragic situation is vividly portrayed in Hosea 4, where the prophet says of Yahweh's unfaithful bride, the Israelites: "A spirit of harlotry has led them away, and they have left their God to play the harlot" (4:12). But the loving and faithful Husband is determined to rescue His bride from her adulterous ways. Hosea's redemption and restoration of his faithless bride becomes a prophetic "action word" through which Yahweh declares to Israel what Hosea said to Gomer: "You must dwell as mine for many days; you shall not play the harlot or belong to another man; so will I also be to you." (Hos. 3:3)

The portrait of Hosea's marriage (chapters 1 and 3) suggests that a monogamous union is under discussion and that such a marriage would be regarded as normative by the prophet's audience. [44] It is beyond doubt that the wife's single-minded devotion to her one husband is called for. And Yahweh's declaration similarly speaks in terms of enduring faithfulness on the part of Israel's "Husband":

> I will betroth you to Me forever; I will betroth you to Me in righteousness and in justice, in steadfast love, and in mercy. I will betroth you to Me in faithfulness; and you shall know the Lord. (2:19-20)

Micah and Covenant Love. — The Book of Micah contains a passage which records a breakdown of proper parent-child relationships. Micah observes: "The son treats the father with contempt, the daughter rises up against her mother, the daughter-in-law against her mother-in-law; a man's enemies are the men of his own house" (Micah 7:6). The lack of justice and love and the breakdown of loyalty and trust in the home cause the prophet to say that "the godly man has perished from the earth" (6:8; 7:2, 5-6). Micah's term for the "godly man" is *chasid,* a covenant term denoting the man of faithful, dependable, unswerving loyalty.[45] The religion of Yahweh as proclaimed by the prophets called for persons who had experienced the *chesed* (the covenant love) of Yahweh to display *chesed* both toward their God and their fellowmen. Micah makes it plain that such *chesed* on the part of children over against their parents in the family circle is required. Micah's statement agrees with the Fourth Commandment and other texts in calling on sons and daughters to show honor and respect to father and mother alike. (Ex. 20:12; Deut. 5:16; Ex. 21:15, 17; Lev. 19:3; 20:9; Deut. 21:18; 27:16)

In the harsh realities of daily life the covenant nation fell short of the requirements of faithful loyalty to its covenant God. Similarly real-life marriage, which prophets like Hosea (chapters 1 – 3) and Jeremiah (chapters 2 – 3; 31:32) used as a symbol of the covenant union with Yahweh,[46] also failed to manifest fully and consistently the requirements of *chesed.* This becomes apparent, for example, from the evidence in the prophetic writings testifying to the practice of divorce during the era of the monarchy. That the legislation of Deuteronomy establishing and regulating divorce procedures (Deut. 24:1-4; cf. also 22:19, 29 in context) was actually implemented in daily life is evident from such prophetic passages as Hosea 2:2 and Micah 2:9 (with less certainty that divorce is here under discussion) and Jer. 3:1, 8. While most of the passages deal allegorically with Israel's relation as the bride of God, they speak all the more forcefully about God's pattern for husband-wife relationships in marriage.

Isaiah's Norm: Wedded Faithfulness. — The later writings of Isaiah, which some Old Testament scholars assign to the post-exilic period, contain three significant passages which may be singled out to demonstrate how this section of the book develops the prophetic motif initiated by Hosea. The pertinent texts are: Is. 50:1-3; 54:1-10; and 62:1-5. Against the background of the legislation in Deut. 24:1-4, Yahweh asserts that no "bill of divorce" was issued (Is. 50:1). Judah is assured: "Your Maker is your Husband" (54:5). The grieving wife will experience the husband's compassion: "With everlasting love (*chesed*=covenant love) I will have compassion on you" (54:8). The renewed marriage covenant between Yahweh and His bride will endure unbroken:

"The mountains may depart and the hills be removed, but My steadfast love shall not depart from you, and My covenant of peace shall not be removed, says the Lord, who has compassion on you" (54:10). This is again the kind of prophetic treatment of marriage which assumes that "the ideal is always to be monogamy" [47] and which holds up for the emulation of husbands the practice of the kind of forgiving love that preserves the marriage covenant unbroken. The same concept of marriage as an abiding union in which forgiving and restoring love is to find full expression also underlies the prophetic portrayal of Yahweh's covenantal marriage to His people in Is. 62:1-5.

Lamentations. — The prophet Jeremiah devotes the first of his five laments to a description of the exiled nation. He pictures Judah as a faithless wife who has been deservedly put away by her husband. She now sits lonely and deserted, "like a widow" (Lam. 1:1), although her "Husband" is not dead. The "lovers" with whom she had committed her adulteries have deserted her (v. 2), and her former beauty has faded (v. 6). She now realizes that it was folly which led her to descend to her low level of immorality and disgrace (vv. 8-9). Passersby ignore her outstretched hands appealing for help, even as her "lovers" close their ears to her appeals (vv. 17-19). Acknowledging that her "Husband" has been "in the right, for I have rebelled against His Word," she has only one recourse; she appeals to Him who loves her still: "Behold, O Lord, for I am in distress, my soul is in tumult, my heart is wrung within me, because I have been very rebellious" (v. 20). The prophet's entire analogy is based on monogamy as God's pattern for marriage.

Ezekiel continues the trend favoring the monogamous design of marriage and the parallel trend supporting the elevation of womanhood in both family and society. His prophetic ministry, both before and after the destruction of Jerusalem, sketches the city's history in the form of an allegory in which Jerusalem is portrayed as Yahweh's wife. Yahweh had first found the city in "the open field" as an unwanted baby girl (Ezek. 16:1-6). Later, when the girl was fully grown, He married her and plighted His troth to her (v. 8). But Jerusalem proved to be an "adulterous wife who receives strangers instead of her husband" (v. 32). Jerusalem's judgment must follow: "I will judge you as women who break wedlock and shed blood are judged" (v. 38). But the divine Husband yearns for His bride and His faithful love will effect her restoration: "Yet I will remember My covenant with you in the days of your youth, and I will establish with you an everlasting covenant" (v. 60). The allegory makes plain that marriage is a covenant to be characterized by love, faithfulness, and indissolubility.

The Book of Malachi has its setting in the postexilic period of reconstruction. A lighthearted attitude toward the permanency of marriage had developed which apparently allowed a man to divorce "the wife of his youth" (2:14), perhaps in favor of another, more youthful wife. The scandalous situation evoked from the prophet a statement (2:13-16) which may be considered the highest expression of the prophetic, covenant concept of marriage. The prophet refers to the people's questions inquiring why Yahweh does not respond to their religious rites and expressions of penitence. The prophet replies: "Because the Lord was witness to the covenant between you and the wife of your youth, to whom you have been faithless, though she is your companion and your wife by covenant" (v. 14). The express use of the Hebrew word for covenant *(berith)* to designate the covenantal relation of the marriage bond is significant.[48]

The Malachi text continues: "So take heed to yourselves, and let none be faithless to the wife of his youth" (v. 15). The RSV footnote offers an alternate translation for the opening words of the verse: "Has He [God] not made one?" Fr. Schillebeeckx has proposed a textual reconstruction on the basis of which he has suggested the tentative translation: "Has not He made them one flesh and life?" [49] Verse 16 begins with the statement of a basic reason for avoiding faithlessness to the wife of one's youth: "For I hate divorce, says the Lord God of Israel." If this rendering of the Hebrew text is valid (and again uncertainty exists), the prophet is here going beyond the permissiveness of the Torah in the matter of divorce (Deuteronomy 24) with this statement, which rules out divorce as categorically contrary to the divine will.[50] For Malachi divorce is a covenant violation. Marriage stands under Yahweh's special protection and is the object of His vigilant concern.[51]

THE FAMILY IN SALVATION HISTORY

Theoretically, it may have been possible for an ancient Israelite to think of marriage as a purely secular institution, but the likelihood of this is small. The simple fact is that all statements regarding marriage and the family which have come down to us in the Hebrew Scriptures at once put marriage and family relationships into a religious context in which they play their role in the Old Testament proclamation of salvation history. We now focus on two major theological concepts of the Old Testament: Creation and Covenant as related to the family.

Marriage and Ongoing Creation

"So God created man in His own image, in the image of God He created Him; male and female He created them. And God blessed them, and God said to them, 'Be fruitful and multiply'" (Gen. 1:27-28a). This basic statement makes the marriage and family structure the context wherein the God of creation carries on His work in human history. It is God who not only guarantees seedtime and harvest (Gen. 8:22), gives food to all living beings (Ps. 104:27; 136:25; 145:15-16; 147:8-9), and governs the heavenly bodies (Is. 40:26), but also creates and forms each new child that is conceived (Job 31:15; Ps. 139:13; Is. 43:7; 44:2; Jer. 1:5) and brings new life to birth (Gen. 29:31; 30:22). It is in the circle of the family that God nourishes and protects the new lives which He creates (Ps. 22:9-11). Genesis 1 and 2 establish the concept of the marriage and family structure as an ordinance of God to carry on through all time His continuing creation of the human family.

Marriage Links Creation and Covenant

God's creation was not an end in itself. It also set the scene for God's dealings with mankind in human history. More specifically, it is linked with the divine covenant God would make with Israel for the benefit of all mankind. "In the deepest sense, God's creation was for the covenant—i. e., it provided both the setting and the foundation for the relationship between God and man which alone gives meaning to man's life." [52] The giving, restating, and eventual fulfilling of the Old Testament covenant promises are all related to the family!

Human life, human sinfulness, and human redemption are bound up in the family. When the first man and woman fell into sin, they were alienated not only from their Maker but also from one another. The result was an altered husband-wife relationship. The wife now stood over against her husband in a position of submission. It was however also in the family that the hope for redemption was centered. In the context of the family the first divine promise of a Redeemer from sin was given (Gen. 3:15). Fulfillment would be through the woman's Offspring: her "posterity" or "seed." [53] The Hebrew term here employed is *zera* (Greek: *sperma*), a singular noun used in a collective sense. This very term links the divine promise of Gen. 3:15 to marriage and the family, since it is through these that human *zera* is assured and perpetuated. The frequency of the term *"toledoth"* (generations, family history) in Genesis further substantiates this.[54]

Chapters 3 — 11 of Genesis delineate the deterioration of the human race, described largely in terms of the inroads of sin on family relationships (between the man and his wife, Genesis 3; between brother and brother, Gen. 4:1 ff.). Sin prompts Lamech to take more than one wife and to boast that he will kill 77 people if anyone so much as strikes him (Gen. 4:19-24). So great was the wickedness of man that God decreed destruction for mankind in the Flood. (Gen. 6:1-8)

On the other hand, it is by means of one family — the family of Noah — that God preserves human life during the Flood and continues the race (Gen. 6:9 — 8:22). The continuation of human *zera* is once more assured as God restates His blessing of "Be fruitful and multiply" on Noah and his family (Gen. 9:1). But even this family is not wholly in unity with God, for shortly after the Flood it too is afflicted with domestic difficulties (Gen. 9:20-28) and rebels against God Himself. As a result people are scattered abroad and their language is confused (Gen. 10:32; 11:1, 7-9). The deterioration which sin had introduced into the first family has now spread to all the families of the earth.

The Role of the Family in Abraham's Blessing

At this point a new section of the Book of Genesis begins. It is introduced by the promise that God will bless "all the families of the earth." The focus narrows to one man, Abraham, and to his descendants. But this does not mean that other men and other nations are forgotten. On the contrary, it is precisely through this one man and his *zera* that God will bring His divine blessings to all mankind. The full text of the divine promise reads:

> Now the Lord said to Abram, "Go from your country and your kindred and your father's house to the land that I will show you.

And I will make of you a great nation, and I will bless you, and make your name great, so that you will be a blessing. I will bless those who bless you, and him who curses you I will curse; and by you all families of the earth will bless themselves" (or: "in you all families of the earth will be blessed" — RSV footnote). **(Gen. 12:1-3)**

Subsequent restatements of this promise assure Abraham that his *zera* will become as innumerable as heaven's stars and that Yahweh's "everlasting covenant" will guarantee "all the land of Canaan for an everlasting possession" (Gen. 15:5; 17:7 ff.). For the Israelite, therefore, marriage and family take on theological significance and are intimately bound up with Israel's faith in Yahweh, its covenant God, and with the fulfillment of His covenant promise.

The Covenant Promise Shapes Old Testament History

In God's promise to Abraham "is to be found the master clue to the understanding of the whole Old Testament history." [55] How true this is may be determined, for example, by studying Psalm 105, in which the worshiping Israelites, in historical retrospect, reviewed and interpreted their entire history in terms of Yahweh's fulfillment of the covenant He made with Abraham (v. 9) and reassured to Isaac and to Jacob (vv. 9-11). It recalls how God sent Joseph to Egypt (vv. 16-24), and later Moses and Aaron, as deliverers (vv. 26-41), because "He remembered His holy promise, and Abraham, His servant" (v. 42). He also gave them the Promised Land (vv. 43-44) and called on His covenant people to "keep His statutes and observe His laws" (v. 45). Thus the psalmist links the covenant made with Abraham to the covenant made with Israel at Sinai, the latter being a development and fulfillment of the former.[56] It was this covenant at Sinai that Hosea and later prophets interpreted figuratively as the marriage covenant between Yahweh and Israel "in the days of her youth . . . at the time when she came out of the land of Egypt" (Hosea 2:15). "The religious use of this figure rebounded upon the idea of marriage." [57]

The Ultimate Fulfillment in Jesus Christ

On the basis of the New Testament, Christian interpretation finds the ultimate fulfillment of God's Old Testament covenant promises in the person and work of Jesus Christ. Old Testament salvation history comes to its culminating conclusions in "Jesus

Christ . . . the son of Abraham." (Matt. 1:1; Matt. 1:2-17; Luke 3:23 ff.; Luke 1:54-55; 1:67 ff.; John 8:56; Acts 3:25-26; Rom. 4:13-25; and Gal. 3:6-29)

These New Testament texts continue the approach of the Old Testament, setting the giving, the renewal, and the eventual fulfillment of the divine promises to Abraham into the context of marriage and the family. In both Old and New Testament declarations marriage and the family are not merely linked theologically to the covenant but are also incorporated into the Scriptures' total testimony that bears witness to Jesus Christ. (John 5:39)

LOVE IN THE OLD TESTAMENT MARRIAGE CONCEPT

The Book of Proverbs bears eloquent testimony to the elevation of the status of woman, specifically the wife and mother. It gives sharp warnings against the harlot and loose woman and calls upon the married man to practice marital fidelity. In passages like Prov. 5:15-23 we see a frank acceptance of sexual morality and the psychology of love. The book closes with a Hebrew acrostic poem praising the virtuous wife, who is "far more precious than jewels" (31:10). "The heart of her husband trusts her" (31:11). In the eyes of her children she takes her place beside her husband as one who deserves their honor, respect, and obedience (31:18; cf. 1:8-9; 6:20; 10:1; 15:20; 30:11, 17). It is remarkable how many of the varied functions of "the virtuous woman" of Proverbs 31 are still roles of the modern woman!

The Song of Solomon is now generally understood as a reflection on the love of a husband reserved exclusively for one wife and vice versa. An examination of this song will reveal that procreation is hardly mentioned and that love is exalted in lyrical effusion. Joyous love is blended frankly and freely with sexual pleasure and heartfelt affection. (1:1-3, 16; 2:6; 4:16—5:1; 7:8-9; 13:14)

> Without the name of God once being mentioned, everything in human love appertaining to the order of creation is hallowed by implicit reference to a divine norm, part of the Israelitic tradition: The monogamous love of two human beings called to become *one flesh* as were the prototype couple.

This is the way Pierre Grelot summarizes the message of the book.[58] The Song has been variously interpreted. It underscores the prophetic understanding of the marriage covenant and calls for a love-filled, joyful fidelity of husband and wife.[59]

This note of joy in love is found in many Old Testament narrations and passages such as Jeremiah 31 and Ezek. 16:8. It goes back to Gen. 2:23, which conveys Adam's enthusiastic and loving response to the joyful discovery of a soul-mate. The joy of the bride and the bridegroom are set forth clearly in the Book of Tobias.[60]

Grelot sees in the Old Testament a progressive, deepening development of the love concept in marriage and family relationships. The emphasis moves from marriage as an institutional concept to a symbol of God's relation to His people, as expressed increasingly by the prophets. It points to the New Testament relationship between Christ and His church in Ephesians 5.[61]

Earlier the Old Testament moral code as civil law allows man a sexual liberty which it refuses to the married or betrothed woman (Gen. 38:15-19, 24). Human affection between marriage partners takes a very subordinate position. The emphasis is on progeny, and love plays a secondary role. Yet love was not absent. It was expressed, for instance, in Jacob's longing for Rachel. (Gen. 29: 17-20, 29-32)

As a consequence of sin, conflict brought new "tragedies" to the family which were dealt with through legislation (divorce code of Deuteronomy 24). But this was a departure from God's original design. Alongside bigamy, polygamy, and the harsh treatment of the woman and the child, there are fine examples of chastity, of a sense of duty, of the expression of love and kindness.

Psalm 45 and the Song of Solomon richly express the love and affection that flourish where *chesed* exists. As God's covenant love for His people became the keynote of prophetic teaching, family goals were raised through the higher ranking of wife and mother and through greater expressions of love, faithfulness, and forgiving grace *(chesed)*.[62] This covenant concept also focused new attention on personal relations between spouses. They represented God's absolute and unalterable values. They gave Israel a new model. As God does not allow even gross sins to annul His covenantal promises, so man and wife were to keep their promises through forgiving love. The love drama enacted by God toward Israel was to be the marriage-family pattern. Unity in love, fruitfulness, and permanence were to be the marks of marriage faithfulness.

These expressions of love cannot be divorced from the creation order of marriage and from the covenant relationship with God, for both are closely linked to salvation history. Israel and God are to be bound not only by the rules of the law but by the ties of the heart.[63]

Speaking of late Judaism and the Book of Tobias, Grelot writes:

Not only does the institution of marriage sanctify love and cover what may be its vulgar features, but the explicit intention of the partners puts it into a religious perspective and integrates it into spiritual life. The basis of the couple's unity is no longer simply the sharing of the marriage-bed, nor even the profound community of their emotional life, but the common sharing of the best that Tobias and Sara possess: their life with God, manifested in prayer.[64]

THE FAMILY IN GOD'S PLAN

Fatherhood and headship in the family are closely related to the fatherhood and headship of God in the Old Testament. Helmut Begemann sees connections at a number of points. The Fourth and Sixth Commandments belong together. "The two together *create* and *protect* the family. . . . By prohibiting incest, Jahwe *institutes* the family and lays the foundation of historical community existence" (italics ours).[65] The social structure of the Old Testament is patrilineal. Children are assigned unilaterally and continuously to the father-son line. The Old Testament speaks of the "God of the fathers" (Gen. 26:24; 28:13; 32:10; 31:53; etc.), perhaps chiefly because God made the covenant with father Abraham. In Biblical language the extended family is related not only to God's Fatherhood but to the Abramitic covenant family in such terms as the "house of Jacob," the "house of Judah," and the "house of David." [66] Yahweh also regulates family affairs (Ex. 20; Lev. 18; Deut. 27). Begemann calls this "God's pedagogy" for His people.[67] Here we have not only the beginning of human history but of salvation history, a line which extends far beyond, even to the New Testament and the present time.[68] Here "the sociological and theological dimensions overlap, appear interchangeable, and set each other in motion." [69] Begemann sees two possibilities: that the social structure was graced with sacred dignity and taken into service by revelation, or that the legal and social preeminence of the male family head was established by divine revelation.[70]

CONCLUSIONS

1. The Old Testament marriage and family structure may be seen embodied in Genesis 1 and 2, where marriage and family are presented not merely as a cultural phenomenon but as divine institutions established by the Creator for man's welfare. Husband and wife are to live together in a monogamous relationship, sharing each other's companionship and sexuality and continuing the Creator's work as they "become fruitful and multiply" under His empowering blessing. The Old Testament recognizes the family as the basic unit of society and the father as its head.

2. The brief accounts in Genesis 1 and 2 do not however allow the drawing of definitive conclusions regarding the relationship of one spouse toward the other. The nature of the relationship is variously interpreted, ranging from male dominance-female submission (superiority-inferiority) to an equality of relationship between husband and wife (partnership). Apart from these views, Genesis 1 and 2 permit a third alternative, namely, superordination-subordination. The superordination-subordination distinction bespeaks a relationship in which the sense of rank does not exist for its own sake but becomes an order in which mutual love and service find fulfillment as the principal consideration.

3. In the state of sin in which mankind lives following the Fall, the relationship between husband and wife is described as one in which the husband "rules over" the woman (Gen. 3:16). Some interpreters regard this as a *prescriptive* divine ordinance, others hold this to be a *descriptive* statement of conditions within marriage as a result of human sinfulness and not a deliberate decree of the Creator. Looking beyond Genesis 3, the overall Old Testament picture shows sin and its effects to be present not only in husbands but also in wives. It is for this reason that other texts, particularly New Testament passages, support the superordination-subordination relationship as one that meets the human situation after the Fall.

4. The writings of the Old Testament demonstrate that in day-to-day living God's plan for marriage and family relationships was not always actualized in the history of ancient Israel. In addition to monogamous marriages among the Israelites and their ancestors, the Biblical records show that their mores included, in varying degrees, such practices as bigamy, polygamy, various forms of

concubinage, divorce, and harlotry. These deviations were explicitly or implicitly condemned. However, the practice of divorce
was, from the viewpoint of life in the community and because of the
"hardness of heart" (Matt. 19:8), tolerated and even regularized by
Biblical law (Deut. 24:1 ff.). Levirate marriages, as stipulated in
Deut. 25:5-10, were meant to preserve the family name and estate
and to provide for the welfare of the widow.

5. The forms of marriage and the patterns of family structure
and authority in various Old Testament eras varied with changing
times and circumstances, revealing not only the cultural influences
of other ancient Near Eastern nations with whom Israel came into
contact but also the impact of social and economic factors in Israel's
own internal development. The fact that a certain marriage or family
pattern appears at a given point in Israel's history (even when not
overtly rejected or criticized by Biblical narrators) does not elevate
that pattern to the status of a divine ordinance expressive of God's
will for all humanity in all times and places.

6. The Old Testament family was patriarchal and patrilineal in
character, with basic authority over family members residing in the
father, as demonstrated, for example, in the father's right to arrange
marriages for the members of his family or his right to dismiss his
wife. The father's authority over the children was, however, shared
with the mother, as seen from the Fourth Commandment and other
legislation which consistently obligated children to honor both
parents. The Old Testament law codes, the historical books, and the
Wisdom literature show that Israelite parents were expected to
manifest love and affection. They were to provide their children
with a general education, religious instruction, guidance and discipline, protection, and the necessities of life.

7. Prophetic covenant theology not only proclaimed Yahweh's
steadfast love *(chesed)* for His people but also called on the people
to practice *chesed* in all areas of life. This had a salutary influence
on the status of women, the home, and the family. While daughters
and wives in earlier periods of Old Testament history were treated
with arbitrary male authoritarianism, the status of women as persons in their own right was elevated under the growing impact of
covenant theology on Israelite life, particularly in response to the
prophetic appeals to reflect God's love in all human relationships.
Prophetic proclamation also strongly influenced marriage in the
direction of the monogamous pattern as originally instituted by

God. The prophets proclaimed, dramatized, and symbolized the personal relationship between Yahweh and His chosen people in terms of the interpersonal relationship of husband and wife in an indissoluble covenant of fidelity and love.

8. Similarly, the attitude toward divorce changed, also apparently under the influence of prophetic preaching. It shifted away from the attitude of permissiveness expressed in the legislation which allowed husbands to dismiss their marriage partners (because of finding "some indecency" or because of "disliking" the spouse, cf. Deut. 24:1, 3) and moved to the attitude of opposition to divorce expressed at the end of the prophetic era. (Mal. 2:16)

9. Marriage and the resulting family relationships are presented as part of God's continuing creation, not only for the protection and development of the human race but also as a part of God's plan for the redemption of mankind through the promised Messiah. Thus the family is clearly related to what theologians call "salvation history."

10. Love and joy in marriage and family relationships are emphasized in such Biblical literature as Psalm 45 and the Song of Solomon. There is a progressive, deepening development as the emphasis moves from a strong desire for progeny to a greater stress (in later Judaism) on love, fruitfulness, fidelity, and permanence of the marriage. This makes marriage comparable to the covenant between God and Israel.

11. We may summarize by stating that prophetic teaching called the Old Testament covenant community back to the pattern set forth in Genesis 1 and 2. In the teaching of the prophets the normative guide for marriage and family structures is Yahweh's covenant with His people. Members of the family, each in his or her own position, are to practice *chesed* toward one another, respect one another as persons, and live for one another in response to the obligations of a mutual love patterned after the divine *chesed* of Yahweh.

NOTES—CHAPTER 2

1. Pierre Grelot, *Man and Wife in Scripture* (New York: Herder and Herder, 1964), p. 37; compare Grelot's article "The Human Couple in Scripture" in *Theology Digest,* XIV, 2 (Summer 1966), 138. See also Edward Schillebeeckx, *Marriage: Human Reality and Saving Mystery* (New York: Sheed & Ward, 1965), pp. 15–16.

2. Gerhard von Rad, *Genesis* (Philadelphia: The Westminster Press, 1961), p. 80.

3. Ilse Bertinetti, *Frauen im geistlichen Amt* (Berlin: Evangelische Verlagsanstalt, 1965), p. 90, n. 53.

4. Ibid., p. 88. Miss Bertinetti, however, argues that the second creation account is of a "legendary character," as opposed to the first account, which is emphatically doctrinal, systematic, and normative. In her view, accordingly, the co-ordination of man and woman reflected in Gen. 1 takes normative precedence over the superordination of the man reflected in Gen. 2. The male superordination of chapter 2, she holds, reflects the conditions of the writer's own social milieu, even as the entire chapter "contains much which derives its origin from the experiences and observations of contemporary man."

5. Grelot, pp. 34–36.

6. Helmut Begemann, *Strukturwandel der Familie* (Hamburg: Furche-Verlag, 1960), pp. 102–103.

7. Ibid., pp. 102–104.

8. On the Hebrew terms see the Hebrew lexicons, especially Francis Brown, S. R. Driver, and Charles Briggs, *A Hebrew and English Lexicon of the Old Testament* (Oxford: Clarendon Press, 1962), under *basar* and *etzem;* also Ludwig Koehler and Walter Baumgartner, *Lexicon in Veteris Testamenti Libros* (Leiden: E. J. Brill, 1958), under *basar.*

9. Compare in this connection the discussion of "one flesh" by Schillebeeckx, who finds in this term not only the idea of woman's being complementary to man and the concept of their physical-marital union but above all the idea of blood relationship within the circle of the family (op. cit., p. 18). See also the discussion of Gen. 2:23 ff. in Umberto Cassuto, *From Adam to Noah* (Jerusalem: The Magnes Press, 1961), pp. 135 ff.; also in Henricus Renckens, *Israel's Concept of the Beginning* (New York: Herder and Herder, 1964), pp. 228 ff.

10. The adversative use of *waw* is common enough to require no documentation. On the use of the *waw copulative* to introduce a concessive circumstantial clause see the Gesenius-Kautzsch *Hebrew Grammar,* 160, a and 141, e; also the Brown-Driver-Briggs Lexicon (under *waw*), p. 253, l, k.

11. See Ch. 1 for comments on the prescriptive-descriptive issue. The Christian places himself under the total Word of God, both Law and Gospel, mindful that "whatever was written in former days was written for our instruction" (Rom. 15:4) and that the accounts of human sinfulness are not to be lightly dismissed, for they are "warnings for us" (1 Cor. 10:6). Helpful is the point stated by Richard R. Caemmerer: "Throughout the Scriptures we read not simply accounts of family life but also a diagnosis of that life as lived with or without God." *Helping Families Through the Church,* ed. Oscar E. Feucht (St. Louis: Concordia Publishing House, 1957), p. 6.

12. This occurred once in Egypt, where Pharaoh took Sarah from Abraham, and again at Gerar, where King Abimelech took Sarah under similar circumstances. See Gen. 12:10-20; 20:1-18.

13. The account is given in Gen. 26:6-11 in a text which offers both textual and historical problems. It is also possible to understand the actions of Abraham and Isaac against the background of marriage customs now known to have existed among the ancient Hurrians, with whom Semites of the patriarchal era undoubtedly had cultural contacts.

14. See, for example, Gen. 20:3, where *ba'al* is used to refer to Abraham and a related feminine form *be'ulath* is applied to Sarah, designating her as a wife (literally, one who is "ruled over" by a ruler).

15. See Gen. 25 for examples.

16. See Gen. 16:1 ff.; 30:3, 9. These three incidents involve a wife's giving a slave girl to her husband as a concubine in the case of the wife's inability to bear children. A very exceptional situation under the ravages of war in a different era is predicted in Is. 4:1, namely, many women taking one husband.

17. See Gen. 38:7-10, for example.

18. Though the men of Sodom refused Lot's suggestion, the narrative nevertheless reflects the kind of authority wielded by a father over children in patriarchal times; see Gen. 19:8.

19. See, for example, Gen. 24:1 ff.; 48:1 ff.; 29:1-28, especially vv. 19, 21, 28; 34:4, 8, 12, 16; 38:6, 11. For further documentation consult Oscar E. Feucht et al., *Engagement and Marriage* (St. Louis: Concordia Publishing House, 1959), pp. 23 — 26. This reference also includes an observation on the relation of Israelite practice to contemporary cultural patterns in the ancient Near East, which were not normative for Israel.

20. Hebrew: *bayith* (house), or *beth 'ab* (a father's house). In sociological terminology this would be designated an "extended family," since it included not merely a single, "nuclear family" consisting of a man and his wife or wives and their unmarried children but also the added "nuclear families" of any of their married children who, as was customary, continued to dwell with or in the neighborhood of the parental home.

21. Hebrew: *mishpachah*.

22. Hebrew: *shēbet* or *matteh*.

23. Hebrew: *zeqenim*.

24. For a discussion of the tribal organization of ancient Israel (especially in comparison with tribal organization among modern nomadic Arabs) see Roland de Vaux, *Ancient Israel: Its Life and Institutions* (New York: McGraw-Hill, 1961), pp. 7 — 8; also the article under *patēr* in G. Kittel, *Theological Dictionary of the New Testament*, V, 959 ff.; also F. Horst's article under *Familie* in *Die Religion in Geschichte und Gegenwart*, 3d ed., 2, 865 ff.)

25. Richard R. Caemmerer, "The Human Family in God's Design," Ch. 1 in *Helping Families Through the Church* (St. Louis: Concordia Publishing House, 1957), pp. 1 — 9.

26. De Vaux, pp. 19 — 61.

27. Synagogs originated during or in consequence of the Babylonian exile. See Edersheim, *The Life and Times of Jesus*, I (Grand Rapids: Eerdmans, 1936), 431. They are usually attributed to the time of Ezra and were well established by the time of the fall of the postexilic temple. See *Encyclopaedia Britannica*, 1960 Edition, 21, 704.

28. The formation of schools for Jewish boys came about 66 B. C. See *Encyclopedia Americana*, 1960, 26, 125. On the education of children see Roland de Vaux, pp. 48 — 50. He indicates there was no Jewish school *system* until about A. D. 63 (p. 50). The "school" was often an annex to the synagog. Isaac Levy, *Synagogue History* (London: Valentine, Mitchell and Company, Ltd., 1963), pp. 19, 23, 44; see also Paul E. Kretzmann, *Education Among the Jews* (Boston: The Talmud Society, 1922).

29. Begemann, *Strukturwandel*, p. 115

30. On the question of child sacrifice in ancient Israel see C. F. Burney, *The Book of Judges* (London: Rivingtons, 1930), pp. 329 — 31.

31. John L. McKenzie in his *The World of the Judges* (Englewood Cliffs, N. J.: Prentice-Hall, 1966) comments on page 158: "The stories present their hero as an amoral giant with uninhibited passions, particularly the passion of anger

and of lust." But he adds: "One should not think that the attitude of Israelite storytellers toward Samson is entirely neutral. . . . Samson is a tragic figure; and possibly the stories are less neutral than they appear."

32. See Gen. 29:15-30; also 26:34-35 and 36:1-14. 1 Chron. 7:4 refers to polygamous marriages in the tribe of Issachar, but the lack of chronological references makes it impossible to state whether the marriages mentioned in that passage precede or postdate the time of Gideon.

33. *Theologische Ethik,* III, No. 2059 ff. (Tübingen: J. C. B. Mohr, 1951). See also Herman Ringling's article "Die biblische Begründung der Monogamie" in *Zeitschrift für Evangelische Ethik,* X, 2 (1966), 81 – 102.

34. Eric C. Rust, *The Book of Judges* in *Layman's Bible Commentary,* VI (Richmond: John Knox Press, 1961), 24.

35. L. Köhler, *Hebrew Man* (New York: Abingdon, 1956), p. 78.

36. Louis Epstein has suggested, on the basis of the incident in 2 Chron. 24:3, that such "moderation" for the king probably "meant two wives and no more, the standard for the common people." *Marriage Laws in the Bible and the Talmud* (Cambridge: Harvard University Press, 1942), p. 12.

37. De Vaux, *Ancient Israel,* p. 25. The assertion that the practice of concubinage largely disappeared during the monarchic period may seem to be challenged by the reference in Jer. 34:8-22 to the release of Hebrew slaves during the early stage of the Babylonian siege in Jerusalem. We cannot positively identify these slaves as concubines.

38. Elsie Thomas Culver, *Women in the World of Religion* (Garden City, N. Y.: Doubleday & Co., 1967), pp. 30 – 34.

39. See de Vaux, Ch. 3 "The Position of Women: Widows," pp. 39 – 40.

40. For a more complete treatment of *mohar* see Oscar E. Feucht et al., *Engagement and Marriage* (St. Louis: Concordia Publishing House, 1959), pp. 19 – 20, 31 – 34, 37, 153.

41. De Vaux, p. 27.

42. R. H. Kennett, *Ancient Hebrew Social Life and Custom* (London: Oxford University Press, 1933 [The 1931 Schweich Lectures]), p. 18.

43. The same background, of course, exists also for such other prophetic passages as Amos 2:7-8; Micah 1:7; 5:13-14; Jer. 2:27; 3:1 ff.; etc.

44. Schillebeeckx comments: "The image of marriage was taken over by Hosea precisely in order to emphasize the exclusiveness of the religion of Yahweh." (Op. cit., p. 37)

45. For a helpful discussion of *chasid* see Norman Snaith, *The Distinctive Ideas of the Old Testament* (London: The Epworth Press, 1960), pp. 122 – 27. Bruce Vawter, *The Conscience of Israel* (New York: Sheed & Ward, 1961), p. 145, translates the *chasid* passage: "The loyal man has perished from the land."

46. For a fuller development of the symbolical use of marriage see Schillebeeckx, pp. 34 – 45; also Grelot, pp. 46 – 68.

47. David Mace, *Hebrew Marriage.* (New York: Philosophical Library, 1953), p. 137.

48. In extrabiblical Jewish usage roughly contemporaneous with Malachi a bride and groom actually executed a "marriage contract" in writing upon entering matrimony. English translations of the Aramaic text of two such contracts stemming from the Jewish colony at Elephantine in Egypt at the middle of the 5th century B. C. are given in J. B. Pritchard, *Ancient Near Eastern Texts* (Princeton, N. J.: University of Princeton), pp. 222 – 23.

49. Schillebeeckx, pp. 20, 93, 96, sees the Malachi text as looking back to the "one flesh" concept of Gen. 2:24 and looking forward to St. Paul's statement in Eph. 5:28. His reconstruction of the text is similar to the reconstruction suggested earlier by Ernst Sellin in *Das Zwölfprophetenbuch* (Leipzig: Deichertsche

Verlagsbuchhandlung, 1922), pp. 533—34. The latter also saw in the Malachi passage reflections of Gen. 2:24 (erroneously cited as 3:24 on p. 553).

50. Robert Dentan comments: "Thus Malachi seems to anticipate by nearly 500 years the position which would one day be taken by Jesus Christ (Mark 10: 2-12)." Introduction to Malachi in *The Interpreter's Bible,* 6, 1120.

51. Since we are not treating divorce in this volume, we can only allude to the "wholesale" separations from "pagan" wives referred to in Ezra 10:18-44, which in the eyes of most commentators constituted a highly exceptional ad hoc procedure to restore the Jewish community and halt a paganizing trend. See Ezra 9:1-2, 10-15.

52. B. W. Anderson in *The Interpreter's Dictionary of the Bible,* I (New York: Abingdon Press, 1962), 729, under "Creation."

53. Contemporary exegetical opinions give a divided answer to the question of whether Gen. 3:15 possesses a Messianic or promissory character. In his Genesis commentary ad hoc Gerhard von Rad states his disagreement with the exegesis of the early church which found a Messianic prophecy here. Alan Richardson on the other hand is representative of those who take issue with von Rad, suggesting that the passage may be read as an allusion to "the ultimate redemption of the human race, and Christians will rightly interpret his [i. e., the author's] unformulated hope as having found its realization in Christ's victory over sin and death." Alan Richardson, *Genesis I—XI,* in the *Torch Bible Commentaries* (London: SCM Press, 1959), p. 75; see also Grelot, p. 46.

54. On the basis of the Hebrew term *toledoth,* employed in Gen. 2:4; 5:1; 6:9; 10:1; 11:10; 11:27; 25:12; 25:19; 36:1, 9 and 37:2, the concept of "family" may be said to serve as a unifying theme not only for the primeval history of Genesis 1—11 but also for the entire Book of Genesis, in fact, also for the entire Bible. According to this term, which gives structural unity to the book, Genesis is literally a book of "family history" (as *toledoth* is actually translated in the RSV at 37:2). The LXX translated *toledoth* as *genesis* and, in apparent recognition of the significance of this term for the structure of the book, this Greek rendition of the term came to be used also as the title of the book. The LXX rendition of *toledoth* is used also in the superscription of St. Matthew's Gospel in phraseology drawn directly from the LXX version of Gen. 5:1. The gospel bears the title "The book of the genealogy [*toledoth,* family history] of Jesus Christ, the son of David, the son of Abraham" (Matt. 1:1). This superscription sees the fulfillment of the covenant promise to Abraham in Jesus Christ. In fact, all genealogical lists—all "family histories"—of Old and New Testaments have their culmination in Jesus Christ.

55. H. J. Kraus, *The People of God in the Old Testament* (New York: Association Press, 1958), p. 26.

56. See, e. g., the exegetical comment on Ps. 105:45 in H. J. Kraus, *Die Psalmen,* in *Biblischer Kommentar: Altes Testament,* II (Neukirchen: Neukirchener Verlag, 1961), 722.

57. Edmond Jacob, *Theology of the Old Testament* (New York: Harper & Brothers, 1958), p. 77.

58. Grelot, *Man and Wife in Scripture,* p. 81.

59. The allegorical approach of early Christian interpreters saw in the Song a figurative representation of the immutable love of Christ for His one bride, the church. The Song makes no reference to Yahweh or His covenant and has, in fact, no explicit religious connotations. Nevertheless, as Schillebeeckx has observed, "the Song was eventually interpreted both by Jewish and by Christian exegetes, as an image of the covenant of grace, that is, as a moving account in image form describing Yahweh's reunion with His bride Israel after the separation of the exile." Schillebeeckx, p. 54; see also Otto Eissfeldt, *The Old Testament: An Introduction* (New York: Harper & Row, 1965), p. 490; and Grelot, pp. 76—81.

60. Book of Tobias in Old Testament Apocrypha: 7:34; 16:9; 25:10. See Grelot, pp. 71 – 74.
61. Grelot, pp. 40, 83, 105.
62. Ibid., pp. 57, 80 – 84.
63. Ibid., pp. 58 – 59.
64. Ibid., p. 73.
65. Begemann, *Strukturwandel,* p. 104.
66. Ibid., pp. 104, 113.
67. Ibid., p. 108.
68. Ibid., p. 111.
69. Ibid., p. 113.
70. Ibid., p. 113.

CHAPTER 3

Family Relationships in the New Testament

HERBERT T. MAYER

The teaching of the New Testament on the family is conditioned by its basic theme that Jesus Christ has brought newness into every aspect of life. This newness affects all relationships in the Christian family. In this chapter, therefore, we shall first discuss the concept of newness as taught by Christ and the apostle Paul, limiting ourselves to the ideas of the kingdom of God, Christian love, and the effect of an eternal perspective on present relationships. Then we shall investigate the chief passages that deal specifically with patterns of family authority and responsibility.

THE TEACHING OF JESUS

The Basic Message of "Newness"

Jesus' teaching on the family must be understood in the framework of His total message, which St. Mark summarized in the words, "The time is fulfilled and the kingdom of God is at hand; repent, and believe in the Gospel" (Mark 1:15). Thus Jesus announced the fulfillment of the former time, or the age of the Old Testament, and the beginning of the new age, the age of God's gracious rule in the hearts of His children through faith. In Him God's kingly rule is present among men, showing itself especially in the free and gracious forgiveness of sins and in the active power of the Spirit, who works constantly to make all things new (Col. 1:9-14; 2:1-23; 3:1—4:1). The newness of God's reign in Christ is revolutionary. It changes every aspect of the lives of those who are in His kingdom.

Christian newness is most evident in the practice of love (agape). It flows from the Gospel, which is God's announcement that He is in the world in Jesus Christ, reconciling the world unto Himself and no longer charging trespasses to those who repent and believe (2 Cor. 5:18-21). Jesus told His followers that they were to love God with their whole being, and their neighbor as themselves. All other dimensions of Christian life are based on this new relationship of love (Matt. 22:37-39). To love God with one's entire being means to live for Him as a slave, to seek to do His will above everything else, to base one's whole life on God, to trust Him to supply every need of body and soul, and, in turn, to offer freely to one's neighbor a love and forgiveness that is patterned after God's. The practice of Christian love creates new relationships among His followers in every situation of life.[1]

The new life in Christ remains imperfectly expressed among His followers, but He has instilled a force in their hearts which drives toward its perfect expression in the future. His followers strive constantly toward this perfection, which they will possess when He comes again. The contrast between the perfect future, which Christians already appreciate because they have seen it in Christ, and their present imperfect state creates a fundamental tension in their lives. This tension is a form of energy which results in continuous change and improvement. (1 Cor. 13:8-13; Eph. 4:13-16; 1 John 3:1-14)

The Contemporary Situation

Jesus was familiar with and, in part, accepted Jewish patterns of family authority and responsibility. He was probably also familiar with the Greco-Roman (Hellenistic) patterns, which were beginning to influence Palestinian home life by His time. These two types were noticeably different. Both were in a state of change and flux brought about mostly by the changing position of the woman in society. The position of the woman in the Jewish home was generally one of marked subordination. According to one tradition, the strict Jewish man spoke a prayer each morning in which he thanked God that he had not been created a Gentile, a woman, or a slave (note the echo of this prayer in Gal. 3:28). The more vigorous antifeminists taught that one should not converse with a woman, not even with one's own wife, for women were greedy eaters, curious listeners, indolent, jealous, and frivolous. In the synagog women were required to sit behind a screen as a sign of their inferior position. The husband could divorce his wife rather easily for a variety of causes, and this usually operated to the disadvantage of the woman. However, the Talmud, or book of Jewish laws, shows that at the same time there were many families in which a relationship of love and tenderness existed between husband and wife and between parents and children.[2]

In the surrounding Hellenistic world the position of women and children was changing rapidly, and the traditional patriarchal family patterns had disintegrated almost completely.[3]

Because many of the Greco-Roman cultural practices were seeping into Palestine, Jewish family structure was also influenced. For our purposes it is significant to note that Jesus never commented directly on specific family patterns. He advocated no changes in family social structures, but accepted the patterns that existed.[4]

Jesus' Ministry to Women and Children

In His actions, as much as in His words, Jesus made plain His conviction concerning the proper regard for woman's place in society, and thus also in the home. He talked with women frequently (John 4) and ministered to their needs repeatedly. He restored several women to useful places in the social order.[5] His deep affection for children also becomes evident as one studies His actions and words.

The Place of the Household in the Kingdom

Much of Jesus' public ministry was directed toward the family, or the household (*oikos*). Helmut Begemann says that Jesus' intention was to show that in God's kingdom ties of blood had been replaced by the spiritual ties of faith, and that in the mission of God's kingdom the family (the *oikos*) is the key unit. For Jesus the Fourth Commandment (honoring parents) remained valid. But in His statements on Christian discipleship Jesus broke down the concept that Jewish biological descendance was sufficient for membership in the kingdom of God.[6]

The *oikos* was of crucial importance to Jesus, further, because it was in the household that Christian education or nurture took place. For both Jew and Hellenist the nurture of children (*paideia*) and the continuing nurture of adults was the primary purpose of life. The Greeks defined nurture as the process of educating man into his true form, the real and genuine human nature.[7]

Both Jentsch and Jaeger stress the fact that Greek and Hellenistic *paideia* was completely man-centered and had as its goal the formation of a man who would live a good and profitable life in this world. While Jesus and the apostles affirmed the central importance of *paideia* in life, they changed its definition radically with their teaching that *paideia* is carried out primarily by God's Holy Spirit and that its basic "curriculum" is the Gospel message of God's grace in Jesus Christ and the free forgiveness of all sins. Its ideal, in contrast to some Hellenistic educators, was the man who placed himself at the service of his neighbor out of his love for God.[8] This Christian education occurs most effectively and most naturally in the Christian *oikos,* the family or household under God.

Begemann devotes a whole chapter to the relationship of the household to the Christian community. The earthly *oikos* (household), he says, is both the prototype and the replica of the heavenly *oikos.* The creation order and social order interpenetrate in the New Testament and are not to be separated. Family fellowship *in Christ* has as its goal the *familia Dei.* This deemphasizes the strictly patriarchal pattern and emphasizes Christian partnership. Begemann sees in the *oikos* an aspect of *Heilsgeschichte.* The New Testament speaks from the new creation concept of a relationship "in Christ." Thus to the creation aspect is added *Gottes Kindschaft* (being a child of God), yet without dissolving the validity of the existing patriarchal pattern, so that "in Christ" there is equality of grace and equal worth *(Gleichbegnadigung und Gleichwertigkeit)* for all in the Christian household.[9] (Gal. 3:28; Eph. 5:21)

The patrocentric social structure of the household was not set aside by Christ and the disciples. Instead, the family structure was acknowledged and put into the service of building the church of the New Testament. The Book of Acts reports that whole families were baptized (Acts 10:24, 48; 11:14-15; 16:15, 31-33; 18:8). This not only testifies to the unity of the household and to the fact that whole families were won for Christ with the Gospel, but also that the housefather became the spokesman of the family before God.[10] (John 4:53; Luke 19:9)

Jesus' Teaching on Divorce

Jesus' teaching on divorce had important implications for family structures. He rejected the patterns of easy divorce; He insisted that marriage was to be a lifelong union created by God. Divorce might be considered only when one party had broken the "one flesh" relationship through fornication. This teaching played an important role in the later history of Christian marriage relations, because it enhanced the dignity and social position of the woman, particularly her position in the family. The stability of the family was, of course, also strengthened.

In His discussion of divorce (Matt. 19:3-12; Mark 10:2-12) Jesus appealed to Gen. 1:27 and 2:24 for His basic argument.[11] It is this recourse to creation in Jesus' teaching which supports the theologian in thinking of an "order of creation."

THE TEACHING OF THE APOSTLE PAUL

Basic Views

The apostle Paul stresses the newness which entered the world through the person and work of God's Son (2 Cor. 5:17). The Father has delivered us, he says, from the dominion of darkness and transferred us to the kingdom of His beloved Son, in whom we have redemption, the forgiveness of sins (Col. 1:13-14). The newness brought by Christ is so different that former distinctions between Jew and Greek, slave and free, male and female are abolished. (Gal. 3:28)

St. Paul summarizes the newness of the Kingdom in his teaching about love *(agape)*. Man's life before God depends solely on God's grace in Christ Jesus. God's love for man begets a similar love in man's heart for God and his neighbor. This new Spirit-created love is the real heart and core of the Christian's life. The Christian shows God's love by placing his life at the service of his neighbor (Gal. 5:13-14). According to Ethelbert Stauffer, brotherly love is the only relevant and forward-looking attitude in this time of anxiety and decision between the cross and the Lord's return.[12]

Paul's Teaching on Christian Families

St. Paul devotes considerable space in his letters to show how the new life in Christ affects patterns of family authority and responsibility. According to the apostle, ties of blood are no longer the primary factor for constituting a Christian family group. Christians belong to the family of God first, in which Jesus Christ is the firstborn Brother (Rom. 8:29). It is the central thesis of Begemann's book that the family or the household *(oikos)* has meaning for Paul only insofar as it serves as a congregation where people are forgiven and then nurtured for their mission work.[13]

Paul combines his teaching about the place of the woman in the church and in the home in a significant way. For example, his teaching on the respective positions of husband and wife is placed in Ephesians 5 into the immediate context of the welfare of the church. This juxtaposition of ideas suggests that Paul saw all questions about woman's position in various relationships as simply different aspects of Gospel newness, like the various facets of a diamond, saying in effect that questions about her position in the social order, or that of the man, must always be seen in relationship to Christ and His church as the family of God.

Mutuality in the Relationships Between Husband and Wife

The New Testament emphasizes a mutuality in the relationship of husband and wife as compared to secular patterns. There is a radical difference between Christian and non-Christian families because the Gospel is working in the Christian home. Paul calls for this new Christian mutuality in passages where the husband is exhorted to love the wife.

Ephesians 5:25-30

Husbands, love your wives, as Christ loved the church and gave Himself up for her, that He might sanctify her, having cleansed her by the washing of water with the Word, that He might present the church to Himself in splendor, without spot or wrinkle or any such thing, that she might be holy and without blemish. Even so husbands should love their wives as their own bodies. He who loves his wife loves himself. For no man ever hates his own flesh, but nourishes and cherishes it, as Christ does the church, because we are members of His body.

In this passage the apostle calls men to love their wives in the unique, Christian way. This love moves the husband to give to the wife that which Christ gave to the church, namely, the grace and strength that enables her to be holy and without blemish, walking before her husband and her Lord "in splendor." It is striking to note that in several passages the apostle calls upon men to love their wives, while wives are never ordered or even reminded to love their husbands.[14]

Begemann observes that "even as" in v. 25 recalls to the reader's mind the full relationship of Christ to His church, for He was both its Master and Servant. It was through His act of love and self-sacrifice that He became Lord and Master of the church. Thus the husband cannot claim to be master over his Christian wife unless he has also given himself for her, as Christ gave Himself. The husband must function as both lord and servant in the family that seeks to live under the Gospel of creative freedom.

As Christ Himself was both Lord and Servant, moving from one role to the other, so the husband exercises both headship and service in the household (Phil. 2:8-9; Matt. 20:26; 23:11; Mark 9:35; 10:43). This Begemann describes as a movement between two poles. They condition each other and operate side by side.[15]

"In Christ"

Another important aspect of the new mutuality of relationship between husband and wife is found in the phrase "in Christ." This phrase occurs some 169 times in the New Testament, the majority being found in Paul's letters. The best summary of this idea is found in Paul's statement that if any man is in Christ, he is a new creature, or better, a new creation (2 Cor. 5:17). "In Christ" is Paul's abbreviated way of saying that when a person is baptized into Christ, he dies to his former way of living; he escapes from the old creation which is perishing; he begins to return to the perfect creation which had existed in the Garden of Eden and will exist again at the end of time (Revelation 21); Christ is dwelling in him to supply him with power through the Spirit; and all who are "in Christ" are united with Him in the body of Christ, which is the church. "In Christ" husband and wife are united with each other even as they are united with Christ. This is the heart of the sacred and mutual relationship between a Christian husband and wife.

This mutuality in the Christian household under the rule of Christ is emphasized by the key verse in the table of duties regarding the family in Ephesians (5:21 — 6:4): *"Be subject to one another out of reverence for Christ"* (v. 21). This has frequently been overlooked.[16]

"One Flesh"

In Eph. 5:31-33 St. Paul speaks of the oneness of man and wife in Christ and quotes Gen. 2:24, which harks back to the oneness of Adam and Eve when God brought them together. "The man and the wife," says the apostle, "are one body." Thus in the space of a few verses in the Ephesians passage St. Paul emphasizes both the spiritual and physical unity of husband and wife, making no essential distinction between the two. This is true, of course, only of Christian marriage. But why does the apostle quote Gen. 2:24 here? In its original setting this passage speaks only of the physical unity, while in Ephesians Paul is deeply involved in the mystery of spiritual oneness and mutuality.[17]

Gal. 3:28 provides the clue for understanding Paul's argument. It reads: "There is neither Jew nor Greek, there is neither slave nor free, there is neither male nor female; for you are all one in Christ Jesus." Many writers take Gal. 3:28 as the Scriptural basis for establishing completely democratic patterns of equality in the Christian home. But this simple interpretation does not do justice to Paul's thought. As we shall see later, the apostle nowhere teaches a complete and unconditioned equality in the modern sense of a 50-50 sharing of all authority and responsibility in the family. Nor does he anywhere criticize or seek to change existing social patterns so long as they are not morally wrong. If Gal. 3:28 is to be understood as a social manifesto of St. Paul, it would be the only example in the New Testament.[18]

The force of Gal. 3:28 is theological, not sociological. It describes the situation which, while it ought to exist among Christians at all times, will exist actually and fully only at the end of time.[19] Note also that the English translation preserves an important difference between the first two clauses ("Jew nor Greek," "slave nor free"), which contain nouns, and the third clause ("male and female"), which contains adjectives. The phrase "male and female" is taken from the Greek translation of Gen. 1:27, which reads: "So God created man in His own image, in the image of God He created him; male and female He created *them.*" The verse speaks of the creation of a single human being in God's image, which act was followed in the creation by the process of "division" of male and female. In Christ Jesus the relationship of perfect unity, which existed in the Garden of Eden, is being restored among male and female Christians who are united "in Christ." They are again becoming ever more fully "one flesh."

The male-female idea appears in the New Testament in three crucial although widely separated passages: Matt. 19:3-12, Eph. 5:29-33, and Gal. 3:28. In Eph. 5:31-33, for example, St. Paul draws an instructive parallel between the church, which is being united more fully with Christ, and the wife, who is being more fully united with her husband. Both unions will be realized fully only at the consummation of the age.

Mutuality of the Sexes

The apostle describes the Christian mutuality of the sexes in still another way in 1 Cor. 11:8, 11-12:

> For man was not made from woman, but woman from man. . . . Nevertheless, in the Lord woman is not independent of man nor man of woman; for as woman was made from man, so man is now born of woman. And all things are from God.

Paul's argument is simple. Man cannot lord it over the woman, for his very existence depends on one woman, his mother. Nor can the woman lord it over the man, for the first woman was taken from the side of man. We shall return to v. 9 later.[20]

In 1 Cor. 7:3-4 husband and wife are told to exercise conjugal privileges and rights in a mutually acceptable manner. The husband cannot demand them, nor can the wife refuse them in a one-sided way.

THE SUBORDINATION OF WOMEN

Most contemporary Christian authorities on family life say that the *correct* understanding of the New Testament teaching on the *subordinate* position of women is all-important. For 1,900 years ecclesiastical writers understood subordination to mean *dominance* of the husband over wife and children in the family. Webster's *Third International Dictionary* reflects this understanding when it speaks of the wife's slavish submission to her husband as a clear example of what subjection means. We shall use the word "subordination" instead of "obedience" or "subjection" to overcome the prejudice of tradition.

The Biblical meaning of subordination cannot be fully understood apart from an understanding of the Greek word *hypotassein* and related words in profane or secular literature. It is beyond argument that the basic meaning of this word-group involves the idea of subordination, either in a sense of dependency or of being lower in a scale of order and rank. But this word-group also has the meaning of arranging things in relationship to other things, in a carefully structured way, so that everything may function well. *Hypotassein* does *not* carry the root idea of slavish and fearful submission, which has become associated with the idea of subordination through the centuries. Thus the word *hypotassein* and related words meant, for example, to be subordinate to the commanding officer, or to be subordinate to the gods (here the idea of "subjection" lurks just below the surface). They are used to describe a disciple who stands in close but subordinate relationship to his master. As a grammatical term *hypostasis* (to stand under) can mean the subjunctive mood in grammar, or it can mean that grammatical relationship in which one clause in the sentence is dependent on the main clause, although it is no less important to the meaning of the sentence.[21]

To say that *hypotassein* and related words usually mean some kind of subordinate relationship expresses only half their meaning in each passage. The subordinate relationship is always established for a specific purpose, and this purpose must be understood if the force and the nature of the subordinate relationship is to be understood. Because every Christian family relationship is established for the benefit of everyone involved, and because it is intended to provide the framework for nurture and to equip the family for its role in God's mission, it follows that subordinate relations serve high and holy purposes.

In contrast to the secular meaning, which has been summarized in the preceding paragraphs, the *hypotassein* word-group has a stronger sense of servile submission in the Greek translation of the Old Testament (Septuagint). Here this word-group is used to translate Hebrew words with such meanings as to be silent, to be dumb or still, to subdue, to bring into bondage, to beat out or to beat down, and so forth. While this force of the word cannot be ignored in the study of the New Testament, it is correct to say that, in general, the meaning of the word-group in the New Testament is closer to the concept "subordinate."

"Subordination," "be subordinate," and related words occur some 37 times in the New Testament. The words describe relationships between people or between people and social structures. The most common meaning is that of subordination of a person to another person or to a social institution such as the government. It is important to determine the reason for the subordinate relationship and its nature and goal in each usage.

In the New Testament *hypotassein* is used to describe the demons being in subjection to the disciples (Luke 10:17-20). It describes the subordination of Christians to God (James 4:7), to His Word and to His law (Rom. 8:7; 10:3; 2 Cor. 9:13; Heb. 12:9). It is used to describe creation subordinated to God (Rom. 8:20; 1 Cor. 15:27-28) or to Christ (Phil. 3:21; Heb. 2:5-8), or of the church to Christ (Eph. 1:22; 5:24). The bishop must be able to keep his children obedient and respectful at all times (1 Tim. 3:4; Heb. 12:9). Children and young persons are to obey their parents and elders (Luke 2:51; Titus 2:8; 1 Peter 2:18; 5:5). Christians are to obey the government (Rom. 13:1, 5; Titus 3:1; 1 Peter 2:13). Paul refused to submit to false teachers (Gal. 2:5). It describes the relationship of mutual subordination which ought to exist among believers (1 Cor. 16:16; 2 Cor. 9:13). In one important passage it describes the relationship of subordination which will exist between the Son and the Father when the Son has completed the work which the Father gave Him to do (1 Cor. 15:27 f.; see 1 Peter 3:22; p. 70). The rest of the New Testament occurrences of the word deal with husband-wife relations. Most of these passages receive fuller treatment later in this chapter. (1 Cor. 14:34; Eph. 5:21-22, 24; Col. 3:18; 1 Tim. 2:11; Titus 2:5; 1 Peter 3:1, 5)

It should be noted here again that *subordination* is quite distinct from *subjection* in its meaning. Subjection carries with it the note of strong domination on the part of one party and servile submission on the part of the other, while subordination merely describes a relationship between a person who is superior in some way and for some reason, and a person who is inferior in that particular relationship.

In the New Testament the relationship of subordination often is established for the benefit of the inferior, rather than the superior, person. The subordination relationship often places a special responsibility on the superior party. The relationship of subordination among Christians is described as one marked by love, hope, and joy. The nature of Christian love and the new life in Christ decidedly affect the relationship of subordination whenever it involves at least one party who is a Christian.

Use in Ephesians

The "be subordinate" concept dominates the section from 5:17 to 6:9. The passage has become one of the chief topics of present-day discussions concerning the role and status of the woman in the family. In verses 17-20 Paul describes the basic attitudes of Christians: They are to be "understanding of the Lord's will, speaking to each other in psalms and hymns . . . singing and making melody . . . giving thanks in the name of our Lord . . ." This passage is a basic and comprehensive description of the new life in Christ. In this context St. Paul introduces the discussion of one specific pattern of the new relationship that exists between the Christian husband and wife (22-24) with a connective verse (21): "Be subject to one another out of reverence for Christ." The Greek text does not have the word for "be subordinate" (be subject) in v. 22, as most English versions do. The translators have borrowed it from v. 21, which refers to preceding (vv. 17-20) and succeeding (22-24) verses and is addressed to both man and wife. This shows the close connection between the two paragraphs. Begemann translates the phrase in v. 21 as "fitting yourselves together in your proper place and order." [22] This is an excellent translation. "Proper" refers to that which is suitable for the new life in Christ.[23]

The call to subordination is clear. Heinrich Schlier speaks of it as the one indispensable factor (the *sine qua non*) in the entire family relationship of those who are in the kingdom of God.[24] Kaehler agrees with Schlier's conclusions and adds the important reminder that subordination and superordination must always be carried out in the love of Christ.[25]

Women in the Church

In 1 Cor. 14:33b-36 St. Paul calls upon women to be silent and "to be subordinate." (Compare the use of the word in vv. 32 and 33a.) This passage has been the center of the discussion in the Lutheran Church about the ordination of women. Those who favor ordination argue that this principle was limited to the social patterns in existence at Corinth. Others argue that all New Testament laws and principles need to be reinterpreted and reapplied, often in drastic fashion, to suit changing situations. Those who oppose ordination maintain that the man and the woman are created with distinct and separate functions and that therefore distinctions are to be maintained. Others argue that social structures which call for patterns of subordination in the congregation and in the Christian home do not interfere with the freedom which the Gospel brings. It seems that the teachings of the New Testament, especially St. Paul's careful treatment of the issues in 1 Corinthians 11 and Ephesians 5, make it clear that we are dealing with relationships which are to be permanent, not only in natural society but also among redeemed children of God.[26]

The Orders of Creation and Redemption

Why does the New Testament teach the subordination of women? Four answers, with many modifications, have been proposed. (1) Woman is subordinate because she was created from man (1 Tim. 2:13). (2) She is subordinate because she sinned first (1 Tim. 2:14). (3) The Christian woman is urged to be subordinate because this was the prevailing pattern among the Gentiles at that time, and the Christian woman is encouraged not to give offense by challenging an ancient tradition. (4) The Christian woman must be subordinate because this is also God's will in Christ for the new order between the crucifixion and the end of time. Our studies have led us to support the fourth reason.[27]

The question can be answered most clearly by distinguishing between Biblical teaching about the orders of creation and the orders of redemption. "Orders of creation" refers to those patterns of relationship which God established in the act of creating; "orders of redemption" is the term used to describe the new relationships established by Jesus Christ. As was pointed out previously, the subordination of the woman rests on both the orders of creation (Matt. 19:3-10; 1 Cor. 11; 1 Tim. 3) and on the orders of redemption (Eph. 5). Christ's work now consists in reestablishing, through the proclamation of the Gospel, the perfection which marked the created order before sin came into the world. On this point, Helmut Thielicke says:

> Though the New Testament recognizes no spiritual subordination
> of the wife to the husband (Gal. 3:28; Eph. 5:23; 1 Peter 3:10),
> it nevertheless upholds this subordination in the earthly affairs
> of marriage.[28]

Rudolf Bultmann affirms that there is no place for the impact of the orders of creation on husband-wife relations in the Christian family. "Since the congregation is withdrawn from the world, this world's distinctions have lost their meaning," he writes. He quotes Gal. 3:28 and 1 Cor. 7:17-24 to support his argument.[29]

Is the subordinate position of the woman the consequence of sin rather than of creation? In 1 Timothy 3 St. Paul says clearly that it is based on both factors. The relationship of subordination was established by the act of creation, and the unhappy features of this relationship, as they affect both the husband and the wife, are the consequence of sin. This double basis of subordination explains why it can be regarded by husband and wife as either a blessing or a curse. When, for example, the husband regards it as a basic order created by God, he rejoices in it and seeks to serve his wife, just because she is subordinate. When it appears as a consequence of sin, one or both parties will be galled by it and seek to overthrow it. It should be remembered that Biblical superordination is as serious a challenge to the husband as Biblical subordination is to the wife. (Eph. 5:24-33)

Today Americans who have been reared in the democratic, equalitarian tradition seem to assume that subordination is somehow evil in itself. Democratically oriented Christians sometimes refer to it as a perversion of the glorious freedom which Christ gained for mankind through His suffering, death, and resurrection. The Christian woman, according to such thinkers, must be the complete equal of her husband in every sense of the word and in every facet of their mutual relationship. However, 1 Cor. 15:28 makes it very clear that there is nothing evil in subordination itself. And they seem to forget that the same apostle who wrote 1 Corinthians 11 and 1 Timothy 3 also wrote 1 Corinthians 13 and Ephesians 5. Even the Son of God will be subordinate to the Father when He has completed all the work assigned to Him.[30] (1 Cor. 15:28)

The subordination of which the New Testament speaks is "for the Lord's sake" and applies to all structures of society — to such relationships as citizen to ruler, servant to master, wives to husbands, husbands to wives. (1 Peter 2:13 – 3:7)

THE RELATIONS BETWEEN PARENTS AND CHILDREN

In his First Letter to Timothy the apostle Paul includes in his guidelines for pastors, deacons, elders, and widows specific suggestions regarding the Christian household. Of a pastor he writes: "He must manage his own household well, keeping his children submissive and respectful in every way; for if a man does not know how to manage his own household, how can he care for God's church?" (1 Tim. 3:4-5). (For other references see 1:11-12; 5:3-4, 9-10.)

Parents and children are related "in Christ" and are called to walk in love, as surely as husband and wife are called to this kind of life. The same ambiguity between subordination and mutuality exists here. This tension, too, will be resolved only when Christ establishes the fulness of His life among us at His second coming. The tables of duties (Eph. 6:1-9; Col. 3:18 — 4:1) make it clear that there is a specific pattern of subordination which characterizes relationships between parents and children, while at the same time stressing the all-important new dimension of love.

The tables of duties deserve careful study by each member of the Christian family. They are not cold rules and regulations made up by the Christian church to pervert the Gospel of freedom which Jesus proclaimed. They are Gospel words which outline the nature of the Christian mission in the non-Christian world.[31]

The tables are not designed to build walls which separate the Christian family from the non-Christian world, but rather to provide directions and patterns for living the Christian life in the midst of the non-Christian world. The tables spell out briefly some aspects of the meaning of the new life in Christ for the Christian family. They provide the general outlines for a genuine ministry of love by which mutual edification and burden-bearing are made possible.

This chapter poses two questions: (1) Isn't there a fundamental contradiction between "life in Christ" and the conclusion about the subordinate position of the woman? (2) If this understanding of the New Testament is correct, how does this "subordination in Christ" work itself out in daily living? To the first question we say: The contradiction is an apparent one rather than a real one. The New Testament affirms this kind of responsible tension in freedom on every page. To say anything less would do injustice to the Gospel and to men and women who are struggling to enjoy the freedom with which Christ has made them free.

To the second question we can only say that some general guidelines have been suggested in this chapter and in other chapters in this book. It is an important and inescapable part of our new life in Christ that we must work out our own application of most evangelical principles. This is small comfort to the puzzled Christian family, perhaps, but this is exactly the way St. Paul trained his friends in Christian living.

CONCLUSIONS

1. The New Testament contains a theology which relates also to Christian family life. The basic emphases in the New Testament are on the radical newness which Christ introduces into every social pattern, on the love and forgiveness heralded in the Gospel, and on the centrality of the family in the global mission program of God.

2. The New Testament does not single out or dictate any specific *sociological* pattern of family structure (patriarchal, small family, large family, the absolute dominance of the husband and father, complete equality between husband and wife, etc.) as the pattern ordained by God for all time.

3. The Christian family is the place where the new life in Christ shows itself most naturally. It is the exercise hall or gymnasium where the attitudes and actions associated with the new life are best developed. It is the place where the basic questions about authority and responsibility are most naturally resolved.

4. The New Testament proclaims a mutuality in the relationship between husband and wife which is new. This mutuality, described most fully in Ephesians 5, calls for husband and wife to regard themselves as one flesh, to live in Christ and in self-giving love toward each other. As Christ is Lord and Servant to the church, so the husband is both lord and servant to his wife.

5. This new mutuality does not do away with the subordinate position of the woman in the home (and in the church). In both the orders of creation and of redemption she is still called to a subordinate position. This subordination is a far cry from the slavish subjection often associated with Biblical teachings, but it is also distinct from the so-called 50-50 patterns of sharing.

6. Parents and children likewise live in relationships of superordination and subordination as part of God's order of creation and also in the new life in Christ. Christ advocated no change in the family social structure.

7. Specific rules and patterns are carefully avoided by Jesus and Paul. The Gospel remains free and creative; thus it can affect family structural patterns in every society and generation. It never becomes identified with one socially conditioned pattern. This creative freedom is an important aspect of the new life in Christ.

8. The New Testament sees a partnership aspect in the Christian family relations as the family expresses its unity and mission "in Christ." Mutual nurture and good functioning of the household are goals of the family under the Gospel as all members of the family are subject to one another out of reverence for Christ.

NOTES – CHAPTER 3

1. The best discussion of love in the New Testament is the article on *agape* by Ethelbert Stauffer in *Theological Dictionary of the New Testament,* ed. Gerhard Kittel and others, trans. Geoffrey W. Bromiley, I (Grand Rapids: Wm. B. Eerdmans Publishing Co., 1964), 21 – 55. Hereafter referred to as TDNT.

2. Stanley R. Brav, *Jewish Family Solidarity: Myth or Fact?* (Vicksburg, Miss.: Nogales Press, 1940), pp. 7 – 10. "The legal status of woman under Jewish law compares to its advantage with that of contemporary civilizations." George Foot Moore, *Judaism in the First Centuries of the Christian Era* (Cambridge, Mass.: Harvard University Press, 1946), II, 126. The Talmud accords high praise to Rabbi Tarfon for his extraordinary filial devotion and affectionate treatment of his mother. Philip Birnbaum, *A Book of Jewish Concepts* (New York: Hebrew Publishing Co., 1964), p. 3. Helmut Begemann, *Strukturwandel der Familie* (Hamburg: Furche-Verlag, 1960), p. 240, fn. 26.

3. Birnbaum. Ch. 4, pp. 1 – 6.

4. Begemann, pp. 121, 123.

5. Albrecht Oepke, *gyne,* TDNT, I, 776 ff.

6. Matt. 12:46-50; Mark 3:31-35. Begemann, pp. 118 – 23.

7. Full discussions of *paideia* are to be found in Werner Jentsch, *Urchristliches Erziehungsdenken: Die Paideia Kyriu im Rahmen der hellenistisch-judischen Umwelt* (Gütersloh: C. Bertelsmann Verlag, 1951, 302 pp.), and Werner Jaeger, *The Ideals of Greek Culture,* trans. Gilbert Highet (New York: Oxford University Press, 1965). Jentsch's definition of *paideia* in Hellenistic usage is on page 82 and that of Jaeger on pages xxii f. Jentsch describes it simply but comprehensively as "the formation of the man."

8. Jentsch, under "Die Gnade als Erzieher," pp. 179 – 87.

9. Begemann, pp. 119 – 42. On the one hand the New Testament lifts all differences (Gal. 3:28) and yet maintains the old order of headship, but sublimates it "in Christ." (P. 130)

10. Begemann, p. 123.

11. It is interesting to note that some of the rabbis taught that both the male and the female person had existed side by side in Adam. He was according to their thinking a "man-woman," an androgynous person. Most responsible exegetes do not agree with this because Gen. 1:27 uses the plural: "Male and female created He them." *The Babylonian Talmud,* ed. I. Epstein (London: The Soncino Press, 1936), "seder Nashim" xvii, 31 – 33. Paul and Elizabeth Achtemeier, *The Old Testament Roots of Our Faith* (Nashville: Abingdon, 1962), pp. 26 – 27.

12. Stauffer, *agape,* TDNT, I, 51.

13. Begemann, pp. 118 – 23. The thesis is correct concerning the family's role in the mission program of the Christian church, but the natural ties are also important for building a strong Christian family and for determining good patterns of authority.

14. Else Kaehler, *Die Frau in den paulinschen Briefen* (Frankfurt a. Main: Gott-helf, 1960), p. 122–23. Miss Kaehler observes that through the centuries men have reverently studied and powerfully preached the command concerning the subjection of wives, but have paid little attention to the full meaning of the command that they are to love their wives.

15. Begemann, p. 135.

16. Ibid., p. 131.

17. Begemann argues that St. Paul is interpreting Gen. 2:24 in what might be called an allegorical way. Paul has in mind Adam and Eve, and is thinking of Eve, who is rightly called the mother of all living. From Eve his thought moves to the wife who is properly called the husband's body because she is the source of his children. Thus, according to Begemann, Paul's point is that the significance of marriage lies in the family. The wife is to her husband as the church is to Christ. Both are agents by whom He creates individuals and groups who will carry out His mission. "The sign made visible of the 'be one flesh' is the child." Bege-mann, pp. 125–26.

18. This does not mean that the Gospel does not have decided implications for social relationships and structures. The leaven of the Gospel has operated continuously to bring about basic changes in many social patterns.

19. Karl Heinrich Rengstorf, "Mann und Frau im Urchristentum," in *Arbeitsge-meinschaft für Forschung des Landes Nord-Rhein-Westfalen Geisteswissen-schaften* (Cologne: Westdeutscher Verlag, 1954), p. 19. Begemann agrees with Rengstorf, p. 130.

20. Some maintain that Paul's comment in 1 Cor. 11:13-16 reflects local Corin-thian social standards. Therefore, the argument goes, this section can have no binding force for today, since the position of women in society and the home has changed. See p. 65 for a discussion of this view.

21. The standard lexica of classical, Biblical, Koine, and Byzantine Greek furnish dozens of examples of the way in which the root meaning of orderly subjection underlies almost every other use and meaning of the members of this word-group.

22. Begemann, pp. 131, 134. Herman Menge translates: *Ordnet euch einander unter, wie es die Furcht [Ehrfurcht] von Christus verlangt.* ("Subordinate yourselves mutually to each other, as the reverence of Christ requires.") Menge, *Die Heilige Schrift Alten und Neuen Testaments* (Stuttgart: Privileg. Württemberg. Bibel-anstalt, 14th ed.). Menge maintains that this verse is the key sentence of the entire section. Many modern translations make v. 21 the beginning of the para-graph dealing with all family relationships, or let it stand alone. (RSV, NEB, TEV)

23. In this passage St. Paul discusses subordination from the viewpoint of the "order of redemption," while in 1 Cor. 11 he argues from the "order of creation."

24. Heinrich Schlier, *kephale*, TDNT, III, 679.

25. Kaehler, p. 123. She refers to Col. 3:18, 1 Peter 3:5, Titus 2:5, and 1 Tim. 2:11 as other clear New Testament statements concerning the subordination of the wife.

26. Sten Rohde, "The Ordination of Women in Sweden," *Lutheran World*, IV (1957–58), 392; "More About the Ordination of Women Controversy," *Lu-theran World*, V (1958–59), 398–400. We agree with Peter Brunner, who observes that subordination in the New Testament is clearly a theological, not a sociological, concept. "Christ says, 'Be subject one to another,' Eph. 5:21. But this in no way means that in Christ the *kephale* (headship) structure (which delegates authority from the Father to Christ to the man and to the wife) given in creation is now cancelled out. On the contrary! In Christ this structure is seen again in its original sense; it is released from the hardness which entered in at the fall, and it receives a content which first came into the world through Christ's reconciling act on the cross and which can be summarized in one word,

agape, love." Peter Brunner, "The Ministry and the Ministry of Women," *Lutheran World,* VI (1959 – 60), 263 – 68.

27. Begemann and Kaehler reach the same basic conclusion, although they travel by different routes and see other implications in their studies besides those that have been adopted in this chapter.

28. Helmut Thielicke, *The Ethics of Sex,* trans. John W. Doberstein (New York: Harper & Row, 1964), p. 150. Eph. 5 also calls for a type of spiritual subordination of the wife to the husband.

29. Rudolf Bultmann, *The Theology of the New Testament,* trans. Kendrick Gobel, I (New York: Charles Scribner's Sons, 1951), 309. Otto Rusz concludes that the new relationship in Christ does away with all earthly or natural relationships. The Christians have a "supernatural" *(übernatürliches)* being or status which is marked by full unity or equality. *Die Briefe an die Römer, Korinther und Galater* (Regensburg: Friedrich Pustet, 1940), p. 270. We do not agree with Bultmann or Rusz.

30. Theologians remind us that 1 Cor. 15:28 means a subordination only with respect to the Son's duties and office. Because He is true and full God, "God of God," He is not subordinate to the Father as far as His godly nature is concerned. But for our purposes here, the point is that subordination will continue in the perfection of heaven.

31. Karl Weidinger is convinced that the tables of duties are Hellenistic perversions of the Gospel. *Die Haustafeln* (Leipzig: J. C. Hinrichs, 1928), p. 3. Karl Heinrich Rengstorf insists that they are fullest Gospel and stand at the very center of the Gospel message. "Die neutestamentlichen Mahnungen an die Frau, sich dem Manne unterzuordnen," *Verbum Dei Manet in Aeternum: Festschrift fur Otto Schmitz,* ed. Herman Obendiek (Wirtten: Luther-Verlag, 1953), pp. 131 – 145.

CHAPTER 4

Christianity and the Family
A. D. 100—1400

CARL A. VOLZ

The family as an institution is obviously not uniquely Christian or limited to the Western hemisphere. But familial patterns as they have existed in the West were shaped by the Christian ethos, and the family structure which 20th-century Europe and the Americas inherited came out of 18 centuries of Christian experience. In this chapter we shall seek answers to the following questions: What patterns of family authority existed in the West when Christianity first appeared? What did the early church say about the family? What can be known about the relationship between husband and wife, parents and children during these formative years? How did environmental factors shape familial patterns? [1]

I. THE ROMAN PERIOD (A. D. 100—500)

The basic unit of early Roman social organization was the patriarchal family, which included not only parents, children, and grandchildren but clients and slaves as well. The father *(pater),* who was its sole legal personality, derived his authority from his religious role as well as from ancient custom. Theoretically the father had powers of life and death. The Roman matron, although subject to her spouse, shared in his authority and dignity. Each patriarchal family was part of a larger unit called the *gens,* or clan. Thus every Roman bore three names: a given name *(praenomen),* a clan name *(nomen),* and a family name *(cognomen).* The only change in this system of names from ancient times to modern is that the *nomen* is no longer used.

As a result of Rome's expansion during the second century before Christ, a transformation of domestic manners and ideals took place. The contrast between the old and new is especially evident in the changed status of women. Cato "the censor" (234—149 B. C.) castigated the independent ways of the women of his day. He warned the senate that "the moment they have arrived at equality with you they will become your superiors," and he urged a return to the old restraints "by which they were subjected to their husbands." [2] But Cato was powerless to stem the tide, and the old solidarity of family life continued to deteriorate. During the late Republic a growing skepticism of Roman religion further undermined the religious base of the family structure.

> In aristocratic circles in Cicero's day divorce was extremely common and a matter of no social concern. Marriages *de convenance* for political or economic reasons were the rule and a large factor in the frequency of divorce. Remarriage was as frequent as divorce. Even the moral Cato divorced his wife to accommodate his friend and remarried her on his friend's death. To live with one woman for thirty years as Cicero did was probably quite unusual among the upper classes, and even he finally divorced his Terentia to marry his young ward . . . . Sulla and Pompey each had five wives . . . . Vespillo (consul in 19 B. C.) said in his funeral panegyric over his wife, "So long a married life as ours, ended by death and not by divorce, is rare." [3]

These tendencies continued unchanged into the Augustan age when Christ was born. Augustus attempted to revive the ancient domestic virtues by enacting the Julian Laws of 19 and 18 B. C., which encouraged marital stability and placed disabilities on unmarried and childless persons. In the Papian Poppaean laws of A. D. 9 precedence was given to fathers among candidates for public office, but a commentary on the effectiveness of this measure is the fact that both consuls sponsoring it were bachelors. Augustus himself divorced his wife, and he found it necessary to banish his daughter because of her flagrant life.

To prevent a distorted analysis of this period, we must admit that practically all the literature on domestic morality from the first century applies to a limited aristocratic circle living in Rome. It is also important to remember that our sources are almost all prejudiced against high society, and occasional lapses from accepted moral standards which have always preoccupied the idle rich made more interesting copy for the masses than did examples of conventional behavior. When all due allowances have been made, it still remains true that the family structure during the early empire was in jeopardy. One index of familial deterioration was the use to which women put their new legal and economic freedom. Martial (died circa A. D. 102) cautioned against marrying a rich woman, for the husband would become her "maid," and Seneca complained that husbands were becoming nonentities while their wives were competing successfully with men in the affairs of state.[4]

It was against this background of family disintegration that Christianity came preaching a message of filial piety and domestic virtue. It may have appeared to be an entirely new social ethic when the enervated Romans heard St. Paul counsel women to be silent in the churches and subject to their husbands, or when St. Peter suggested a similar relationship of male priority in the home. Certainly the notion of parental responsibility for the training of children was an innovation in a society which had usually regarded this as a responsibility of slaves. These concerns of New Testament writers were pursued further by the early Christian Fathers.

Voices of the Church

As early as A. D. 110 we have evidence that the church was adding its blessing to the marriage ceremony. In that year Bishop Ignatius of Antioch wrote: "It is right for men and women who marry to be united with the bishop's approval. In that way their marriage will follow God's will and not the promptings of lust. Let everything be done so as to advance God's honor." [5] Late in the same century Clement of Alexandria defended marriage against the attempts of the Gnostic sects to discredit it:

> Therefore we must by all means marry, both for our country's sake,
> for the succession of children, and as far as we are concerned for
> the perfection of the world; since the poets also pity a marriage
> half-perfect and childless, but pronounce the fruitful one happy.[6]

He points out that marriage results in an act of cooperation with the Creator: "Thus man becomes an image of God insofar as man cooperates in the creation of man." [7] Perhaps his most lofty statement on matrimony is his commentary on Matt. 18:20: "Who are the two or three gathered together in the name of Christ, in whose midst is the Lord? Are they not man, wife, and child, because man and wife are joined by God?" [8] Clement regarded the married man as superior to the single since he was disciplined by his responsibilities and did not have the leisure to fall into temptation and so fall from faith. This same Father is the author of the earliest extant Christian hymn. Its theme deals with Christian education, and it is known today as "Shepherd of Tender Youth."

A few years after Clement, Tertullian, that impetuous North African (d. ca. 230), extolled the merits of celibacy to such extremes as to be labeled a misogynist. Yet even he conceded that "the union of man and woman, blessed by God, is the seminary of the human race and devised for the replenishment of the earth." He continued by denouncing those who claimed that Christ's advent abolished marriage. "They separate one flesh into two and deny Him who first made the female from the male and then recombined them in the matrimonial union." [9]

These lofty conceptions of the marital estate and family life meant little to those families in which only one or two members became Christian. Such (mixed) marriages often resulted in a great deal of pain and anguish for both parties. Justin Martyr (d. 165) wrote: "The father, the neighbor, the son, the friend, the brother, the husband, the wife are imperilled; if they seek to maintain discipline, they are in danger of being denounced." [10] Clement of Alexandria warned: "If anyone has a godless father or brother or son who would be a hindrance to faith and an obstacle to the higher life, he must not associate with him or share his position." [11] In the *Recognitions* of Clement we read: "When differences arise in any household between a believer and an unbeliever, an inevitable conflict arises, the unbelievers fighting against the faith and the faithful refuting their old error and sinful vices." [12] Tertullian stated that heathen husbands were accustomed to keep their Christian wives in subjection by threatening to denounce them to the government officials.[13] Justin records that an aristocratic couple was leading a profligate life, but when the woman became a Christian she divorced her husband, who in turn succeeded in having her Christian teachers put to death for alienating his wife's affections.[14]

Many are the scenes of domestic pathos in times of martyrdom. Perhaps the most celebrated is the account of the Christian woman, Perpetua, and her pagan father. He first tried to make her recant by force and then besought her with tears and entreaties. "Have pity on your father's white hairs. Pity your tender son." But she replied, "He has God, and God is able to have pity on His own." In the same account we read of Felicitas, who gave birth to a baby girl while awaiting martyrdom. After the mother's death the child was brought up by the "sisters." [15] It was possibly due to these unhappy family divisions caused by the intrusion of Christianity that the Fathers were led to denounce mixed marriages. Bishop Callistus of Rome (A.D. 217–222) decreed that henceforth aristocratic Christian women would be permitted to marry lowborn Christian men rather than be party to a mixed marriage. This is the earliest example of the church creating ecclesiastical law which went directly in opposition to the laws of the state. When entire Christian families became implicated under persecution, they often encouraged one another to remain steadfast. We have the famous account of Origen, who though only a young teen-ager wrote to his imprisoned father, "See that you do not change your mind on our account." If Eusebius is correct, it was only through the expedient of hiding his clothes that Origen's mother prevented him from joining in his father's martyrdom.[16]

Apostolic Constitutions

By the fourth century Christianity had successfully withstood the pressures of persecution, and under Constantine the church became a favored institution. This century witnessed the beginning of large-scale literary activity by Christian writers, who occasionally dealt with questions of the family. In most cases the Fathers called for a return to the ancient Roman disciplines under the authority of the father, although the patriarchal role was to be tempered with Christian love and mercy. The *Apostolic Constitutions,* written ca. A.D. 380 in Syria, offer these suggestions to Christian fathers:

> Fathers, rear your children in the Lord, bringing them up in the nurture and admonition of the Lord (Ephesians 6:4), and teach them arts that are serviceable and befitting this Word, that they may not, waxing wanton through prosperity and remaining unpunished by their parents, find license unseasonably and rebel against the good. Therefore do not hesitate to reprove them, chastening them with severity; for by correction you will not slay them, but rather will save them, as Solomon says in his Wisdom (Proverbs 29:17), "Correct thy son and he shall give thee rest; even so shall he fill thee with good hope." Thou shalt beat him with the rod and deliver his soul from death (25:14)." And again the same sayeth thus (13:24), "He that spareth his rod hateth his son," and again we read (Ecclesiasticus 30:12), "Smite his loins sore while he is

little, lest he become stubborn and rebel against thee." So he who forbears to exhort and chasten his son hateth his own child. Teach your children the word of the Lord, straiten them even with stripes and render them submissive, teaching them from infancy the Holy Scriptures, transmitting to them your words and God's words and all divine writings; not permitting them to exercise authority over you against your judgment, nor allowing them to foregather for carousal with their equals in age; for in that way they will be diverted into disorder and fall into fornication. And if they suffer this by their parents' heedlessness, those that begat them shall be responsible for their souls. If the children, by reason of their parents' sloth, consort with licentious men, though they have sinned, they alone will not be punished, but their parents shall be brought to judgment on their behalf. Therefore give heed that you contract betimes to join them in wedlock, that in the burning heat of youth habits of fornication may not ensue, and you shall be held to account by the Lord God on the Day of Judgment.[17]

Already during the late Republic the old patriarchal form of family life had given way to the nuclear form, that is, the husband, his wife, children, and in some cases, servants. This type of structure is reflected in Chrysostom's (d. A.D. 407) comments on the hierarchy of authority in the family.

Further, in order that the one might be subject and the other rule; (For equality is wont oftentimes to bring in strife); He (God) suffered it not to be a democracy, but a monarchy, and as in an army, this order one may see in every family. In the rank of monarch, for instance, there is the husband; but in the rank of lieutenant and general, the wife, and the children too are allotted a third station in command. Then after these a fourth order, that of the servant. For these also bear rule over their inferiors, and some one of them is oftentimes set over the whole, keeping ever the post of the master, but still as a servant. And together with this again another command, and among the children themselves again another, according to their age and sex; since among the children the female does not possess equal sway . . . Therefore even before the race was increased to a multitude, when the first two only were in being, He (God) bade him (Adam) govern and her (Eve) obey. And in order again that he might not despise her as inferior, and separate from her, see how He honored her, and made them one, even before her creation . . . But that she on the other hand might not be elated, as being granted him for help, nor might burst this bond, He makes her out of his side, signifying that she is a part of the whole body. And that neither might the man be elated therefore, He no longer permits that to belong to him alone which before was his alone, but effects the contrary to this, by bringing in procreation of·children, and herein too giving the chief honor unto the man, not however allowing the whole to be his.[18]

Chrysostom and Augustine

This same Chrysostom was author of an interesting tract entitled *An Address on Vainglory and the Right Way for Parents to Bring Up Their Children.*[19] The education of the child, he maintains, is the primary responsibility of the father, and its goal is the virtuous life (Chs. 16 — 18 and 67). The child's soul is like a city or a kingdom over which the parents draw up rules, establish disciplines, and seek its welfare (Chs. 23 — 26). As to corporal punishment: "Have not recourse to blows constantly, and accustom him not to be trained by the rod," but in extreme circumstances the rod may be used (Ch. 30). Inculcate good habits, for it takes only two months for bad habits to grow (Ch. 33). Chrysostom offers a number of examples for storytelling, since these excite the imagination and strengthen the bond between parent and child. When telling a story, preferably a Bible story, the father should ask the child to repeat it to make certain that he understands it (Chs. 39 — 41). The father should also "go and lead him by the hand into the church. You will see the child rejoice because he knows what the other children do not know" when he hears a familiar Bible story (Ch. 41). An interesting opinion of Chrysostom concerns the naming of children. He deplores the custom of naming them after their parents or grandparents, because in this way pagans seek to perpetuate themselves in their children. Since Christians believe in the resurrection of the dead, it is not necessary so to perpetuate oneself, but rather name them "after the righteous — martyrs, bishops, apostles. Let this be an incentive to the children. Let one be called Peter, another John, another bear the name of one of the saints" (Ch. 47). He also placed much value on a child's exposure to the influence of his pastor. "Let him often see the head of his church, and let him hear words of praise from the bishop's lips" (Ch. 83). Throughout this delightful essay one characteristic feature which recurs is a warning against mixing the sexes in education. The young boy should be shielded from all contacts with girls, and the story of Joseph should be told him frequently (Chs. 60–62). As the lad grows to puberty, however, Chrysostom warns that parents can expect him to become more interested in girls than before. "The medical guide tells us that this desire attacks with violence after the fifteenth year. How shall we tie down this wild beast? What shall we contrive? How shall we place a bridle on it? I know none, save only the threat of hellfire!" (Ch. 76). On the marriage ceremony he suggests: "Let us celebrate the marriage feast without flute or harp or dancing; for a groom like ours is ashamed of such absurd customs. Nay, let us invite Christ there, for the bridegroom is worthy of Him. Let us invite His disciples; all things shall be of the best for the groom. And he himself will learn to train his own sons in this way, and theirs in turn, and the result will be a golden cord." (Ch. 88)

Like Chrysostom, Augustine of Hippo compared the father's role to that of a ruler of a city and related the peace of the city to peace and good government in the family. The family was the basic unit in a stable society and ordered state.

> The human family constitutes the beginning and the essential element of society. Every beginning points to some end of the same nature, and every element to the perfection of the whole of which the element is a part. Thus it becomes evident that peace in society must depend upon peace in the family, and the order and harmony of rulers and ruled must directly be actualized from the order and harmony arising out of creative guidance and commensurate responsibility in the family.[20]

These Christian fathers did not suggest a dictatorial role for the father as head of the family, but following New Testament imagery, they assumed a relationship between husband and wife as one reflecting that between Christ and the church. Victorinus Afer, a fourth-century African Christian who wrote in Rome, in commenting on Eph. 5:25 ff., urged the husband to be ready to suffer all things for his wife, just as Christ loved the church and gave Himself for it. The wife is to serve her husband, who is her head, just as the church is to serve its head, but the husband is also to love his wife as his own flesh. The husband, who represents the spirit, and the wife, who represents the soul, are to be indivisibly joined in marriage as Christ and His church.[21]

CONCLUSIONS

The foregoing excerpts lead us to make the following observations concerning Christianity's attitude toward and influence on the family during the first four centuries:

1. Inasmuch as Christianity demanded an entirely different life-style from that of the Roman pagans, mixed marriages resulted in considerable domestic tension.

2. The church sought to restore the father to a position of primary authority in the family. However, his authority was to be exercised in love, and his relationship to his wife was to reflect that between Christ and the church.

3. Education of the children was the primary responsibility of the parents, who were to be assisted by the church.

4. The family was considered to be the basic unit of society and the state.

5. Since marriage was believed to be instituted by God, bride and groom were urged to receive the church's blessing on their nuptials. Because of its divine origin, marriage was good, and according to some Fathers, to be preferred above celibacy.

6. Although the lofty ideal of Christian family life (like all ideals) was never fully realized in actual practice, the ideal served as a benificent counterforce to the decadent Roman family ethic under the empire.

II. THE MEDIEVAL PERIOD (A.D. 500—1400)

From the sixth to the eighth century Christianity, having won the Mediterranean basin, expanded northward into Europe and the British Isles. Here the Christian evangelists met a Teutonic familial structure which closely resembled the old Roman patriarchal system, with the nuclear family providing the base, a cluster of families forming the clan, or *Sippe,* and an aggregate of clans comprising a tribe. Tacitus at the end of the first century and Salvian in the fifth contrasted the virtues of the Teutons with the vices of the Romans, but both writers may have exaggerated for effect. Tacitus' account is the fundamental literary source for early German family life.

> They believe that the sex [woman] has a certain sanctity and prophetic gift, and they neither despise their counsel nor disre-

gard their answers . . . . [At age 14] in a full assembly one of the chiefs or the father or relatives of a youth invest him with shield and spear. This is the sign that the lad has reached the age of manhood. Before this he was only a member of a household, hereafter he is a member of the tribe . . . . [The men engage in fighting] while the hearth and home and care of the fields is given over to the women. . . . Their marriage code is strict, and in no other part of their manners are they to be praised more than in this. For almost alone among the barbarian people they are content with one wife each . . . . The wife does not bring a dowry to the husband, but the husband to the wife. The parents and relatives are at the ceremony and examine and accept the presents — gifts not suited to female luxury nor such as a young bride would deck herself with, but oxen, a horse and bridle and a shield together with a spear and a sword . . . . The bride is admonished that she is becoming the partner of her husband's labors and dangers, destined to suffer and dare with him alike in peace and war.[22]

Tacitus continues by stating that the wife hands on her dowry to her daughters or daughters-in-law. He maintains that adultery is rare, and its punishment is immediate and severe. "They accept one husband, just as they have one body and one life. Their love is not for the married state but for the husband. To limit the number of children or to put any to death is considered a crime, and with them good customs are of more avail than good laws elsewhere." [23]

Modern scholarship has both confirmed and denied Tacitus' secondhand observations, though the balance tends to favor his essential accuracy, with the qualification that by the fifth century the seminomadic German tribes of former years had settled to a more agricultural style of life. The *paterfamilias* resembled his older Roman counterpart in many respects, although his authority was tempered by the council of tribal elders. The father could dispose of his daughter in marriage, and he represented unmarried daughters in court. Wallace-Hadrill comments on the role of women in Teutonic society:

The *mundium* was the dominion or protection exercised by the family, the husband or the king over women, and thus the value or price of women, or of any person not a slave in civil law. A free woman could no more be without her *mundium* than she could be without her soul. When she married her husband acquired it, at a price, from her family. The *mundium* was certainly a woman's or a slave's effective defense; but it was also an affirmation of the superior right of the family, or in its absence, of the king over the individual. It could be a very hard right, and the instinct of the Church was against it.[24]

As to Teutonic succession, the general practice allowed a share of the inheritance to each man, woman, and child, including illegitimate offspring. Ripuarian Frankish law of the fifth century regulated inheritance up to the sixth degree: "If the sixth male be alive, let not the female succeed." [25] Salian Frankish law stated: "If a man dies without male heirs, let his father and mother succeed him; if the parents are dead, his property should pass to his brothers and sisters." But if all of these are dead, "let the nearest heir of the father succeed; as regards Salian land, let it not pass to a woman but let all the land be given to males." [26] While these legal codes tend to exclude a man's wife and daughters from the inheritance, they also reflect a strong family cohesion which included uncles, aunts, and grandparents. The purpose for excluding women from the inheritance was evidently conditioned by the fact that property usually had to be maintained and defended through physical arms — an activity not suited to the distaff side. Some law codes limited the inheritance to the eldest son (primogeniture), while the Anglo-Saxons distributed it equally among all sons (gavelkind). By the High Middle Ages, however, it was not unusual for the youngest son to inherit the father's property.

Under the Merovingian dynasty (5th to 8th century) the barbarian tribes became assimilated with the earlier Gallo-Romans in Gaul, and the tribal structures of the Germans became less pronounced. Although the tribes retained certain characteristics and settled in geographically circumscribed areas (Burgundians, Franks, Swabians, Lombards, Saxons, etc.), the relationship between the parent tribe and the nuclear family grew more tenuous.

Feudalism and the Family

In order to understand familial patterns in the Middle Ages, it is necessary to grasp the concept behind feudalism. According to this system of landholding, no one really owned land. The king held his land from God, in trust, and he in turn permitted his vassals the use of large tracts of land in return for services. These services almost always included military obligations in addition to goods or rents. These nobles in turn granted the holding of smaller bits of land to lesser nobles under terms of contract for services, and so on down to minor lords who held only a few acres. The feudal contract was expressed in an oath of fealty and loyalty or in an act of homage. Thus all wealth was calculated in terms of landholding. It was basically an agrarian society with a closed, self-sufficient economy. Feudal noblemen were in actual practice farmer-warriors. On the lower level of the farms and manors the serfs who actually performed the work in the fields were also bound to perform services and give goods or rents to their lord. The serf was "bound to the soil," which meant he could not be moved from one manor to another, but he and his family were an integral part of the holding. In theory, therefore, manorialism reflected a static condition, but in practice there was considerable mobility among the serfs nevertheless, not only horizontally from place to place but vertically in society as well.

It is clear that the feudal system profoundly affected marriage and the home. When a vassal died, his lord was naturally interested in the new husband of the widow, since he would in all probability receive the holding. This was especially true by the 12th century, when a woman's right to inherit her husband's property was fully recognized. "Widows were not left time to weep for their husbands, inasmuch as it was imperative that the fief should be managed by a man, so that in feudal amours sentiment had no part." [27] Therefore lords usually reserved the right to choose, or at least approve, a widow's new husband, but in some cases widows were able to gain free choice by payment of a fee. The same economic interest prevailed in the marriage of a vassal's daughter, especially if she was the principle heir of property. Once women's rights of inheritance became established, it was only natural to view them more in terms of land value than for their person, and they became pawns on the feudal chessboard. Occasionally there were bethrothals between infants who were still in the nursery, and marriages between girls of 12 and boys of 14 (the legal ages) were commonplace. It is not difficult to understand the medieval saying, "Land marries land." Because of this cavalier approach to marriage, divorces were also common among the nobility. To have three or four spouses was a minimum. The slightest motive might cause a man to repudiate his wife. Grounds for annulment recognized by the church were only three: (1) if the groom had been ordained prior to the marriage, (2) if the parties were related within prohibited degrees, and (3) for impotence. However, in practice the church often sanctioned divorce for other reasons, and thanks to the complicity of the clergy, marriages could often be broken as easily as they were entered into.

The feudal system, based as it was on military service and rustic occupations, did little to encourage refinement of domestic virtues. "What, after all, was the chateau [castle]? A military post, a barracks, and it has never appeared that barracks were a very suitable place for the creation and development of delicate morals, and of sentiments of courtesy founded on the respect for women." [28] Husbands did not refrain from using physical violence against their wives. Luchaire recalls an incident involving the king of France. The queen, Blanchefleur, took it upon herself to counsel the king in an important decision. "The king heard it and anger showed in his face: he raised his fist and struck her on the nose, so hard that he drew four drops of blood. And the lady said, 'Many thanks; when it pleases you, you may do it again.' " [29] Numerous other literary sources indicate that striking a woman on the nose was a favorite method of reproof. One cannot help but conclude that a courteous attitude toward women was rare in feudal society.

The wife or daughter of the serf was obviously in a poorer position to determine her destiny than was the noblewoman. The following medieval account from Britain reflects her lot:

> A servant woman is ordained for the wives' rule and is put to office and work of travail, toil, and drudgery. She is fed with gross and simple meat, and is kept under the yoke of thralldom and service. And if she conceives a child, it is taken from the mother's arms to servage [a condition of servitude]. And if a serving woman be of bond condition she may not take a husband of her own will, and he who marries her, if he is free, he is made a bondman after the marriage. A bondwoman is bought and sold like a beast . . . . Fear makes bond men and women meek and low, but love makes them proud.[30]

The Church and Family Relations

The influence of the church was omnipresent during these years, and its power was exercised chiefly through the sacramental system. By elevating marriage to the position of a sacrament it underscored the sanctity of the estate. Popes and bishops did not hesitate to pronounce excommunication on adulterous lords. Pope Nicolas I (d. 867) forced Lothair II of Lorraine to receive back his divorced wife, and he deposed two archbishops who had connived at his bigamy. King Phillip II of France was excommunicated for the shameful way in which he had treated his wife, Ingeborg, and King Philip I was likewise placed under the ban for his behavior. Medieval chronicles abound in examples of ecclesiastical efforts at upholding the sacredness of marriage. Changes in marriage customs cast further light on the increasing influence of the church. Originally the barbarian ceremony was civil, consisting of two parts: the betrothal, or *beweddung,* which was simply the payment of money to seal the contract, and the *gifta,* in which the bride was given away by her father. From the 10th century on the church added its blessing to these practices, and the rite was performed at the church by the priest.[31]

> Both in books and sermons the Church loved to praise marriage; she looked upon it as sacred and indissoluble. Jacques de Vitry [d. 1240] went so far as to say that married people "also belong to an Order, the Order of Matrimony." . . . And the Dominican, Henry of Provins, pointed out that, "At the time of the Deluge, those whom God preferred to save were married people." . . . Theologians and canonists produced a whole body of legislation which occupies a large section of the present *Codex.* Marriage [was considered to be] a sacrament, but in what exactly did it consist? The canonists replied: "Its essence is the consent of the parties. They themselves administer the sacrament." The priest, they maintained, acts as witness on behalf of God and blesses it. . . . The Church set her face against feudal marriages whereby a man gave his daughter to some vassal whom he desired to invest with land. They were marriages lacking genuine consent, and were therefore considered invalid. The Church forbade clandestine marriages and required the presence of witnesses.[32]

A caution is in order, however, when one undertakes an analysis of medieval institutions. For too many years the odium cast upon these centuries by men of the Renaissance has influenced our own attitudes to the point where "medieval" has become synonymous with oppressive, tyrannical, and benighted. This is also true of assessments of the medieval family. These centuries were filled with contradictions, and for every act of violence it seems possible to offer an example of mercy. For example, an early 12th-century chronicler has left us a description of the pious family in which the father, Ailsi, "was a good and holy man . . . who begat and brought up his children in the fear of the Lord." [33] Despite the accounts of male cruelty, it was still necessary for a man to win the love of his wife. "Before the wedding the groom thinks to win the love of her that he woos with gifts, messages, and presents, and the promise of much more. To please her he must engage in deeds of arms, might and victory. He speaks pleasantly to her, and notices her cheer, and tells her openly his intentions in the presence of her friends." [34] Examples of tender love such as between Heloise and Abelard abound. One poignant letter from a wife to her ailing husband reveals a more exemplary side of domestic life: "Dear husband, I desire heartily to know of your welfare, thanking God that you are mending from the great disease you have had, and I thank you for the letter you sent me, because mother and I were heartsick from the time we heard of your sickness. . . . If I had my way you would be home. I pray you when father comes to London that you would come home, if you can ride, for I will keep you as tenderly as those in London. . . . May almighty God have you in His keeping." [35]

Manorial Domestic Life

Life on the manor involved the entire peasant family in the work of farming. Like agriculture until the advent of modern technology, it was always a familial venture. The housewife concerned herself with sewing and spinning, with the hens, and with tending the small cottage garden with its cabbages, beans, and peas. The children played in the nearby woods or on the common meadow. Although we read of tyrannical lords or stewards of the manor, it was always to their advantage to treat the serfs with consideration. Often close ties of friendship and loyalty existed between them. Serfs were under contract, and in case of a lord's violation of trust every serf had the right to air his grievances in the monthly manor court, where cases were reviewed by his peers. Jay Williams offers us a glimpse into manor domestic life.

> While it was true that highborn ladies gave a great deal of attention
> to their clothes, just as women do today, the lady of the manor had
> many duties to perform which kept her endlessly busy. If her hus-

band kept his eye on the work of the tenants, her domain was the castle, or manor house, and its servants. She had to oversee the work of the household, supervise the dairy, the gardens, the kitchen and the bakery. She saw to it that clothes were made, and might herself weave or sew ... Many gentlewomen could read; they encouraged the composing of poetry and music. Most important, when her lord went off to war the lady took his place as chief of the estate, responsible for its administration and welfare. . . . Accustomed to hunting, riding, and hard exercise, the noble lady was often strong-willed, tough, domineering, and like her father or her husband, used to giving commands and having them obeyed.[36]

Although women were theoretically inferior to men, as indicated above, in actual practice we read of any number of aristocratic women leading extremely active lives in the world of politics and intrigue. While Louis IX was away on a crusade, his mother not only ruled France for four years, but she succeeded in quashing an armed rebellion as well. The very fact that women were often pawns in the feudal system gave them an advantage in a seller's market. Eleanor of Aquitaine, queen of half of France, shrewdly married herself to the king of England. Otto I of Germany first interfered in Italian affairs by answering the pleas of the beautiful Adalheid, who thereby succeeded in becoming the empress. Henry IV of Germany was almost vanquished by the intrigues of Matilda of Tuscany. During numerous regal and ducal minorities large parts of Europe were ruled by women, whose influence did not subside when their sons reached their majority, which was age 14. Although it is probably true that these aristocratic women may have been exceptions to the rule, a painting in the British Museum depicting a peasant woman of the 12th century beating her husband with a distaff seems to indicate that not all women were content to accept a passively subordinate role in the home.[37] Indeed, our numerous literary sources indicating the inferiority of medieval women are all of male authorship, and sometimes they seem to reflect more wishful thinking than actual conditions of the time.

By the 12th century a commercial revolution had taken place in western Europe which signaled the decline of feudalism. An increase in trade prompted the rise of cities, and the corresponding influx of capital made the old, landed, self-sufficient economy impossible to maintain. Serfs hired themselves out for wages, and in the new urban centers there arose a breed of men, merchants and craftsmen, who had no lord except the king. This new bourgeois attitude also affected family life, most noticeably in the emancipation of women from the restrictions of the feudal way. The 14th century abounds in handbooks of instructions to housewives, all written by men, who constantly urge the good wife to be more submissive. Evidently these guidebooks were considered necessary. In the towns women found work as weavers and in other crafts or ran businesses of their own (brewing was almost entirely in the hands of women), and some formed guilds of their own and demanded a voice in the affairs of the town. In 1322 a woman doctor was brought before the ecclesiastical authorities of Paris and charged with unlawfully practicing an art reserved for men. The consensus of the judges was that "it is better and more becoming that a woman clever and expert in the art should visit a sick woman . . . it is better that she be permitted to make visits than that the sick should die." [38]

Just as agriculture involved an entire family in a common pursuit and so contributed to family solidarity, so also prior to the industrial revolution entire families were often engaged in a single craft. "Whereas in a modern town most husbands go out to work while their wives stay at home, in a medieval town the family tended to remain centered for most of the day in the home. On the ground floor the master of the house with his apprentices and sons would work in the shop or sell from the stall which opened directly onto the street. Upstairs the mistress with her daughters, and the servants — if she was rich enough to have any — did the housework." [39]

Chivalry and Women

The late Middle Ages witnessed the emergence of a genre of literature which extolled courtly love and the chivalric ideal. Chivalry refers to the idealization of the virtues required of the medieval knight, most notably those of loyalty, defense of the church, and the protection of women. Alongside this development went the elevation of women's status in society. Knights chose a "lady love," usually a married woman, whose cause they championed and whose favors they occasionally received. A 12th-century writer has left us a treatise, "Rules of Courtly Love," which counsels in part: "Marriage is no real excuse for not loving . . . . He who is not jealous cannot love . . . . No one should be deprived of love without the very best of reasons . . . . Nothing forbids one woman being loved by two men or one man by two women." [40] French and Provencal literature tended to stress illicit liaisons. Walther von der Vogelweide, a 13th-century German minnesinger, tended to extol the virtues of the married life: "He happy man, she happy woman, whose hearts are to each other true; both lives increased in price and worth; blessed their years and all their days." [41] The prevalence of this literature is further evidence of the emancipation of women in the late Middle Ages, but where courtly love was assiduously pursued, it cannot but have been detrimental to domestic tranquillity. On the ecclesiastical side, this phenomenon found expression in increased devotion to the Virgin Mary, as evidenced in poetry, in the Dominican institution of the rosary, and in the flood of churches dedicated to Notre Dame. Numerous women mystics in the Rhine Valley produced literature, notably Elizabeth of Schonau, Hildegard of Bingen, Mary of Ognies, Liutgard of Tongern, and Mechtild of Magdeburg.

The Church and Women's Status

Officially the church played a generally conservative role as she reacted to capitalism and the changes it brought. Thomas Aquinas, who followed Aristotle in many respects, insisted on the natural inferiority of women to men. He viewed woman primarily as an instrument of procreation. "St. Thomas reiterates the opinion that man represents in himself perfection, while woman stands for the imperfect, and that nature at all times is bent on the production of the male and produces the female only when it is thwarted by inner or outer factors." [42] Thomas believed that nature inevitably progresses from the imperfect to the perfect. Hence marriage, which has its origins in human nature, advances in Christianity to a moral sphere, producing offspring, faith, and the sacrament. He stresses the ideal of mutual love between husband and wife, parents and children, but at the same time he believes that the personality of the woman is absorbed by that of her intrinsically superior husband. Aquinas believed that celibacy was to be preferred above marriage, but he also observed: "Although the state of virginity is better than the state of matrimony, a given person may still be more perfect in the married state than another in that of virginity." [43]

Alongside this conservative position, which echoed many of the attitudes of the early Fathers, was that of William of Ockham, who maintained an equality between the sexes. "According to the Epistle to the Colossians there is neither male or female. And therefore wherever the wisdom or goodness or power of women is essential to the treating of the faith, which is the especial concern of a General Council, a woman must not be excluded from such a General Council." [44] Neither the early Fathers nor the apostles themselves were willing to permit women this much authority in the church. Although attempts were made to regulate domestic life through the growing body of canon law, the 14th and 15th centuries experienced a wave of skepticism in matters of faith, and society became increasingly secularized as the church spent its energies on the papal captivity at Avignon and on the subsequent schism.

The Christian leaven which entered Europe during the early Middle Ages unquestionably provided society with an organization and a stimulation for dynamic change. The commonly held Renaissance dictum that Rome's fall somehow was catastrophic for the West has been challenged by virtually every contemporary medievalist. [45]

During this millennium the church provided a noble theory of domestic stability based on Christian love. The fact that theory and practice were found at times to be at variance is not a fault peculiar to these times. Henri Daniel-Rops has summarized the church's attitude toward marriage and the family in the medieval period.

> The church, then, was at pains to honor marriage as it deserved. She likewise undertook the training of mankind in love, and laid down rules wherever there was danger that instinct might break loose. Important consequences followed, of which two in particular should be noted. The first of these concerned the family, which would infallibly have been ruined by lustful imagination and unbridled passion if Christianity had not stemmed the tide. By this means the very framework of society was strengthened in such a way as to endure for centuries, and it is no exaggeration to say that the enormous increase of population during the Middle Ages was partly due to the Christian view of marriage. The church's attitude towards human love had another consequence which made a deep impression on the minds of Europe, and helped to distinguish Western civilization from those, say, of India, China, and Islam. This was the raising of women's status, a truly remarkable phenomenon . . . . The church obliged man to respect the dignity of woman, who ceased to be his property, the plaything of his passions

or his interests . . . . The church effected a complete reversal in the order of values, making woman, weak and helpless though she remained, no longer dependent on the warrior but the object of his veneration.[46]

CONCLUSIONS

We offer the following conclusions regarding the church and familial life from A.D. 500 to 1400:

1. The patriarchal family structure of the Teutonic tribes gave way to a nuclear pattern brought by Christianity from the Mediterranean basin.

2. Both pagans and Christians emphasized the inferior status of women in society. However, they also both insisted, in contrast to the imperial Romans, that women were to be treated with dignity and respect.

3. The medieval church sought to enhance the institution of marriage and the family by providing penalties for those who disrupted domestic life. It elevated marriage to a sacrament, and by supporting the ideal of chivalry sought to refine men's attitudes toward women.

4. Despite woman's theoretically passive role in society, numerous examples from literature indicate that many women refused to accept a submissive role.

5. Patterns of family life were influenced by nontheological forces, e.g., feudalism and capitalism, and by theological forces such as the philosophy of Thomas Aquinas and a statement of William of Ockham.

6. During this millennium the church provided a noble theory of domestic stability based on Christian love.

NOTES—CHAPTER 4

1. A basic bibliography on the history of family organization will include the following works: Mary B. Messer, *The Family in the Making* (New York: G. P. Putnam's Sons, 1928); Willystine Goodsell, *A History of the Family as a Social and Educational Institution* (New York: Macmillan Co., 1915); Carle C. Zimmerman, *The Family of Tomorrow: The Cultural Crisis and the Way Out* (New York: Harper & Brothers, 1949); George G. Howard, *A History of Matrimonial Institutions*, 3 vols. (Chicago: The University of Chicago Press, 1904); Edward Westermark, *The History of Human Marriage*, 5th ed., 3 vols. (New York: Alerton Book Co., 1922); Joseph Kirk Folsom, *The Family*

and *Democratic Society* (New York: John Wiley and Sons, 1943); Ruth Nanda Anshen, ed., *The Family: Its Function and Its Destiny,* rev. ed. (New York: Harper & Bros., 1949); for early church, see Shirley Jackson Case, *The Social Triumph of the Ancient Church* (New York: Harper & Bros., 1938).

2. In Livy, *History,* XXXIV, 1–8, as quoted by Albert A. Trever, *History of Ancient Civilization,* Vol. II, *The Roman World* (New York: Harcourt, Brace and Co., 1930), 140.

3. Trever, p. 280.

4. Ibid., p. 445.

5. Ignatius to Polycarp 5:2 in *Patrologiae cursus completus,* ed. J. P. Migne, Series graeca, 5, col. 724. Hereafter Migne will be referred to as *PG* (Series graeca) and *PL* (Series latina). Immediately preceding this section Ignatius counsels: "Tell my sisters to love the Lord and to be altogether contented with their husbands. Similarly, urge my brothers in the name of Jesus Christ, 'to love their wives as the Lord loves the Church.' If anyone can live in chastity for the honor of the Lord's flesh, let him do so without ever boasting. If he boasts of it he is lost; and if he is more highly honored than the bishop, his chastity is as good as forfeited."—Jean Danielou and Henri Marrou, *The First Six Hundred Years* (New York: McGraw Hill Book Co., 1964), pp. 175–77, comment: "The Christians, adopting the notion of Roman law, regarded consent as constituting marriage. They also kept the practices accompanying the pagan celebration of marriage: the importance of the veil, the reading of the contract, and the joining of hands. They removed only what was specifically idolatrous: sacrifice and the reading of horoscopes. At the beginning of the third century the Christians had no liturgical celebration of marriage, but they realized that they were being united before Christ, as we see in bas-reliefs where Christ is represented crowning the bride and joining the couple's hands . . . the child received instruction in Christianity in his own family."

6. Clement of Alexandria, *Stromateis* 2:23, in *PG* 8, col. 1089.

7. Clement of Alexandria, *Paidagogus* 2:10, in *PG* 8, col. 505.

8. Clement of Alexandria, *Stromateis* 3:10, in *PG* 8, col. 1172.

9. Tertullian, *To His Wife* 1:3, in *PL* 1, col. 1391. Elsewhere in the same treatise he speaks of Christian marriage in this fashion: "How can we describe the happiness of this marriage which the Church approves, which the oblation confirms, which the blessing seals, which the angels recognize, which the Father ratifies?" 2:6, in *PL* 1, col. 1410. Here we find the elements of an early Christian marriage liturgy.

10. Justin Martyr, *II Apology* 1, in *PG* 6, col. 443.

11. Clement of Alexandria, *Who Is the Rich Man Who Can Be Saved?* 22, in *PG* 9, col. 628. He continues (Ch. 23) by warning: "Suppose it is a lawsuit. Suppose your father were to appear to you and say, 'I begot you, I reared you. Follow me, join me in wickedness and obey not the law of Christ,' and so on, as any blasphemer, dead by nature, would say."

12. *Recognitions of Clement* 2:29, in *PG* 1, col. 1263.

13. Tertullian, *To His Wife* 2:5, in *PL* 1, col. 1408.

14. Justin Martyr, *II Apology* 2, in *PG* 6, col. 443.

15. *The Martyrdom of Saints Perpetua and Felicitas,* ed. and trans. Anne Fremantle, *A Treasury of Early Christianity* (New York: Viking Press, 1948), pp. 219, 224.

16. Eusebius, *Ecclesiastical History* 6:2, in *PG* 20, col. 522. Adolf Harnack, *The Mission and Expansion of Christianity* (New York: Harper & Brothers, 1962), p. 397, n. 2: "Cp. Daria, the wife of Nicander, in the Acts of Marcianus and Nicander, who exhorted her husband to stand firm. Also the Acts of Maximilianus, where the martyr is encouraged by his father, who rejoices in the death of his son; and further, the Acta Jacobi et Mariani, where the mother of Marianus exults in her son's death as a martyr."

17. *Apostolic Constitutions,* ed. F. X. Funk (Paderborn, Germany, 1905), 4, 11.

18. John Chrysostom, *Homily 20 on Ephesians,* in *PG* 62, col. 148. Cf. Arthur Repp, "John Chrysostom on the Christian Home as a Teacher," *Concordia Theological Monthly,* XXII (December 1951), 931 – 48.

19. The edition here referred to is edited by M. L. Laistner, *Christianity and Pagan Culture in the Later Roman Empire Together with an English translation of John Chrysostom's Address on Vainglory and the Right Way for Parents to Bring Up Their Children* (Ithaca, N. Y.: Cornell University Press, 1951).

20. Augustine, *The City of God,* 19:16, trans. Ruth Nanda Anschen, *The Family: Its Function and Destiny* (New York: Harper & Bros., 1949), p. 2.

21. Victorinus Afer, *Commentary on Ephesians,* in *PL* 8, col. 1287.

22. Tacitus, *Germania,* in Donald A. White, ed., *Medieval History, A Source Book* (Homewood, Ill.: The Dorsey Press, 1965), p. 49. Cf. Salvian, *On the Governance of God,* trans. Jeremiah O'Sullivan, in *Fathers of the Church* series, ed. Ludwig Schopp et al. (New York: Cima Pub. Co., 1947).

23. Ibid.

24. J. M. Wallace-Hadrill, *The Barbarian West* (A. D. 400 – 1000) (New York: Harper Torchbooks, 1962), p. 59. The term *mundium* comes from the old German *Mund,* meaning "Hand, Schutz, Schirm." It denotes a guardianship *(Vormundschaft)* as exercised for children, the weak, and wives. *Deutsch-Amerikanisches Conversations-Lexicon,* Alexander J. Schem (New York: Commissions-Verlag von E. Steiger, 1872), Vol. VII.

25. *Monumenta Germaniae Historia,* Leges V, 240, as cited by Jeremiah O'Sullivan, *Medieval Europe* (New York: Appleton-Century-Crofts Inc., 1943), p. 496.

26. Ibid. – Ranulf Glanville, a 12th-century English jurist, stated that a woman's person passed into that of her husband. A summary of Glanville's views is given by Florence Buckstaff, "Married Women's Property Rights in Anglo-Saxon and Anglo-Norman Law and the Origin of the Common-law Dower," *The Annals of the American Academy of Political and Social Science* (Philadelphia, 1894), p. 252.

27. Achille Luchaire, *Social France at the Time of Philip Augustus* (New York: Harper Torchbooks, 1967), p. 363. (King of France – b. 1165, d. 1223)

28. Ibid., p. 351.

29. Ibid., p. 355. – Jay Williams, *Life in the Middle Ages* (New York: Random House, 1966), p. 47, quotes a late 14th-century account of a woman who scolded her husband in public, whereupon he "smote her with his fist down to the earth, and then with his foot he struck her in the visage and brake her nose, and all her life after she had her nose crooked . . . for her evil and great language."

30. "The Servant's Lot," in G. G. Coulton, ed., *Social Life in Britain from the Conquest to the Reformation* (New York: Barnes and Noble, repr. 1968), p. 339.

31. For a complete study of the development of medieval marriage customs see George G. Howard, *A History of Matrimonial Institutions,* 3 vols. (Chicago: The University of Chicago Press, 1904).

32. Henri Daniel-Rops, *Cathedral and Crusade,* I (Garden City, N. Y.: Doubleday and Co., 1963), 363 – 64. Roman Catholic canon law was much occupied with the essence of marriage rather than family relationships.

33. "A Pious Family," Coulton, p. 221.

34. "Man and Wife," Coulton, p. 441.

35. "Wife to Husband," Coulton, p. 442.

36. Williams, p. 76.

37. Ibid., p. 49.

38. Gui de Chauliac, *The History of Surgery,* cited in *The Portable Medieval*

Reader, ed. James Ross and Mary McLaughlin (New York: The Viking Press, 1960), p. 640.

39. Williams, p. 46.

40. Andreas Capellanus, *The Rules of Courtly Love,* in *The Portable Medieval Reader,* p. 115.

41. Walther von der Vogelweide, *Unter der Linde,* as cited in Henry O. Taylor, *The Medieval Mind,* II (Cambridge: Harvard University Press, 1951), 57. — Daniel-Rops, op. cit., p. 367, "There is a well-known and apposite remark of Charles Seignobos, 'Love? An invention of the twelfth century!' And Gustave Cohen, an expert on the medieval period, is of the same opinion. 'Love,' he says, 'is a great discovery of the Middle Ages, especially of twelfth century France. Before that time it had not savored so fully of eternity and spirituality.' Here we meet a question which has produced two fascinating but widely different interpretations: How far was this metamorphosis of love, or rather this appearance and impressive growth of love-passion in Christian consciousness due specifically to Christian influence?"

42. Hans Meyer, *The Philosophy of St. Thomas Aquinas* (St. Louis: B. Herder Book Co., 1944), p. 207.

43. Daniel-Rops, p. 363. — Modern scholars find discriminatory statements about woman's status in scholastic theology as reflected in Roman Catholic canon law.

44. "Women and General Councils," William of Ockham, *Dialogues,* in Coulton, p. 457. Evidently this churchman was referring not to Colossians but to Galatians (3:28).

45. For instance, William C. Bark, *Origins of the Medieval World* (Stanford: Stanford University Press, 1966), p. 69: "The primary thesis of this chapter, and indeed of this work as a whole, is that something new, distinct, and essentially original began in the Western portion of the Roman Empire; that its elements are distinguishable by the fourth century. This something is perhaps best described as a new attitude toward life . . . . Perhaps the worst menace [to an understanding of this period] is the preoccupation with the vast epic of the decline and fall [of Rome]; the 'authoritative' conviction that the early Middle Ages were a time of superstitious ignorance and general lethargy, enlivened only by fitful flashes of barbaric violence and cruelty . . . . All the old views [of the Middle Ages] are products of ignorance and bias. All are primarily negative. All are quite wrong."

46. Daniel-Rops, p. 365.

CHAPTER 5

Family Ethos
in the Light of the Reformation

EDWARD H. SCHROEDER

The previous chapter discloses the medieval data on the *family* strictly speaking. Concern for "family" in the Christian Middle Ages focused on marriage and the issues of sexuality, the relations of the sexes to each other inside and outside of marriage, and the celibate alternative to marriage. Insofar as the children figured in the consideration, the view was something like this: Family is a marriage to which children have been added. Medieval theology emphasized marriage by making it a sacrament and at the same time rated celibacy above marriage. Nothing so sacral was predicated to family. That fact itself is curious. Every man in his own biography finds himself first of all in a family. He is initially in biological relation to the other humans—father and mother—who brought him to life. Why was this basic datum of human existence so unattended in medieval Christian theology? Whatever the reasons may have been, the opposite was true for Reformation theology.

The Gospel and the Family

At the heart of the Reformation was of course the rediscovery of the Gospel—not the rediscovery of the family. Yet in the case of Luther himself the latter (the disclosure of what God is doing in families) came to be seen related to and yet distinct from the former (what God is doing in the Gospel).[1] The Reformation insight into the Gospel was precisely this, that in the cross and resurrection of Jesus Christ God was doing a work that was distinct from and at one fundamental point contrary to *all* His other works in creation, including His work in the human family. In the Gospel God does indeed create a new man; but this creation — via forgiveness — is distinct from the way He creates and preserves human babies. The one point where the Gospel is "clean contrary" is at the point of forgiveness; it is contrary to all the critical evaluation God makes of mankind via the normal structures of the creation wherein He criticizes man for being a sinner. In Luther's own rhetoric God's operations in the "normal" contours of parent-child relationships were subsumable under the caption of God's left-hand kingdom: His twofold work of creation and criticism. He could also sum up this double work under the single word "law." [2]

THE FAMILY: GOD'S CREATION IN ACTION

It is patent especially to us moderns that the "laws" of biology and genetics are operative in the procreation of children. We know even better than the Reformation age did how the "laws" of psychological and sociological interaction give shape to children and parents as they live together in family units. To call this the work of God's law is to see that God's "law" encompasses much more than just God's legislation. [3] For Luther it was an obvious way of making sense — contemporary and practical sense — out of the First Article of the Christian creed. This primordial biological operation is the agency whereby "God has created me . . . has given me and still sustains my body and soul, all my limbs and senses, my reason and all the faculties of my mind." [4] The family is the agency whereby I am created and then preserved for the first 10, 20, or more years of my life. God does this for every man via his parents. This operational sequence is part of the Creator's law.

Thus family is the operational and functional relationship of parents and children. It is a process of God's creation in action. It has validity in that God Himself keeps it going, and does so apart from any linkage to Jesus Christ and His Gospel. Even where Christ and the Gospel are unknown, God still keeps families happening. He continues to work through this medium. But then that raises the question: What all is God up to in this medium?

We have already touched on the fact that families are the agency for the continuation of God's human creation. In his expanded explanation of the First Article of the Creed and the Fourth Commandment of the Decalog in the Large Catechism, [5] Luther spells out how I am the recipient of my own existence (in fact, my identity) via my parents. The biggest gift my parents bestow on me is *me!*

God through them gives me my existence, and once given, He through them keeps it going.

The Family "Places" Us

But there's more to it. By means of this channel God does more than just bring me into existence somewhere in the cosmos. He puts me via my family ties into a specific place. Existence bestowed via parents is *placement,* God's placement. God places me in a particular family, with a particular father and mother whose particular hereditary qualities transfer to me. He may place me with particular siblings, and with this goes particular placement in the "stepladder" of this particular sibling group. I am placed into a particular century, a particular race and nation, a particular economic and social class, and so forth. All of that is "given" to me by the "accident" of my birth.

Luther's own German words for this placement were *Ordnung* and *Stand.* He uses them practically as synonyms. So does the Augsburg Confession when it speaks of them as "ordinances of God," "orders of God," and "stations of life." [6] They constitute the actual space where God has placed me in my particular life, the "estate" where God stations me. In English we still talk about the "estate" of marriage. For Luther the family was also an estate, as were the other placements into which God moves people by the natural operation of the laws of human society.

God's "Order" for His Work

But God is doing more than just putting me down in a particular place in His creation. Having given me placement, He calls me to work — to work for Him. Operating from my particular station, I am called to be God's own operator performing His *opus,* His work. And now the term "order" helps give shape to the work I do in my stance. Order means that the context in which I exist is not unspecified, is not completely at random, is not first of all to be created by myself. I come into the world already placed in a family order, a sibling order, a racial and national order, and so on. Whether these orders are themselves healthy or not is secondary to the inescapable fact that they are indeed in operation — in operation upon me.

Luther did not envision the orders as primeval standard blueprints or organizational chart boxes into which God places people. Rather his own focus was on their dynamic operational character —

for good or ill—to give concrete shape to the particular placement, and that means the particular biography that every man has. It is via these particular orders, in short, that God has made me, and has made me the particular, peculiar, unique individual being that I am. The orders are the instruments of the Creator in bestowing concretion to my own creaturely existence. And above all they are the framework in which God calls me to carry out His work.[7]

The actual shape of one of the orders which is God's instrument for concretizing my existence, is variable. Nevertheless what God is up to in the national, social, economic, familial, and matrimonial orders—that does remain constant. He is keeping His creation going, concretizing and criticizing it. The historical shape of any given order is open to historical development simply because it is a piece of history.[8] The key question of any order, whatever shape it has, is: Is God's law in its twofold work being carried forward in creation?

The family as order and as placement for doing God's work in the world, along with all the other orders in which God places every man, stood in sharp contrast for Luther to another kind of "order" in particular: the specious religious and monastic orders.[9] Apart from their works-righteous piety, perhaps their second most objectionable characteristic was that they were an order of "self-chosen works." This criticism Luther levels throughout his treatment of the Ten Commandments in the Large Catechism, but it is especially explicit in his treatment of the Fourth Commandment.[10] Here he chastizes the works which the monastics think up for themselves to do (shaving their pates, going on pilgrimages, etc.) in place of the "work" God calls them to do as responsible children of their own parents and responsible parents for the next generation. Both responsibilities they escape by virtue of their entry into the monastic "order." When God originally placed us in the order "family," He thereby ordained much good and terribly urgent work for us to do.

How God Orders the "Orders"

But where is it that God ordains this work for us? How does He "order" it? Simply in the Bible? In explicitly worded commands and prohibitions? Although the monks laid claim to Biblical injunctions for "leaving father and mother" and avoiding the anxiety of family affairs, Luther did not go to the Bible to get specific "orders" for whatever work is to be done in the world. Luther's natural orders are not patterned ways in which God, so to speak, "gives orders," as a police officer issues traffic orders, "ordering" drivers to do this and that. This is not at all what Luther means by the "orders which God commands." A better rendering of this might be "the orders which God *ordains,* institutes, establishes." By virtue of God's natural placement of us in this order, He assigns us our work – often without a word of command or a moral injunction so much as uttered.

Take the order of marriage. How does God get young people to do His continuing creating "work" of falling in love, marrying, having intercourse, and the like? By giving them Biblical injunctions to this effect? Hardly. Do Christian young folks court and marry each other and have babies because God once said in the Book of Genesis, "Be fruitful and multiply and replenish the earth"? Not really. What prompts them to do this creational work is the way God has arranged them. He put them in "order," one male and the other female, with powerful sexual drives and romantic interests and mutual attractiveness. (The Lutheran Confessions emphasize this point very earthily.) [11] Only the moralist would pretend that a "Christian view of marriage" must mean a Christian set of marital prescriptions and advice. Because so much of this is simply "doin' what comes natcherly," Luther's orders are indeed the "natural orders," as opposed to the moralistic monks' "*self-chosen* orders."

The same sort of "naturalness" is operative with respect to parent-child relationships, where the work assignments likewise emerge, often enough without specially revealed commandments from God – right out of the already existing child-parent relationship. For many a vexing parental problem Luther would say: The place to go for help is not the Bible, but some wise, experienced Christian mother. Moral injunctions already presuppose a prior, highly complex set of orderings. This is very obviously true of the Fourth Commandment. "Honor your father and your mother" takes for granted that I already *have* a father and mother, indeed that there already is an "I" brought into existence by this father and mother. We can be sure that Bible-passages and Christian moral advice were not the prime movers in bringing this about. [12]

The role which the Biblical commandments *do* play in Luther's view of the family must still be discussed. We shall do so later, after looking at the critical element of the twofold work which God gets done via His natural orders in creation.

THE FAMILY: GOD'S CRITICISM IN ACTION

In Luther's model all the orders of creation were lumped together under the rubric of God's left-hand kingdom. This kingdom, like its correlative kingdom of God's right hand, is not viewed as territory or as a particular location, but as the regnant action which God Himself is taking with all the valid, authorized authority that a human king has in rightly reigning over his subjects. Thus as Luther portrays it, the kingdom of the left hand is not only a kingdom for getting God's creating done but, simultaneously, for getting sinful creatures *accused.* "The law *always* accuses," [13] and so does God's left-hand kingdom, very concretely and life-relatedly. Accordingly, by seeing the left-hand kingdom as the regime of an accusatory law, Luther's understanding of "calling" and *Stand* can be seen at a still deeper level of meaning than we have exposed above.

Up until now we have seen order, calling, *Stand* (Luther himself often uses them interchangeably) as the placement where we are concretely put, and put to work, or at least called to go to work for God. A man's calling is not just his being called to do godly work and to give godly witness through his labor, both in his professional vocation and in the multiple wageless works he does for people in the various natural orders where God has placed him. No, his calling is also his being called to *account,* and this by *God.* That is his *Stand,* his witness stand. And it is precisely by these flesh-and-blood human relationships that a man, as father or as son, is bound. They serve as God's prosecuting attorneys against him.

The "Critical" Function of Families

A man's own children are the accusing finger of God for him. Their protestations of injustice ("Daddy, that's not fair!"), their retributive responses, or their silent, twisted personalities are God's law in action, evaluating the work of one of God's ordered parents. Not from somewhere on high but from one's children come the scales that weigh, approve, or find wanting a man or woman as God's agent for fathering or mothering one of His creatures. And of course the same critical action operates in the opposite direction. God's critical (judgmental) evaluation of children occurs through His fatherly and motherly workmen who call these children to account — and call them to account not just in general, but in that particular order which links both of them to each other. What are they criticized for? For not obeying mother's instructions to clean up their room? Yes, but more than that. For being unloving to their parents? Yes, but more than that, too. Finally, if parents in the family order really are instruments of God's always accusing law, then they are accusing these people (to be sure, "their own" children) of what God accuses them, namely, of *sin*. Parents are God's agents for accusing these God-created children of being sinful sons and daughters. Accusing a person of sin does not, of course, mean carping at a person for his mistakes, but passing on to him the verdict that he is not the person God wants him to be.

To be sure, parents as prosecutors, who are themselves equally and mutually prosecuted by their children, may well distort the purity with which they carry out their role as God's prosecuting attorneys, since they too are sinful also in their prosecutors' role. Nevertheless, even though they are prosecuted prosecutors, they convey God's accusation of sinners: "You are not the persons I wanted you to be in this particular placement where I put you, that is, linked to these parents whom I called you to serve as their sons, and to those siblings whom I called you to serve as brothers. You are not sinners in general, but in this particular ordered relationship you are sinners — sinners as sons." Father and mother likewise get accused by their own offspring functioning as God's prosecuting attorneys to pass on them His verdict: "You are not just a sinner in general, but a sinner-father, a sinner-mother, and your works do follow you."

God's Left-Hand Kingdom and His Inscrutable Forgiveness

What does God have in mind with this left-hand kingdom and its multi-ordered regime of criticism and accusation? That question, of course, is no minor issue. The fact is: It is *the* question of the universe. Just what is God up to in the whole of His creation — not only in the galaxies and among the planets, but also in human history, in families and in marriages, and in the intimacies, intricacies, agonies, ecstasies, and the mortality of human existence? Perhaps we could have deduced His creational and critical work in the world by careful and keen observation and analysis. St. Paul thinks so in the opening chapters of Romans. But that doesn't yet give us any answer to the question: What for? Yes, what is the kingdom of the left hand for? For just keeping the wheel of creation going but then, as far as man's sphere is concerned, critically cutting it down to size, finally to the size of a box that's buried six feet under? There is a rationale to that; it does make sense, the kind of retributive legal sense that operated when Adam and Eve were evicted from God's garden. But why continue creation and criticism, if the upshot of it all is that all God gets out of it is one disobedient sinner after another?

In Luther's own career it was the writers of the Old Testament Psalter and the apostles John and Paul in the New Testament who were his major mentors in getting an answer. St. Paul said: "For God has consigned all men to disobedience, that He may have mercy upon all. O the depth of the riches and wisdom and knowledge of God! How unsearchable are His judgments and how inscrutable His ways!" (Rom. 11:32-33). The incredible thing that no one would ever have guessed is that God is really out to *redeem* His incriminated world. What makes this so incredible is that this is in substance the exact opposite of what He is actually executing via the left-hand operation of His orders of creation.

There is no unambiguous evidence in creation itself that redemption is what God is really up to. And if it weren't for one thing, there would be no grounds at all for such an incredible conviction. That one thing, of course, is the cross and resurrection of Jesus Christ. Incredible (for Paul, at least) is not the "minor" miracles associated with Jesus' life and ministry, but the major "coup" that God Himself executed when He let His Son be executed in the immutable operation of His own divine criticism. In that very event He executed the agents for criticism themselves: His own judgment of sin, His own wrath, His own verdict of death. That's what Paul is marveling at in the verses cited above. "How inscrutable!" (Rom. 12:33). Who would ever have guessed it? Who would have thought that God would trump the cards in His left hand with the Person who sits at His right hand (Christ), and do it in that deep, inscrutable way? [14]

It is this insight into the Gospel that was at the basis of Luther's way of relating the two kingdoms (God's ambidextrous works: the creational criticism of His left hand and the Christ-centered forgiveness of His right hand) to each other. [15] The distinctions between these two kingdoms is for Luther fundamental for his understanding of families. The family as God's creation is God's work, but it is not Gospel. Therefore it is the work of God's left hand. What makes the left-hand kingdom left-handed is not its structured character (as is sometimes erroneously ascribed to Luther), in contrast to the notion that the right-hand kingdom operates without structure, by means of some sort of grace-full osmosis or just at random. No, it is not the family's structuredness that makes it left-handed, in distinction from God's right-hand operation. Rather it is the fact that the family is a *family,* which puts it into the kingdom of the left hand. What makes it left-handed is the sort of things that happen in it: the creating and preserving of human life, the factual inequality and subordination of one human being to another, the mutual criticism and retribution that are carried out, the legal modes that operate to generate and preserve life.

The Left-Hand Kingdom and the Right-Hand Kingdom

After looking hard at the Gospel, Luther's eyes see more clearly what the end of all things is — all things already now in operation in God's creation. The family is God's work, but it is not Gospel. It is a component of the "heaven and earth [which] shall pass away." Family life as such is for Luther's eschatology [16] a strictly interim arrangement; it is strictly provisional. In the new kingdom of the *right* hand, *which is already present* though far from consummated, there is neither male nor female. In it people will neither marry nor be given in marriage. There are no distinctions there of parents and children. This is reflected in Gal. 3:28 and Matt. 12:46-50. Families, like the left-hand kingdom to which they belong, are in that sense a makeshift.

But this does not mean that in the right-hand kingdom there is no "structure." For example, this right-hand kingdom's very essential "order" of brotherhood and mutual forgiveness [17] is for Luther a highly structured thing. In fact, it is the kind of new and revolutionary structure which is already at work in, with, and under the structures of the left-hand kingdom, ultimately to *subvert* them. It doesn't only support them and help fulfill them. Grace doesn't only enable us to "keep" the Law. It also begins to undermine the Law and its whole vast order of judgment. For example, in the family the distinctions between husband and wife, parents and children operate not only to provide for and sustain one another, but also to keep each in his or her place ("Stand"), thereby to identify each one's unique responsibilities and thereby, in turn, to expose each one's sin. But when, say, a father repents to his daughter for having been unreasonable with her and she absolves him of his sin —

perhaps even absolves him in the name of the triune God—behold what "subversion" is going on! Now already the whole legal order of subordination and superordination is giving way.

At first it sounds incongruous to talk about subverting and undermining God's left-hand kingdom with His right-hand one. Worse yet, it sounds impertinent. And indeed it would be so if men set about doing that on their own. But the one who initiated this subversive revolution is God Himself. In Jesus Christ God Himself is at work turning His own left-hand worldly operation upside down. Christ is the one who really initiated the leveling of important, lawful differences. What a "threat" His forgiveness is to the whole authority structure! See how one whole kind of authority—and a God-ordained authority it is—is being subtly revolutionized into a new and opposite kind of authority, one which *ultimately* makes the family and all other natural orders obsolescent.

This subversion (literally, "turning under" one reality for the sake of another) is not complete until the consummation of God's eternal plan, the *eschaton*. But then it will indeed be complete. And the slow phasing out of all the old left-hand orders has already been in process for two millenia. Luther's revolutionary eschatology saw marriage, family, state, and all the rest already being marked for replacement, precisely by the way in which Christians *lived* in these orders. Christ's people do not jump out of the left-hand orders once they've been grafted into Christ's new order of love and forgiveness. But they cannot and do not treat the left-hand orders as ultimates. They have a foot in the new age, and what they still have in God's left-hand old age is had "as though they had none. . . . For the form of this world is passing away" (1 Cor. 7:29 ff.) [18]

TWO SPECIFIC EMPHASES

This is the foundation for Luther's perspective on the order of the family. One needs to comprehend this larger picture in order to make sense of specific elements in his rhetoric on the family. We shall look at two such specifics. The first is: What are the implications for family life of Luther's (that is, the Scripture's) view of God as "Father" and of human beings as His "children?" The second is: What does Luther do with the Fourth Commandment in his catechisms?

God as Father

There's really nothing very obvious about casting God in the masculine gender, except insofar as God is thought of as man's progenitor, ancestor, creator. But who, especially today, would pick the metaphor of "father" to describe God's compassion and His forgiving love? Today, if we picked our God-metaphor from family life at all, we'd be more apt to think of "mother" as more suggestive of love, mercy, and kindness. More likely, we'd look outside the parent-child relationship altogether, perhaps to the love-relationship of courtship and marriage: the "lover," the "bridegroom," the "husband."

The trouble with these metaphors, Biblical as they also are, is that they fail to convey how God is *superior* to us, especially in view of our egalitarian way of thinking nowadays about husbands and wives, namely, as equals. And what makes the mother-metaphor deficient is that, for Luther's time at least and of course for Biblical times, it did not sufficiently convey the implication of divine *authority*. (In our own more matriarchal society it may be that the mother attains more and more to the authority-figure once represented by the father.) For Luther "father" helps to describe God, because within family organization the father is presumably the one who has the last word, so to speak, as the household magistrate or judge.

But then, notice what it does mean to call a *loving, forgiving* God "Father." He is not forgiving in the sense that He is nonjudgmental. He is unstintingly judgmental. His forgiveness is not an *absence* of criticism. No, it is the *overcoming* of His criticism, the *trumping* of His judgment with His love. This characteristic of what Luther understood to be the real depth of fatherly love—the father not ignoring the fault of the children but chastising it, yet in such a way that the chastisement itself could then be upstaged, one-upped, superseded by the father's forgiveness—is of course primordially demonstrated in God's relation to the death of Jesus. Here God and Jesus are related as "Father" and "Son." And so also in the human family the "apple" is to the "rod," not as a weakening of the punishment or a balancing of it, but as Easter is to the Cross—as a *victory* over the rod! That sort of dialectical interplay between judgment on the one hand and forgiveness on the other—not just *both* forgiveness *and* judgment, rather forgiveness as the *triumph* over a likewise valid judgment—had real implications for

Luther's view of familial superordination and subordination. Because the father was the family *judge* par excellence, his love was the family's *love* par excellence because of what all this fatherly love overcame in its opposite: fatherly judgment. Luther's favorite way of describing the conflict between divine criticism and divine mercy — and a conflict it was, not just a nice, pragmatic balance — was as "this very joyous duel." [19] When he spoke this way, his thoughts about the parallels with human fatherhood in the Christian home were often near at hand, as his illustrations prove.

Another example of how Luther's view of the family, especially the father-child relationship, is derivable from his doctrine about God appears in the way Luther finds the doctrine of justification by *faith* being expressed in the Johannine part of the New Testament. Luther finds John describing "faith" often enough as "love." Our faith in Christ can also be expressed as our love for Him. But how does such love, that is, such faith, justify us before God? Well, God is to Jesus as a father is to his only son: very fond and very proud of him. And as also happens with such fond fathers, they warm up to people who have the good judgment to admire their sons. (Just see how much the baby-buggy-pushing father likes you when you stop to compliment his young offspring!) Accordingly, the Johannine writer sees the disciples as "loving" this only Son of God, and the Son's Father likewise loves them *as* lovers of His Son, even though the very same disciples (as Luther marvels) are accused by Jesus as being in all other respects "sinners." [20] In connecting this view of the divine Father and His divine Son to *human* father-son relationships, we might smile and say: How daringly anthropomorphic Luther was willing to be in his picture of God! But that is only half the story. The other half is the way in which Luther was willing to see some of the features of *human* behavior, for example, a father's fond pride in his son, as a reflection of the *divine*.

The Fourth Commandment

Luther's exposition of the Fourth Commandment in the Large Catechism is an extensive and intensive treatment of the family.[21] Fatherhood and motherhood are here designated "estates." The persons standing in these estates are "God's representatives," and they deserve to be treated as such. This is not to deify them or to idealize away their failings, but to recognize what God is doing for children through them, in short, to reckon with the "hidden majesty [sc. God's own] within them."

Luther laments that in his day this divine vocation which parents execute is "despised and brushed aside, and no one recognizes it as God's command or as a holy, divine word and precept." This is the "commandment in its full glory," but that glory has been unseen, and the counterglory and "order" of the monastic life, so rampant by the end of the Middle Ages, is evidence enough for Luther that this commandment is not understood. It is not the insubordination of children to parents that is at issue. Instead it is the "work" God wants done in the world. Here Luther contrasts "their self-devised works" with the family task "that God has chosen and fitted you to perform . . . so precious and pleasing to him." He paints the picture of the monks on the Last Day, who shall "blush with shame before a little child that has lived according to this commandment and confess that with the merits of their whole lives they are not worthy to offer him a cup of water."

A superficial observer might read Luther's lament as a typical oldster's complaint about the generation gap. But he is really aiming at what we today call cultural criticism. Although the Middle Ages had sacramental things to say about marriage, it had lost its antenna for the godly character of the family.

> No one will believe how necessary is this commandment, which in the past was neither heeded nor taught under the papacy. These are plain and simple words, and everyone thinks he already knows them well. So he passes over them lightly, fastens his attention on other things, and fails to perceive and believe how angry he makes God when he neglects this commandment, and how precious and acceptable a work he does when he observes it.[22]

Luther's point is not that children are flagrant Fourth-Commandment breakers. Instead his analysis shows him that the medieval heritage has left parents in the lurch by not showing them God's work via the family. Thus since no set of parents had themselves been shaped by such a family ethos at the time when they were children, "one fool trains another, and as they have lived, so live their children after them." And yet Luther notes that it ought to be a most obvious fact to common-sense observation that "God feeds, guards, and protects us and how many blessings of body and soul he bestows upon us" through the family order. "But here again the devil rules in the world; children forget [this estate of] their parents, as we all forget God." If it weren't for that, the commandment would never need to have been given. But this "perversity of the world God knows very well. By means of commandments, therefore, he reminds and impels everyone to consider what his parents have done for him. Then everybody recognizes that he has received his body and life from them and that he has been nourished and nurtured by them when otherwise he would have perished a hundred times in his own filth."

What about the promise attached to this commandment, and to this one alone: "that you may have long life in the land where you dwell"? This promise is not like the promise of the Gospel. This promise is valid, to be sure, but it applies only to those who perform the qualifying conditions. Such a promise in fact is implicit in all the commandments. If you keep the commandments, you will be rewarded. But the hidden hook in this promise is its inversion for those who are commandment-breakers. Long life for commandment-keepers, but "penalty for him who disobeys." And the ultimate penalty is the antithesis to the promised reward, namely, "the grim reaper, Death! This, in short, is the way God will have it."

What we see in this survey is Luther's clear statement that the family is an operation of God's left-hand kingdom, a reign of law, where a man gets what he's got coming. Even promise and reward are his only if he fulfills the stipulations. In the human-to-human realm of family operations Luther is not so pessimistic as to doubt that reward situations ever arise. They do, and he acknowledges them. He is much more graphic, however, in sketching the way penalties for nonperformance are executed in the normal operations of multi-ordered daily life.

The Fourth Commandment's promise of long life, of course, is not to be confused with God's own gift of life in His Son. That life no one merits by performance in any case. That life God gives not to people who have fulfilled the performance prerequisites, but to those who have not, to sinners. And the reason He *does* do it is "for the sake of Jesus Christ."

Authority and the Parental Office

As Luther concludes his treatment of the commandment, he moves into the subject of authority. Here we see the grounds for his earlier affirmations about the "special distinction . . . which God has given parenthood above all estates that are beneath it." Concerning the multiple placements we have with fellowmen, "the first and greatest" is that of our family ties to our parents. Life in lefthand kingdom relationships is lived in authority—authority under which we stand and authority which we exercise in our manifold placements. "Out of the authority of parents all other authority is derived and developed." [23]

Human existence in the world depends on the valid operation of authority in all the ordered placements where God locates us. Authority does not mean dictatorial tyranny. It is the authorized operation of God's own representative in a particular order. But life under authority must be learned. Another way of saying it is that obedience (not servility) must be learned. Man needs to learn to live on the receiving end of someone else's valid authority. Both, the one exercising authority and the one obeying it, are called into this placement and to this work by God Himself.

When he sounds his jeremiad on the general state of public affairs ("the world now so full of unfaithfulness, shame, misery, and murder"), Luther sees the cause of it all in the fact that "everyone wishes to be his own master, be free from all authority, care nothing for anyone and do whatever he pleases." In short, people don't know the Fourth Commandment. Apparently for Luther it is in the family—and perhaps here alone—that authority can be learned. Here parents have a workable given context for practicing their authority. And above all, here the matrix of love and trustworthiness on the part of the authority figures can be experienced by the children as they learn to live with authority in both its creational and critical functions. For the recalcitrant one, who refuses obedience to valid authority, God's agencies—in extreme cases, the hangman—can by physical power enforce authority anyway. But a man finally delivered to the executioner can hardly be said to have learned to *live* under authority.

But are all such authority figures as "fathers by blood, fathers of a household, and fathers of the nation" inclined to carry out *God's work* with their authority? Or are they, too, tempted to exercise it in their own self-chosen works? Indeed they are so tempted, and they do succumb. So Luther devotes his concluding paragraphs to that very problem. He does not conclude on a very cheerful note. Indeed the whole kingdom of God's left hand by itself does not conclude cheerfully either. Any order, when populated by sinners, will not balance out to be total good news. Nevertheless a family can function well as God's left-hand agency without any Gospel or Gospel-trusting people in it. But what happens when Christ's people are present in a particular family? That we must yet examine.

Is There a "Christian" Family?

God's redemptive purposes, His right-hand work, realized in the cross and resurrection of Christ, are much less patent than the worldwide operations of the divine left hand. But they are not inoperative in, with, and under the orders of the left hand. Yet they operate only when they are concretely inserted by some agent for God's right hand. For wherever there stands a Christian — in family, marriage, economic, or political "order" — there God's right-hand kingdom has its agent present. It authorizes him to operate right within the contours of the orders of the other hand. A Christian uses his left-hand kingdom station — the factual placement and concrete linkage with people that are given him — as the platform for initiating and, if it has already been begun in the person he is linked with, for continuing *the new order of God's own love and forgiveness.* In short, he injects Christ into the operating creational-critical order and assists God in generating the new creation at that very spot.

Consequently for Luther one must be careful in talking about a "Christian" family. As family it is God's left-hand kingdom work. It is, as it were, "non-Christic." When Christ has become "all in all," the "natural" family will have passed away. What Luther can comprehend under the combined terms of "Christian" and "family" is one or more Christians bound to one another in the natural order of a family. But then, strictly speaking, what is on the scene is not a new kind of family, but the operational body of Christ, the new creation, the new order of God's love and forgiveness. This new order uses the interpersonal linkage which this particular family configuration (an old order) provides, but uses it ultimately for nonfamily purposes — for tying people into Jesus Christ, and thereby tying them into the family of their heavenly Father.

There are no resources in the normal family "order" for doing this. The only resources anywhere are the means of grace that come from the Lord of the cross and of the empty tomb. So the only necessary perceptible difference between a family where Christians are present and one where they are not is this: In the former the

Gospel will be "happening," Jesus Christ will be talked about and commended to family members and His forgiveness exchanged, even as the normal critical operations of the parent-child vocations expose the sinner still functioning in the other member. That is the only palpable difference that Luther would see as necessarily present in a "Christian family." He would expect, as does Christ, that the exchanged forgiveness would work to "subvert" other facets of family operations. but even if this subversion were scarcely palpable, the new creation is there in that particular order of the old creation. It is there because Christ is there, insofar as even one or two (or more) are gathered at that placement *in His name,* naming Him as Lord and talking His name to one another.

CONCLUSIONS

1. In Reformation theology the family is seen to be the work of God, related to, yet distinct from, God's final word and work in the Gospel. In the distinction between Law and Gospel, between God's kingdom of the left-hand and kingdom of the right hand, the family always belongs to the former.

2. The family is the primordial agency for God's placing a human being into His creation, and doing so with specific concretization—temporally, spatially, relationally. In this placement (order) the individual is given his station (*Stand*) and is called to work *(Beruf)*.

3. The work of God to be carried out in these placements (the family is only one of the many placements every man has) is twofold: God's continuing *creational care* and His *criticism of sinners.*

4. The inscrutable character of this circle of creation and criticism is resolved in the cross and resurrection of Jesus, God's right-hand Man, through whom God trumps the twofold work of His own left hand.

5. The right-hand work of God in Christ brings a new order and structure into the old orders of the creation. This new order is the order of God's Gospel of love and forgiveness. The important element in this new order is Christ, the Head of the body, from whom the whole structure lives and grows. The Gospel lifts life to a new order.

6. In this new order, as in the old ones, God's agents for His operations are people. The operations differ by virtue of what the agents are administering, whether God's law or God's Christ.

7. Because of the very character of God's right-hand operation, the orders of God's old creation are relegated to penultimate, provisional, makeshift significance. They are components of "the form of this world," which by God's own new action in Christ "is passing away."

8. When the grace of Christ operates in a person whose placement is in the family order, he is not only being supported in fulfilling the work of this order, but is also ultimately subverting the very order itself. This "subversion" begins when the Gospel is operative, and it comes to completion with the consummation of all things in eternal life.

9. For Luther the word "father," when applied to God, evokes both the image of authority (for God's creational and critical work) and the image of forgiveness (God's action in Christ trumping judgment with mercy).

10. Luther's exposition of the Fourth Commandment in the catechisms illustrates many of these theses.

11. Any Lutheran discussion of the "Christian family" must reckon with the fact that these two words are on opposite sides of the line that distinguishes God's two kingdoms.

NOTES – CHAPTER 5

1. Curiously enough, much of the secondary literature on the *family* in Reformation thought neglects to draw the picture in relation to the specific impact of the Gospel in Reformation theology. In addition, the family is often actually relegated to secondary consideration while the subjects of marriage and sexuality dominate the discussion. This is true, e. g., of the chapter, "Reformation Perspectives on Family Issues," in Roy W. Fairchild and John Charles Wynn, *Families in the Church: A Protestant Survey* (New York: Association Press, 1961), and even of William H. Lazareth's *Luther on the Christian Home* (Philadelphia: Muhlenberg Press, 1960). An exception to this is Helmut Begemann, *Strukturwandel der Familie* (Hamburg: Furche Verlag, 1960), who draws on Luther's "two regime" view of God's actions to analyze what happens in human family structures. Central for the perspective on Luther reflected in this chapter are the works of Werner Elert, *The Structure of Lutheranism* (St. Louis: Concordia, 1962), pp. 59 ff., and *The Christian Ethos* (Philadelphia: Muhlenberg, 1957), pp. 81 ff.

2. The twofold function of God's law: preserving and continuing creation while at the same time exercising the divine criticism upon it, represents Luther's

standard exegesis whenever he addresses the subject. Yet both of these functions of the Law are distinguished from the novel function of God's Gospel. See, e.g., his commentary on Galatians in *Luther's Works* (St. Louis: Concordia Publishing House, 1963 and 1964), Vols. 26 and 27, passim. A concise summary both of the Law's twofold function and the Gospel's alternative is Werner Elert, *Law and Gospel*, (Philadelphia: Fortress, 1967).

3. The extensiveness of the territory covered by the term "Law" in Luther's theology is documented by Gerhard Ebeling in his *Word and Faith* (Philadelphia: Fortress Press, 1963), pp. 391 ff.

4. From the explanation of the First Article of the Apostles' Creed in the Small Catechism. *The Book of Concord*, ed. Theodore G. Tappert (Philadelphia: Muhlenberg, 1959), p. 345. – Cf. Werner Elert, *The Christian Ethos*. In Ch. 3, "The Natural Orders," Elert clarifies the term "orders": "The orders which the Decalog presupposes in its command and prohibitions are orders designated as orders of creation. We belong to them by 'nature' through our creatureliness. In His relation to these orders God is not so much a lawgiver as a creator and ruler. The term 'order,' however, is somewhat ambiguous and requires clarification before we continue to use it" (p. 77). "The order of creation is not a product of the creative but the regulative activity of God, it is existential situation." (P. 78)

5. Ibid., pp. 379 ff., 411 ff.

6. Ibid., pp. 37 – 38.

7. See Elert's treatment of the orders in Luther's ethics, *The Christian Ethos*, pp. 77 – 81.

8. It may well be that Luther did not enunciate this as clearly as we historically conscious moderns would wish to have it. Nevertheless Luther has no theological investment to protect by denying the mutability of the orders. See the section "Die Familie" in Elert's as yet untranslated Vol. II of *Morphologie des Luthertums* (Munich, 1953), pp. 80 – 124. *(The Structure of Lutheranism* referred to in n. 1 is Vol. I.)

9. See the recent work by Bernhard Lohse, *Mönchtum und Reformation: Luthers Auseinandersetzung mit dem Mönchsideal des Mittelalters*, (Göttingen, 1963).

10. Tappert, pp. 380 ff.

11. Ibid., pp. 51 f., 239 ff., and passim.

12. Elert, *Ethos*, pp. 81 ff.

13. Tappert, p. 112.

14. This is the way Luther regularly preaches on this text, the standard Epistle for Trinity Sunday. See, e.g., St. Louis edition of *Luthers Sämmtliche Schriften* (1883), XII, 637.

15. Luther's two-kingdom teaching is very likely the most debated item in recent Luther scholarship. The view taken in this chapter is that of Elert, *Ethos*, pp. 289 ff., of Ebeling, pp. 386 – 406 ("The Necessity of the Doctrine of the Two Kingdoms"), and most recently of Ulrich Asendorf, "Die Lehre von den beiden Reichen und die Theologie der Revolution," in *Jahrbuch des Martin Luther Bundes*, ed. Johannes Schulze (Erlangen & Rothenburg ob der Tauber: Martin Luther Verlag, 1969), pp. 34 – 51. Spokesmen for a considerably different view of Luther's teaching on the two kingdoms are, e. g., E. Wolf and J. Heckel.

16. See Ulrich Asendorf, *Eschatologie bei Luther* (Göttingen, 1967). See also Begemann, Ch. 7.

17. See Elert's treatment of "The Order of Love and Forgiveness," *Ethos*, pp. 345 ff.

18. The author here is using "subvert" not in the modern, negative sense. From the human point of view we may use the terms "convert" or "turn around." The

Gospel takes over as the ethos of the person living under God's grace. This is imperfect in this life; it comes to perfection only at the consummation of God's eternal plan. (The editor)

19. *Luther's Works,* 26, 164.

20. See. e. g., Luther's sermonic exegesis of John 14:21 ("He who loves Me will be loved by My Father"), *Luther's Works,* 24, 145 ff.

21. All the citations in this section are from Tappert, pp. 379—89.

22. Tappert, p. 384.

23. Fairchild and Wynn (p. 6) reflect this thought, although they do not reflect Luther's two-kingdom theology, as we have sought to do in this chapter, when they say: "In its own distinct way, the family serves as an educational institution without peer throughout our culture. It is indeed, as Martin Luther named it, 'a school for living.' But the educational process of the home is seldom instruction as such; it is nearly always in terms of nurture. The home specializes in informal education. The nurturing process is found in the ordinary daily life of the home. It begins with supplying the baby's physical needs, and continues as members of the family communicate their way of life, their bases for making decisions, and their interpretation of values. It is here, in fact, that the rudimentary beginnings of faith are to be located: an understanding of what love is, of forgiveness, of relationships with persons, and gradually a relationship with God. These grow out of home life."

CHAPTER 6

Family Relations in North America

HERBERT T. MAYER

Family structures do not change abruptly. We always carry much of the past into the present and on into the future. Thus the spiritual, social, economic, and political patterns of the Middle Ages moved into the Reformation period. Similarly Roman Catholic, Reformed, and Lutheran traditions were transferred from the European homeland to the new American frontier. Church doctrine and tradition played an important role in maintaining old patterns and in adjusting to new developments in American family life.

Patterns of authority and responsibility in American family life are surprisingly complex. On first impression it may appear that the story can be told very simply, namely, that family life in America changed from a strong patriarchal pattern to a more democratic equalitarian pattern from the beginning of the 17th century to the middle of the 20th century. However, there are too many significant variants to permit us to be content with such a simple summary. We shall, therefore, in this chapter deal especially with three historical periods: from approximately 1600 to 1790, from 1790 through 1865, and from 1865 to the close of World War II.

Three factors helped to determine family patterns in early American life. One of these was the sometimes complex inheritance from the medieval age handed down from generation to generation and brought by emigrants from Europe to America. The second factor was the transition from feudal landlordism to industrial capitalism. And the third was the influence of the American frontier and its new independence on family living. These are not dissimilar from the three concomitant social structures related to the 17th and 18th centuries, namely, the dominance of the organized church on the entire Christian community, the close relationship between landowner and family inheritance, and the extension of commerce due to the development of industry beyond the confines of the home and family.[1]

Many historians see in this change a shift from mutual person-to-person concern and service to greater individualism and the development of a strong profit motive. As capitalism increased, human values declined. Some indicate that during this period family control passed from a dominant church-centered ethos to a dominant society-centered ethos. Marriage, once under the full control of the church, became more related to political authority and responsibility. (Some attribute this to a misunderstanding of Luther's teaching on marriage.) Thus, for instance, the civil marriage act of 1563 in England, which forbade the church to have anything to do with marriage rites, was reflected in the New England colonies. It was not until 1773 that Rhode Island gave ministers permission to perform weddings.[2]

Puritan theology dominated the culture of colonial New England, and preachers were not slow to remind feminine hearers of their place of inferiority. Yet this was not so exclusive that there were not also sermons which advised husbands to revere, respect, and show affection for wives and daughters. So while the austerity seemed to be clearly voiced, it was modified to a degree with admonitions to Christian love and mutual service. Historians see the Puritan influence as a more or less direct derivation from the emphasis on piety and the church-dominated civil righteousness found in John Calvin's concept of the church-state.[3]

The American frontier also played a significant role. Frontier life is largely antisocial. The resourcefulness and strength of the individual take precedence over the role of and responsibility to the social group. In another sense family solidarity was certainly strengthened by the frontier, where the whole family was united in making a living and in self-defense against all of its foes.

FROM DISCOVERY TO THE REVOLUTION

In the New England colonies (Massachusetts, Connecticut, Rhode Island, New Hampshire, Maine), founded by the Pilgrim Fathers and the Puritans, controlling of wives by husbands and of children by wives was the order of the day. The husband and father considered himself responsible for the entire household. There were examples of mercenary marriages and, as late as 1756, Connecticut recognized the right of parents to choose mates for their children. These general attitudes were reflected in family structure, authority, and homelife.

There was a strong reliance on Mosaic laws. Following the norms of the Church of England, divorce statutes did not exist in many states. Goodsell summarizes this period as follows:

> The first settlers made every attempt to safeguard the institution of matrimony and to prevent thoughtless persons from entering into the contract carelessly and without due formality. Parental consent, given to the town or county clerk personally or in writing, was everywhere required; due notice of the marriage by banns or posting or, in default of banns, by license from the Governor, was demanded in all the colonies; the solemnization of marriage was regulated by law; and, finally, registration of the marriage in town or county clerk's office, or, in colonies where the Church of England was established, by the parish clerk, was a universal requirement.[4]

There was austerity on the frontier, but it was not divorced from genuine attachment and love between husband and wife. John Winthrop refers to his mate as "my deare, my chief love in this world, my sweet wife," and Cotton Mather's description of the last hours at the bedside of his dying wife makes most evident the mutual love and deep affection that must have prevailed in the family.[5]

With regard to the place of children, they were to be seen, not heard, and home discipline was stern and arbitrary, compelling obedience and submission. Once again also the opposite is evident in Cotton Mather, who gave this view of child training: "I first beget in them a high opinion of their father's love to them, and of his being best able to judge what is good for them . . . My word must be their law . . . . I would never come to give a child a blow except in cases of obstinacy or some gross enormity." [6]

The middle colonies (New York, New Jersey, Pennsylvania, Delaware) had a more heterogenous population with a strong mixture of Dutch, German, and Scotch-Irish immigrants whose family life was a bit more independent and free. Women and children were more fully educated. Washington Irving's stories provide vivid and accurate portraits of the husband-wife relationships in the Dutch colonies. Greater freedom was given older children, as well as the right to seek their own life's partners. One writer says that an extreme affection obtained between parents and offspring, that marriage was always very early, and very often happy.

Among the Germans in Pennsylvania home discipline was rigid. Children received diligent home training. They were taught early in life to work, especially to learn trades. The practice of binding children out to service so that they might learn trades was followed quite generally in Old Germantown, Pa. Parents loved their home and children and made homelife attractive.[7] The Swedes in Delaware brought along a similar family tradition, as did also the Norwegian immigrants who settled in the Midwest during the 19th century.

The story is somewhat different in the Southern colonies (Virginia, Maryland, North and South Carolina, Georgia). Life was influenced by French and English traditions. The larger plantations tended to develop the patriarchal family clan and a degree of aristocracy. Agricultural and climactic situations fostered something like European feudal patterns. Some historians have compared the Southern family to the old Roman *familia,* since the landowning family played the dominant role in the South. The education of Southern women was in some cases excellent, and their role in society was strong.[8]

In the colonies children were carefully educated in the catechism and were very early familiarized with the ritual of the church. Religious groups, such as the Society of Friends, enjoined upon all parents the painstaking education of their offspring in the principles of morality and religion. This training was most severe among the Puritans of New England. Cotton Mather was highly critical of the harsh methods of the schoolmasters.[9]

The theory of marriage as a civil contract prevailed. Marriages were usually solemnized by civil magistrates. No divorces or legal separations were granted in the Southern colonies throughout the colonial period.[10] The canons and rules of the English and European churches were respected with regard to marriage and divorce.

The family in 18th-century Virginia continued to be patriarchal, with a strain of English aristocracy that continued into and beyond the American Revolution. In South Carolina marriages were preceded by financial and property settlements properly drawn up and by the publishing of banns. The Salzburgers of Ebenezer, Ga., wrote to their homeland asking for unmarried women with a genuine fear of God and an exceptionally honest life. Among most of the colonists the family altar was the means of giving Christian nurture to the children. Religion had a profound influence in the Southern colonies; most families had and used the Bible.[11]

Thus a number of factors contributed to early American family life. Much depended on the economic resources and the religious, physical, mental, emotional, and social contributions brought to the family by the marriage partners. Husbands and wives represented the traditions of the families from which they sprang, carrying forward the patterns they knew as part of their tradition.

FROM THE REVOLUTION TO THE CIVIL WAR

The American Revolution produced some of the social changes associated with war, but on a rather limited scale. Because men were absent from home for military campaigns, a greater responsibility in farm and business management devolved upon women. A democratic spirit was developed by the struggle for independence and by the new freedom set forth in the Declaration of Independence. It also developed a greater sense of responsibility in individuals and families.

After the war there was a growing disposition to grant individuals their rights. Much effort was devoted to developing the new republic and its institutions of free government. This was the new challenge toward nationhood; and families rallied to the challenge of building a distinctly American society out of old traditions from Europe and out of new insights from colonial experiences.

Independence from English rule signified no fundamental change in social life; the colonial tradition passed on unbroken into the folkways of the new American republic. Until the Civil War the population was distinctly rural, and urban sophistication did not penetrate the standards and habits of most of the people. The pioneer spirit was still in its prime. Domesticity was supreme, and the family was the one substantial social institution.[12]

After the Revolution came the westward movement of colonists and of thousands of new immigrants from Ireland, England, Scotland, France, Germany, and the Netherlands. They came for many reasons, some to escape military service, some for the sake of religious freedom, and most of them to build strong families and find new fortunes. Wave upon wave of families moved westward to the Appalachians, to what we now call the central states, to the prairies west of the Mississippi, to the Rocky Mountains, and on to the California and Oregon coasts.

The influence of the frontier increased noticeably during the great move to the West. Early marriages and large families were the rule. Grandmothers in their thirties were not uncommon. In the Ohio Territory anyone willing to work hard could establish ownership of 100 acres in three or four years and thus economically establish his own family. According to Calhoun, the whole weight of the frontier freedom conspired with the modernist individualism imported from Europe to effect that family disintegration, whose later phenomena are so conspicuous today.[13]

On the frontier the woman could scarcely get along without a partner. The wife was valuable for her labor and companionship, serving also as the mother of numerous sturdy workers. There was an abundance of unoccupied land, and the pioneers found large families desirable. Marriage was early, with the church teaching a patriarchal family pattern as God's ordinance.[14]

The New Frontier Life

Frontier life called for greater participation on the part of women in tilling the land and building houses. This led to greater democratization of family life. Affection replaced money as the chief consideration in the choice of a mate. Social rank was considered of less importance than among European forebears. Both women and children enjoyed higher social status. This helped children achieve greater self-reliance and emotional maturity. All this led to a sense of greater familial partnership. The trek to the Midwest and Far West brought many hardships and called for new sacrifices by men, women, and children. It also meant isolation from relatives and greater self-dependence as families occupied or acquired new land (homesteading). The challenge and conquest of the new frontier developed greater equality between man and wife.[15]

European observers of American life in the first half of the 19th century were impressed with the freedom accorded children and with the surprising maturity they evidenced. Calhoun explains that this is an inevitable development in a land where resources are far greater than population. "In a new world, men face the future and worship, not ancestors, but posterity." [16] He also maintains that by its very nature political democracy must emphasize the importance of the individual rather than the family. Most historians see a direct connection between a democratic political structure and the democratizing of the family structure.

Patriarchalism and Women's Rights

Various family structures ranging from the patriarchal to the democratic and equalitarian have continued to coexist through various periods of history to our modern times. But they have done so in diverse ratios or degrees as the authoritarian pattern declined and the partnership patterns increased. In all of these periods we must not assume a lack of respect and love between husbands and wives and between parents and children. Thus Calhoun asserts that by the time of the American Revolution man was taught by experience "to understand aright the reverence due to the nobleness, the purity, the gentleness of woman. He was learning to accord his wife the unstinted and sincere homage that her character deserved." Chivalry was taught in the home and in the schools.[17]

The growing disposition to grant each individual his rights grew naturally out of the political doctrine that "all men are created equal." General education for all children, girls as well as boys, in elementary schools as well as high schools, led to the founding of the first women's colleges (Oberlin in 1833; Mount Holyoke in 1837). The women's movement of 1840 had as its aims legal rights for women, higher education, full political rights, and marriage as an equal and permanent partnership. Already at the opening of the Civil War a dozen states had given wives the legal right to own and manage property.[18] Suffrage was granted to all women in the United States by the passage of the 19th amendment to the Constitution in 1920. But voting rights had been granted to women by some states much earlier, for instance, Wyoming in 1869, Utah in 1870.

In the post-Revolution period the American family was a closely knit institution holding its members together by economic, legal, and religious bonds, as well as those of affection and authority. Still patriarchal in type, the family was governed by the husband and father, whose power over wife and children was not yet challenged. Law, religion, and public opinion united in support of father-power; and unquestionably this centralization of authority in the father was a factor in maintaining family solidarity. However, this power was undermined by a number of factors, such as the extension of the frontier farther and farther into the wilderness of the West, the rapid development of machine industry, the powerful influence of liberalism and democratic ideas, and the weakening of dogmatic religion.[19]

FROM THE CIVIL WAR TO THE WORLD WARS

The war between the Northern and the Southern states over the question of slavery brought sharp separations of opinion which also involved families and a whole social system. Church bodies as well as political communities split over the slavery-freedom question. Negro families, both free and slave, bore the brunt of this social conflict. Chapter 8 of this study includes a summary of the structure, roles, and relationships of the Negro family then and now.

Various observers of the American scene from 1860 to 1960 give us their impressions of the family. Philip Schaff in 1855 observed that family devotions and the observance of the Sabbath were almost universal in America.[20] Alexis de Tocqueville in *Democracy in the Family* writes: "The father exercises no other power than that which is granted to the affection and experience of age; his orders would perhaps be disobeyed, but his advice is for the most part authoritative." [21]

In 1887 Samuel W. Dike in *Perils to the Family* spoke of the home turning over its former work to the shop, the school, and the church. He reported that new emphases, tending to weaken the family structure, were appearing in print. Clergy and church were referred to as moral guardians of the family.[22]

Writing in 1905, Frank N. Hagar in his book *The American Family: A Sociological Problem* expressed the opinion that "for over 200 years in the colonies and the early republic no essential weakening or impairment or degeneracy of the family appear." [23] A German writer, George von Skal, in 1907 stated that he discovered in America greater recognition of the individual's rights, mutual love and respect, and the expectation of honest obedience, not as the result of compulsion but of honesty and mutual respect.[24]

Horace Bushnell

New ground was broken in the seminal study by Horace Bushnell entitled *Christian Nurture*.[25] Bushnell spoke of the need for strong parental and paternal roles. He traced the authority of the father to the religious fact that he is the natural and moral image of

God. He includes the mother in the task of making God present to the children.

In his chapter on "Family Government" Bushnell speaks of the home as "a little primary bishopric under the father," a domestic state "where love has authority, and presides in the beneficent order of law." He refers to family government as a "vice-regent authority, set up by God." "The parents are to fill, in this manner, an office strictly religious; personating God in the child's feeling and conscience, and binding it, thus, to what, without any misnomer, we call a filial piety." He asserts, "The government will then have a genuine authority and power, because the rule of God is in it."

Regarding the husband-wife relationship he says the unity and harmony between them is a precondition of authority. They are to be "so far entered into the Christian order of marriage, as to fulfill gracefully what belongs to the relation in which they are set, and show them to their children as doing fit honor to each other." He quotes a statement from a treatise on Christian family life: "A wife cannot weaken the authority of the father without undermining her own, for her authority rests on his, and if that of the mother is subordinated to that of the father, yet it is but one authority."

With regard to child guidance Bushnell writes: "For as the law of God is a schoolmaster to bring us to Christ, so there is a like relation between law and liberty in the training of the house." "Punishments should be severe enough to serve their purpose; and gentle enough to show, if possible, a tenderness that is averse from the infliction." "If you assert the law, as you must, then you must have your Gospel to go with it; your pardon judiciously dispensed, your Christian sympathies flowing out in modes of Christian concern, your whole administration tempered by tenderness." [26]

Other Voices from the Churches

The Roman Catholic segments of the population were partly assimilated and partly isolated from the mainstreams of American culture. As a consequence of this, patterns of family authority among Roman Catholics were of various types. Both the "Old Immigration," which had consisted largely of German and Irish families, and the "New Immigration" of Polish and Slovene nationalities were characterized by various types of patriarchal structure. National priests contributed to the continuation of these patterns as they, in many cases, sought to preserve national identity. The administration of canon law, with its restriction of women's rights and its medieval thought, supported European customs of relationships between husband and wife and between parents and children.[27] At midcentury Catholic writers speak about the chaotic condition in family structures, roles, and relationships.

In a textbook prepared for Catholic schools, Edgar Schmiedeler affirms the dominant position of the husband. He writes:

> Down through the centuries the husband and father has been recognized as the head of the family. That is really to say that it is the common view of mankind that he should be the head. That, too, is the view of the great philosopher-theologian of the church, St. Thomas Aquinas. While maintaining the equality of man and woman, of husband and wife, St. Thomas insists that for the proper functioning of the family the wife should be subject to her husband, for here — as in society — without such a leadership the society could not exist and life in it would be burdensome.[28]

While family relations have always been a concern of the churches, it was in the midtwenties of this century that church denominations set up separate family life departments and developed curricular materials for parents, adult study groups, and youth dealing with broad areas of family living. This new interest grew out of concern for the stability of the family and out of a desire for a constructive approach to Christian family living. It intended to meet effectively the many changes affecting the family in the 20th century.

In 1910 a special committee of the Presbyterian General Assembly referred to the decay of family religion in some portions of the church.[29] In 1911 the Federal Council of Churches' committee on family life spoke of the home as the foundation of human welfare and "the place where all that builds up or pulls down in the social order does its final work. . . . Many are coming to see in the home the very crux of the social problem." [30]

It is impossible to identify in this period a representative Protestant position on family authority and responsibility. But a review of some two dozen books and pamphlets prepared by influential Protestant churchmen shows several distinct trends of thought. Some writers endorse the emerging egalitarian marriage structure. Leland Foster Wood, a nationally recognized leader of the Federal Council of Churches in matters of family life, argued that nothing was more likely to make marriage difficult than for one to try to dominate the other, as had been the pattern in the tradition of marriage. "Not dominance and obedience but a common mind is the mode of cooperation for mates." [31]

Wood urged that children be given a new place in the family circle, saying, "The family is a natural group in which each member is to be in the center at times." He said that the other side of the commandment, "Thou shalt honor thy father and thy mother," calls on parents to "reverence the developing personality of your children." [32] Many churches espoused the establishment of the family council as a means of developing good parent-child relationships. The insights of psychology as well as fellowship in Christ were being recognized.[33]

Several writers emphasized the importance of discipline and parental authority in the home. Mark Fakkema, representing the evangelical strain, urged a strong discipline in the home because parents "as responsible guardians, must ever uphold and insist upon [God's righteousness] with compelling urgency." "If you follow the instruction herewith given," he wrote, *"your children will grow up to be obedient children."* He cautioned against the extremes of training by brute force or by giving every possible freedom.[34]

Lutheran theologians in the 19th and first half of the 20th century endorsed a European *paterfamilias* relationship. The wife was subordinate according to the will of God. Her place was in the home. The husband was to love his wife as Christ loved the church (Ephesians 5). Children were to occupy a subordinate place in the family structure, while parental love provided for their upbringing. In marriage the husband obligated himself to provide a home for his wife and to support her. The father's responsibility was to provide for the physical needs, while the mother served as the keeper and maker of the home.[35]

On the subject of family authority and responsibility a General Council (Lutheran) publication in 1899 contained a typical statement: "As the headship of Christ is in God; so the headship of the woman is in the man. As Christ is subordinate to the Father in one sense and yet equal to God at all times; so the woman is subordinate to the man, and is equal to the man. . . . The principle laid down by the apostle is as binding today as it ever was. The married woman is to show in public that she is bound to a husband and that she reverences him. . . . At no time did this headship mean un-limited rule. At no time as a Christian could he dictate that his wife must do the work, while he enjoyed the wages. . . . At no time could he exercise violence upon her person. His will is not to prevail in an arbitrary manner in the household."

With regard to the church's stand on the so-called democratic family, a United Lutheran Church in America publication in 1944 stated that family life has become less autocratic and that home democracy is workable, asserting: "If their love is intelligent, their life one of sharing, and their differences settled by discussion and compromise, they are on the way to the highest type of family order." [36]

In his lecture on Christian ethics (printed in 1897) Gisle Christian Johnsen (1822 – 1894), a Norwegian professor of theology, included in his 10 theses on marriage the following:

> Hence it is necessary that it [marriage] be founded upon mutual love and respect; that the husband and wife conduct themselves in a Christian manner toward each other; that the divine order be preserved wherein the husband is the head of the wife and she his help-mate, the husband not ruling over his wife as a tyrant, and she not attempting to assume a master-role over him. The leveling, controlling and reconciling factor is to be love, mutual love. This love thus manifests itself on the part of both husband and wife in a form which corresponds to the actual objective relationship. On the part of the husband it appears as a *leading love,* which will not lead in a selfish, arbitrary manner, but in the *name of the Lord,* according to His will, to His honor, and on the wife's part, as an *obeying* love, in which she is subject to her husband as unto the Lord, not submitting herself to another person in a cowardly, slavish fear, but under the will of the *Lord* in willing obedience.[37]

The teaching of The American Lutheran Church is summarized in the following paragraphs:

> The husband is to be the head of the household, the wife to be submissive to her husband. Each of these relationships carries with it the overtone "as to the Lord," for the husband is not tyrant over his wife nor does the wife meekly grovel before her husband. The teaching emphasizes the importance of orderly human relations, in which, for the sake of good order there must and can be only one head, the husband.

The church has not taken a stand against the "democratic family," which term does not imply indiscriminate equally divided authority. Through the Commission on Social Relations it accepts the idea of the family partnership in which each member has responsibilities and privileges in relation to his capacities for contributing to the family unity. A paper on "The Family Council," advocating this idea of sharing family experiences and family planning in relation to the growth and maturity of the members, was circulated to all pastors in 1946, and drew only one critical letter in objection to the view taken.[38]

The White House Conferences

Significant for any study of family relationships in this period are the White House Conferences on Children and Youth held between 1909 and 1940. The first (1909) dealt mainly with the physical and material needs of children. The second (1919) devised standards for health, education, and welfare. The third (1930) considered the adjustments of the child to his parents, his brothers and sisters, the community, and society at large. The fourth (1940) focused on the place of the child in a democracy and equipping him for life in a complex world. It said: "Development of spiritual values in the home requires attention; the hope of democracy rests not only on scientific inquiry, technical progress, and social organization, but above all upon personal and social integrity."

A keynote of the conference with regard to family life and the child was expressed as follows:

> The vast majority of children are members of families. Their world opens up in a family, and they continue to spend most of the hours of the day in or about the home, even after school and playmates have begun to claim a large place in their thoughts and activities. Home and family are the first condition of life for the child. They are first in importance in his growth, development, and education.[39]

A Sociologist's View

M. C. Elmer calls attention to the extension of modern education to roughly 20 years, and to the fact that the child cannot be broken up into parts with various agencies responsible for various parts. The family must be the integrating agent. He writes: "The continual acceptance of religious beliefs which embody the family's ethical principles and philosophy of life lends tone and direction to the practices of the family and makes it a most important factor in social control." And this he considers all the more necessary as more and more functions of the family are taken over by the community.[40]

In the economic depression of the 1930s, in World War II, and since then the oft raised question has been: Is the family disorganizing? Elmer says:

> The family is not being disorganized. We are just entering a period of social development when the family is being reorganized on the basis of a new set of social values. Instead of economic activity, ownership of flocks and herds, occupation or titles, political prestige or genealogical facts or fabrication, mutual affection and sympathetic understanding are becoming the basis of family organization.[41]

By mid-20th century American family life had become strongly wife-and-mother-centered and child-oriented. The child had a more favorable place. But he was too often left without adequate guidance in moral and spiritual matters so important to personal integrity.

As the families moved to the cities in rapidly growing numbers and as fathers and children, and in many cases also mothers, were separated from each other for 10 or more hours per day, family structures were radically altered. The authority of the father declined rapidly. A decidedly more democratic pattern began to emerge as a viable option.[42]

Elmer observes that the demand for the elimination of child labor did not make adequate provision for the years between childhood and maturity, and that families assumed that schools, churches, and other agencies were taking care of certain aspects of the child's education. The result was a lessening of family responsibility for children. Other agencies stepped into the breach, many a one of which "failed to recognize that it represented merely one of the many spires on the structure of which the family and its members constituted the base." [43]

Shift of Emphasis

Between World War I and World War II scholars shifted the emphasis from biological and historical origins to functions the family must perform in society, especially the psychological and sociological functions. Many spokesmen expressed strong misgivings as to whether families can perform their indispensable functions without religious and moral fortifications. "The principal function of the family," says one authority, "will remain the rearing of children, *for their own sake!*" [44]

In the past the family as an economic unit was needed to operate the farm, the workshop, the business. Success depended on the solidarity of the family. The headship of the father was needed as manager. To some degree even in the modern family this is still the case. Therefore Max Horkheimer writes:

> In spite of these important changes, the moral and religious ideas, the spiritual images, derived from the structure of the patriarchal family still constitutes the core of our culture. Respect for law and order in the state appears to be inseparably tied to the respect of children for their elders. Emotions, attitudes, and beliefs rooted in the family account for the coherence of our system of culture. They form an element of social cement. It appears to be imperative that society keep them alive, for it is a question of the life and death of civilization in its present form. The idea of the nation has not been able to fulfill the functions of the family in this respect. [45]

Thus the Judeo-Christian family traditions with some modifications continued to be dominant through three millennia until we come to recent times. The events marking the first half of the 20th century—two world wars, an economic depression, the advent of the scientific age, and developments in industrialization and urbanization—account for the greatest changes, both in theory and practice, regarding marital and family roles, relationships, and authority patterns. From his present vantage point the historian cannot predict what new patterns are apt to be dominant in the future.

CONCLUSIONS

1. Patterns of authority and responsibility in American families have been largely determined by folkways inherited from the past and by economic and political developments. Economic changes have altered certain functions of the family, while democratic influences have altered modes of operation.

2. The Puritan ethic furnished the most important religious motivation for family structures for most of our period. This approach emphasized the dominant role of the husband and saw the Bible primarily as a book of rules and regulations.

3. Both in husband-wife and parent-child relations some degree of authoritarianism existed. But we must also conclude from the record that love and affection were taught and expressed. "If you assert the Law . . . you must have your Gospel to go with it." Moreover, the frontier helped to develop a family partnership.

4. The 20th century witnessed the extensive transfer of traditional family responsibilities and activities to other social agencies.

5. Roman Catholic, Protestant, and Lutheran churches emphasized a patrocentric structure and the subordinate position of the wife and children. The Roman Catholic views were shaped by the principles of canon law. Protestant and Lutheran theologians drew largely on the statements of the New Testament. The churches' teachings often exhorted the husband to love and cherish the wife, and urged both husband and wife to bring up their children in an atmosphere of discipline combined with affection. Support for more egalitarian husband-wife relationships and child-centered structures began to appear in Protestant circles.

6. The teachings of the churches have probably been understood by their members in the light of their own family traditions. A husband from a strong *paterfamilias* tradition found in the churches' statements warrant for a strong assertion of his domination of wife and children and vice versa.

7. In general the churches during this long period favored the existing patterns in the family. In the period prior to World War II they had little to say about actually adjusting to meet new needs and new family problems.

8. Various family structures from the patriarchal to the democratic and equalitarian have continued to coexist through 300 years in America, with the partnership type becoming more and more accepted. The moral, spiritual, and economic outlook and the background and resources each mate brought to the marriage determined family structures, roles, and relationships.

NOTES—CHAPTER 6

1. The best general history of American family life is Arthur W. Calhoun, *A Social History of the American Family,* 3 vols. (New York: Barnes and Noble, 1917, paperback ed., 1960)—hereafter cited as Calhoun, *History.* See also Willystine Goodsell, *A History of Marriage and the Family* (New York: Macmillan, 1934), Chs. 9—13.

2. Andrew G. Truxal and Francis E. Merrill, *The Family in American Culture* (New York: Prentice-Hall, 1947), p. 61. For a detailed study of the importance of church-state relations in the area of marriage, see George Elliott Howard, *A History of Matrimonial Institutions,* 3 vols. (Chicago: University of Chicago Press, 1904), II, 121 – 37.

3. Mary Sumner Benson, *Women in Eighteenth-Century America: A Study of Opinion and Social Usage* (New York: Columbia University Press, 1935), pp. 104 – 106, 122 – 24, 223 – 24; Bernhard J. Stern, *The Family, Past and Present* (New York: Appleton-Century Co., Inc., 1938), p. 186; Perry Miller and Thomas W. Johnson, *The Puritans* (New York: Harper, paperback), Ch. 1.

4. Goodsell, pp. 367, 391, 355 – 427.

5. Ray E. Baber, *Marriage and the Family* (New York: McGraw-Hill, 1939), pp. 91 – 112; M. F. Nimkoff, *The Family* (Boston: Houghton Mifflin Co., 1934), pp. 160 – 78; Joseph K. Folsom, *The Family and Democratic Society* (New York: John Wiley and Sons, 1947), pp. 116 – 44.

6. Calhoun, *History,* I, 109, 113 – 14.

7. Ibid., p. 203.

8. Arthur W. Calhoun, "The Early American Family," *The Annals of the American Academy of Political and Social Science,* clx 1932, pp. 7 – 12.

9. Goodsell, pp. 414 – 15.

10. Ibid., p. 395.

11. Calhoun, *History,* I, 252, 281; II, 331 – 34.

12. Calhoun, *History,* II, 11.

13. Ibid., p. 28.

14. Ibid., pp. 11 – 15, 68.

15. M. F. Nimkoff, *The Family* (Boston: Houghton Mifflin Co., 1934), Ch. 5: "The Modern American Family," pp. 179 – 83.

16. Calhoun, *History,* II, 51 ff.

17. Calhoun, *History,* I, 275, 282.

18. Goodsell, pp. 461 – 69.

19. Ibid., pp. 457 – 58.

20. Calhoun, *History,* II, 463 – 64.

21. De Tocqueville, *Democracy in the Family* (Century Co., 1898), II, 241.

22. Calhoun, III, 171, 283.

23. Ibid., p. 165.

24. Ibid., pp. 170 – 71.

25. Horace Bushnell, *Christian Nurture* (New Haven: Yale University Press, originally developed in 1847; reprinted in 1947 with an introduction by Luther A. Weigle, Sterling Professor of Religious Education). Available also in a 1966 paperback.

26. The quotations in the above paragraphs may be found on pp. 269 – 73, 276, 280, 285, and 288 of the 1947 reprinting.

27. John L. Thomas, *The American Catholic Family* (Englewood Cliffs, N.J.: Prentice-Hall, Inc., 1956), pp. 108 – 147; H. A. Ayrinhac, *Marriage Legislation in the New Code of Canon Law,* rev. by P. J. Lydon (New York: Bentziger

Bros., Inc., 1949), pp. 10 – 11; Alphonse H. Clemens, *Marriage and the Family: An Integrated Approach for Catholics* (Englewood Cliffs, N. J.: Prentice-Hall, Inc., 1957), pp. 74 – 75.

28. Edgar Schmiedeler, *Marriage and the Family* (New York: McGraw-Hill Book Co., Inc., 1946), p. 115.

29. Calhoun, III, p. 315.

30. Ibid., pp. 309 – 10.

31. Leland Foster Wood, *Growing Together in the Family* (New York: Abingdon-Cokesbury Press, 1935), pp. 22, 99, 71 – 73. Similar views are to be found in two 1935 publications of the Federal Council of Churches: *Building the Christian Family, A Program for the Churches* and *Safeguarding Marriages.*

32. Wood, pp. 71 – 73.

33. Joe W. Burton, *The Church and Family Life* (Nashville: Broadman Press, 1948), p. 16.

34. Mark Fakkema, *How to Teach Obedience* (Chicago: National Association of Christian Schools, 1947), pp. 5, 8 – 9, 12, 14, 17.

35. August R. Suelflow, "Research Summaries," prepared for this study; based on "Documents and Manuscripts of The Lutheran Church – Missouri Synod" (St. Louis: Board of Parish Education, The Lutheran Church – Missouri Synod, 1953), unpublished report.

36. "Research Summaries" (unpublished report, 1953), prepared for this study by Harold J. Maleske. The General Council was one of the Lutheran bodies combined into the United Lutheran Church in America in 1918.

37. "Research Summaries" (unpublished report, 1953), prepared for this study by Prof. G. M. Bruce of the (Norwegian) Evangelical Lutheran Church.

38. "Research Summaries" (unpublished report, 1953), prepared for this study by Carl F. Reuss, executive director of the Commission on Research and Social Action of The American Lutheran Church.

39. M. C. Elmer, *Sociology of the Family* (Boston: Ginn and Co., 1945), pp. 504 – 05.

40. Ibid., Ch. 7: "The Family and Religion," pp. 109, 212.

41. Ibid., pp. 227 – 28.

42. Ibid., pp. 250, 504 – 508.

43. Ibid., pp. 506 – 508.

44. N. W. Foote, *Encyclopaedia Britannica*, 1960, IX, 63.

45. Max Horkheimer in Ch. 18, "Authoritarianism and the Family Today," of *The Family: Its Function and Destiny,* ed. Ruth Nanda Anshen (New York: Harper & Bros., 1949), p. 361.

CHAPTER 7

The American Family in the Midst of Socioeconomic-Technological Change

ROSS P. SCHERER

Previous chapters covered eras in which both societies and families were closely related under the aegis of the church. Such societies, particularly in the period preceding the Renaissance and Reformation, tended to be static, directed to the past, and family-like in their structures. A person's age and sex pretty much determined his roles and spheres of responsibility. We now turn to the modern period when the economic, political, and intellectual sectors became autonomous from the church, and when religious life and organization itself became pluralistic. The family, in turn, also changed to accord with the needs of the new society. During the great medieval period the church tended to question and to slow down the changes which were to produce the new urban industrial society. Generally speaking, as mankind moved into the modern scientific age, the influence of religion was, at worst, a kind of rearguard action; at best, it not only contributed to the formation of the new order but was also a factor in lessening the human costs of industrial change.

The theme of this chapter is that the parallel development of modern industry, modern cities and metropolitan areas, complex organizations and bureaucracies, and new forms of everyday logic and belief produced a modern social order which in turn demanded a new kind of family to be compatible with it. These processes of industrialization, urbanization, bureaucratization,[1] and ideological change are not radically different in Europe or the rest of the developing world; however, the United States development appears to be the most advanced. The family in the U. S. thus became adapted to the needs of the new "open" society, with concomitant shifts in the patterns of mate selection, authority structure, role for women, the character ideal for children, and husband-wife relationships. About a generation ago Ernest Burgess summarized all this in designating the change as one "from familism to individualism." [2] Burgess cautioned that the process of shift is seldom complete in any one place, since "familism" and "individualism" are "ideal" or exaggerated types. Pure familism (the subordination of personal interests to the values and demands of the family), in fact, seems to exist in very few places—it did exist in precommunist China. Similarly pure individualism is found perhaps only in a colony of "hippies," if such an enterprise really exists for very long. Nevertheless, as a society we have moved from a position somewhere short of familism to a present position somewhere short of total individualism. As a matter of fact, the American family shifts from familism to individualism and back again as it goes through various phases in its cycle of aging. In other words, continuity in both society and family demands that the process be mixed, or else we will have no society at all.

Daniel Bell in a recent article poses the dilemma of modern society succinctly:

> The simple and crucial result for the individual is that no longer will any child be able to live in the same kind of world his parents and grandparents inhabited.
>
> For millennia, children retraced the steps of their parents, were initiated into stable ways and ritualized routines, and maintained a basic familiarity with place and family. Today, not only is there a radical rupture with the past, but a child must necessarily be trained for an unknown future. [3]

The break in continuity required by modern society thus poses a tremendous burden for the modern family. It is the source of much modern strain. Yet few today would choose to return to a "pre-industrial society" if it would mean giving up our wonderful mechanical servants, the excitement of being in touch with so many diverse cultures and the consequent new learnings, and the new possibilities for total honesty and openness. Thus, though the new society presents problems and strains, it also presents new opportunities. The family, while exhibiting many symptoms of strain, also demonstrates remarkable resilience as it continues to perform various functions essential to both the corporate and individual needs of mankind. Many writers have pointed to the removal of certain non-core functions of the family with industrialization. However, it is difficult to imagine the removal from the family of those functions which have to do with man's biological phasing, as childbearing, socialization or child-rearing, basic personal maintenance, and aging or maturing. In other words, the requirements of population replacement, the helplessness of the immature, the existence of sex and maleness and femaleness, and the transmission of the heritage all require something like the family, even though the form itself may change.

Thus the residual and unique contributions of the family in society appear to be certain old ones: reproduction of new human beings, fitting such human beings to take their places in society, daily physical maintenance — feeding, clothing, sheltering, equipping — and a new one: daily supporting and restoring individuals psychologically by means of primary group life.[4]

While the gratifying-restoring function must always have been present, it looms much larger in modern society with its impersonality and with the removal of the functions of economic production, education, and even religious training. While the family finds it difficult within itself to bridge the gaps of racial and class diversity, it does incorporate within itself persons of different sex and age, and so provides some healing of the gender and generational gaps. For many parents, having children is the equivalent of taking dozens of courses in continuing education, even into old age. In all this the hardest task parents have is preparing their children for their own self-actualizations, for making their own marks in a world whose next frontier is outer space.

The shift from a medieval to a modern social order has been variously described. We could say that we have moved from a society which was manually powered, local, seniority-based, traditional, and familistic to one which increasingly is technological, industrial, cosmopolitan-total, achievement-based, rational-scientific, individualistic, and bureaucratic in nature.

The rest of the chapter will examine these major determinants of the modern social order in more detail, particularly in relation to family structure and process. The current chapter, for simplification, will relate the discussion to the middle-class suburban family in the U. S., since this is the model most normative for the

U. S. and is the one assumed in the mass media. It seems to be especially characteristic of America with its stress on equality, optimism, future orientation, and activism.

Technological and Industrial Change

It is difficult to consider the rise of modern industry apart from its technology. Undoubtedly much of industrial development has been pragmatic and the result of chance insight, even though these uninformed individual decisions have led to what is now our modern industrial "system." Some writers argue that the story of modern industry is the story of its technology, although the roles of the modern economic market, motivation and belief, and organizational genius must also have been indispensable in the emergence of the modern order. Some have pointed to the compounding nature of inventions, whereby inventions breed inventions. A fuller history of a changing technology would have to include changes in energy sources, processing and handling by machines, transportation and communications, calculating and computing devices, and use of various "mechanical servants."

The Industrial Revolution is said to have begun in England in the textile field roughly around 1750 [5] and was later imported to the U. S. The major consequence for the family as an institution was the removal of production from the home and the removal of the father from the family for most of the day. In the agricultural situation the father's role as parent was reinforced by his role as foreman of the work. With the decline of cottage industries and the "putting out" system (raw materials were "put out" into the homes and picked up as finished products) and the aggregating of workers in factories, the family member went to work primarily as an *individual*. For a time the spending of the incomes of individuals continued to be subject to family control. The tradition of family identification with work continued in certain occupations: skilled crafts, small proprietorships and businesses, and certain "independent" professions. These exist to the present day.

For most families, however, the emergence of industry meant employment of the breadwinner in nonfamily, non-worker-owned factories. The shift to the more hierarchical and impersonal factory involved a decline in confidence and pride in workmanship—skill shifted from the worker to the machine. Also, at the beginning at least, factory work meant the dehumanizing of the worker, heavy and often dangerous labor, exploitation of workers (including women and children), and the centralizing of workers and their families in unhealthful and unsanitary slumlike conditions in "coketowns." [6]

In the long run, of course, industrial development meant a great uplift in the human standard of living. The increase of modern "consumer goods" made a reality of the wildest dreams of pre-industrial man. In the *short* run, however, industrialism meant for the early laborers in industry a new kind of slavery and a real decline of leisure. (Medieval man did not work nearly as hard or as long as did men in the early phase of the Industrial Revolution.) [7] Especially difficult must have been the need to accommodate to factory scheduling and group discipline for 12-hour days, as contrasted with the much more freely paced conditions of self-employment.

The Industrial Revolution reached a belated climax in the U. S. in the early 20th century with the creation of the assembly-line concept in Detroit in connection with automobile manufacturing. If in previous machine shops the worker was confined for long hours, he now found himself paced by the machine and even treated like one.[8] On the other hand, concomitant with this dehumanization was the elevation of public conscience as seen in the child labor laws and limitations on women's work. Aiding in this was also the industrial union movement which grew out of the depression of the 1930s. Furthermore, the assembly line itself meant mass production, and mass production meant a higher living standard. The assembly line, while taking the joy out of work, put joy into life by means of the wider distribution of consumer goods; it made possible a low-priced automobile for each family in the U. S. The joylessness of the job increased the desire to be creative elsewhere in the increasing leisure hours. Man's increasing "alienation" in industrial work pushed him into finding stimulation and meaning for his life in the increasingly longer weekends and vacations.[9]

With the 1950s came a further step in industrial development: the introduction of partial "automation" whereby some of the heavy handling of materials and dangers were reduced. In some industries a more complete type of automation could be introduced, namely, "continuous process" industries—those where the product is in fluid or continuous form (paper, chemicals, petroleum).[10] In its fullest, or "cybernetic," sense automation means the monitoring of machines by machines. While the introduction of partial or full automation meant unemployment for some, for more workers it has meant a shift to cleaner and more stimulating work with less drudgery. It has also meant a continually rising standard of living and working, split partly into higher wages and partly into a shorter work week.

Concomitant with this "second industrial revolution" — the monitoring of machines by machines — has been the transformation of the clerical sector. With the decline in agriculture as a source of work, and with the increasing efficiency of the productive sector, our society is experiencing a redistribution of workers to the service, distribution, and administration sectors. Modern economic problems are becoming less the problems of production and more the concerns of service and human relations. We are currently experiencing a revolution in credit operations. The most recent and immediate applications of the new "hardware" technology of computers is in the credit field, namely, check sorting, bank credit cards, billing. This "credit revolution" has all sorts of consequences for our society and especially for the modern family.

Effects of the Industrial Revolution on the Family

Let us recapitulate the discussion of the effects of industrial developments on the family. The Industrial Revolution meant the removal of production from the family circle, where such productive activity had been a means for integrating it. It also meant that husbands and fathers, sometimes even the children, would be involved in hard, monotonous work for long hours. Family members lacked a basis for joint identification. Thus these developments were detrimental in the short run. In the long run, however, industry meant an elevation of the standard of living. It freed most men from manual drudgery. It permitted the rise of leisure industries — the automobile, travel, camping, television, and various other electronic or mechanical sources of pleasure.

The removal of the father from the family involved a whole train of consequences, including effects on educational and familial functions. Generally speaking, the wife and mother fulfilled an important economic function, but this was within the family. However, in the later stages of industrial development, as the service and administrative sectors of modern life became more developed, women began to enter the labor market in force. The city homemaker had fewer economic duties than the farmer's wife. Clerical and secretarial work was less arduous and more befitting women's nature.

Over half of all married women, age 25 and older, participated in the labor force in the U. S. in 1966 (many of these part time, of course), in addition to 71 percent of single women.[11]

A *demand* for women's services has obviously been a prerequisite for their entering the labor force. However, a number of other factors have served as important stimuli or attracting forces: the opportunity for creativity outside the family, individualism, the effect of medical technology on infant mortality and longevity, the possibility of birth limitation and contraception. All these factors have transformed the entire family cycle – the staging and phasing of the various major events in the family from marriage to death of the spouses. Glick demonstrates the dramatic nature of these changes by means of hard facts, based on Census data, in the accompanying table.

TABLE 1: MEDIAN AGE OF HUSBAND AND WIFE AT SELECTED STAGES OF THE LIFE CYCLE OF THE FAMILY, FOR THE UNITED STATES: 1890 TO 1980

STAGE	1890	1940	1950	1959	1980
Median Age of Wife at:					
First marriage	22.0	21.5	20.1	20.2	19.5 – 20.4
Birth of last child	31.9	27.1	26.1	25.8	27 – 28
Marriage of last child	55.3	50.0	47.6	47.1	48 – 49
Death of husband	53.3	60.9	61.4	63.6	65 – 66
Median Age of Husband at:					
First marriage	26.1	24.3	22.8	22.3	22 – 23
Birth of last child	36.0	29.9	28.8	27.9	29 – 30
Marriage of last child	59.4	52.8	50.3	49.2	51 – 52
Death of wife	57.4	63.6	64.1	65.7	68 – 69

Source: Paul C. Glick, David M. Heer, and John C. Beresford, "Family Formation and Family Composition: Trends and Prospects," in *Sourcebook in Marriage and the Family*, ed. Marvin B. Sussman (Boston: Houghton Mifflin Co., 1963), p. 37.

Over the period of years the reader can note the earlier ages for first marriage, birth of last child, and marriage of last child, but the later ages for death of spouse. The earlier staging of events is especially dramatic for the husband, involving a drop of 10 years from 1890 to 1959 for age at marriage of last child. Note, however, that for the decades ahead of our present situation, date of birth and marriage of children is expected to come slightly later. These changes can be directly related to the greater likelihood of women working in the future. The telescoping of the period of childbearing and of launching grown children into their own family lives, as well as the postponement of death, makes for a longer period in which the wife could work and a greater period of solo companionship for husband and wife. The longer potential period for work has a bearing on the woman's period of schooling, especially during the college period. If a woman could be employed for a longer time after her children are grown, then a heavier investment in her education is warranted, and this in turn creates a greater desire to cash in on the investment in college, if made. So by a constantly changing set of circumstances more women enter the labor market, and a new type of family situation is created. Such a progressive emancipation of women from the home occurs within the limits placed by child-bearing and comes as a result of the technological, social, and cultural changes noted above.

The "new leisure" can have a dissipating effect on personal and family life. However, it can have an energizing and renewing effect as well. The new leisure resulting from the continuing industrial revolution can provide the means for wider travel, more time for joint family participation, and more continuing education for the grown members of the family. It can mean more time for family participation in the nonwork sectors of life, including specifically religious activities. Modern man is increasingly freed from the biological and economic necessity of large families and from the drudgery of mere subsistence activities. This means that parental concentration can focus on child-rearing, on assisting the children to learn skills for diagnosis, creativity, management of change, and "self-actualization." [12] (A recent study gives definitive evidence on the handicapping effects of overly large families.[13]) Thus, in a sense, the modern family structure must be functional so as to enable parents to help the children outgrow and possibly out-distance them. While the children can never match the wisdom of their elders until they themselves are old, their educational and intellectual development may continually outpace that of their parents, especially in the newer sciences.

Earlier it was said that the modern direction of life has been "from familism to individualism." However, it was also observed that this is only a *relative* shift. Actually the American family operates during the family cycle (family founding, childbearing, child-rearing, "child-launching," and empty-nest stages) between the two poles. The family undoubtedly is the most individualistic as the unmarried pair are in the process of forming their own family.

Familism goes into fast effect with the period of childbearing and child-rearing, especially when the wife and mother does not work outside the home. Later, as the children go into high school and college and the mother again enters the labor market, individualism again increases. Recent research indicates also that there is a considerable amount of mutual aid extended by the collateral branches of the middle-class family.[14] This aid is welcomed but not necessarily expected or mandatory.

The authority pattern in the modern family becomes less dogmatic and more pragmatic, in keeping with the future-oriented nature of modern child-rearing and -launching and also with the newer family function of mutual support and restoration. While the chief breadwinner is separated from the other family members, his economic contribution provides leverage and a source for authority when needed. As women enter the labor force in greater numbers, their supplementary earnings provide a basis for further independence. Economic authority, while more pragmatic than traditional or legalistic authority, is apt to be more functional in the long run and is apt to exist less for itself. Some thinkers worry about the merging of roles and spheres of the sexes, although thus far such merging appears to be more apparent than real. However, the "feminizing" of men and the "masculinizing" of women bears watching.

Urbanization and Suburbanization

The rise of modern industry precipitated the development of another environing influence for the modern family: the contemporary metropolitan community. As countless books on ethnic history have shown, earlier cities in the U. S. were populated largely by ethnic stocks from northwestern Europe, with the rural hinterlands in the Midwest being peopled by those from northern and north-central Europe. When the time came, however, for the development of the great metropolitan centers in the East and Midwest, toward the latter part of the 19th century, the newcomers tended to come from eastern, southern, and southeastern Europe.[15] While the earlier newcomers came at a time when the U. S. was largely rural and so adopted farming as an occupation, the later newcomers (Italians, Poles, Eastern Jews, et al.) had little choice but to become urban laborers. The result was a greater cultural heterogeneity in the developing urban areas.

The Industrial Revolution operated to exert both a "push" and a "pull" with regard to rural migrants to the cities. The pull was provided by the developing city factories which needed unskilled labor; the push was provided by the declining need for farm labor as farming gradually became mechanized and more scientifically efficient by means of the new discoveries in agricultural science. By the 1960s, however, it began to look as if the drain of labor from the farmlands had reached a point of depletion. In 1900 U. S. farm workers comprised over 37 percent of the active labor force. That figure dropped to 6 percent by 1960 (even less by now).[16] Much of this decline occurred in the last two decades. Conversely, the proportion of those in white-collar work increased during the same period from about 18 percent to over 42 percent. One effect of this is the decline of the "family farm" as a way of life and the conversion of the remaining farmers into small- to medium-size businessmen or commercial farmers (commonly termed "agribusiness" now).

Cities in the Northeast and the Midwest grew first and reached their major growth prior to World War I. New York City reached its first million by about 1870.[17] Cities of the South and West are still maturing, although most of our major older cities have reached a point of saturation and are even declining in their populations. Since World War II the major metropolitan growth has been in the outer ring, in the suburbs and on urban fringes. About two thirds of the population of the U. S. is now found in the 212 Standard Metropolitan Statistical Areas, areas which are essentially counties having a central city of 50,000 or more.[18]

Suburban development began originally in the period prior to World War I, when the commuter railroads were built. However, the major growth of the suburbs had to await the end of World War II with its backlog of postponed satisfactions, expressways, Federal home financing, mass-produced building, outlying shopping centers, and a resurgence of "familism." [19]

All this means that Americans are migrants. A Bureau of Census survey in the early 1950s reported that "nine out of every 10 Americans had moved at least once in their lives. About one out of every four had moved in the 15-month period preceding the survey, three out of every four had moved since 1941, and four out of every five since 1935. Persons always living in the same house constituted only 9 percent of the population." [20] This means, of course, that some hardly ever move, and others every few years. Many move from suburb to suburb as the husband and father is transferred or upgraded in the executive hierarchy of his corporation. Some move from inner or outer city areas to the outer suburban ring, partly to upgrade themselves through a higher standard of housing and other amenities, but also to some extent to escape what they regard as blight and decay and what they perceive as a threat to their all-white neighborhoods.[21] Some corporations report increasing resistance from families, especially wives, to overfrequent transfers. Yet this is part of the rational approach of corporations to the problem of executive deployment within a market situation.

As was mentioned earlier, the American family long ago lost its function of economic production and has now, under the influence of advertising agencies and the mass media, become one of the principal national agencies of economic "consuming." U. S. productive capacity has become so great that distribution, service, and leisure have become more and more important as employment sectors. What is some people's play becomes other people's work. Thus it is important for the contemporary American family to teach its children skills and sophistication in the important area of consuming: shopping, evaluating, and purchasing. The many mail-order catalogs, shopping centers, consumers' guides, and the like can make this quite a game of wits, ethics, and values. The school can help develop a protective shield against the false blandishments of the TV hucksters, but perhaps the family can teach this best.

One criticism that is made of the mass-produced suburb is that families there are cut off from collateral kin and seem to be buried in a homogeneity of their own class and ethnic makeup. William Whyte, as a matter of fact, has maintained that the new suburb is not guilty of patriarchy or even matriarchy but of "filiarchy," or the rule of the community by children.[22] It may be, however, that as communities age, they become more heterogeneous and thus no different from the older neighborhoods of the city itself. One sociologist, for example, maintains that neighborhood areas must be seen in relation to their stage in the process of community aging and also to the particular stages in the family cycle of the majority of residents.[23] Furthermore, like an iceberg perhaps, the mutual-aid activities among collateral kin often are not visible in the case of the suburban middle-class family, although research shows they are there.[24] The picture is not completely clear, but as suburbs age they tend to become more heterogeneous and more representative of the entire population of the region, hopefully including blacks.

Thus the suburban community provides some of the intimacy of the small town of yore, with adjacence to the cultural institutions of the large city. It provides competition and stimulation for child-rearing with high standards. However, its atmosphere may be somewhat artificial with the absence of its males during the day, with the frequent rarity of older couples, and with the absence of diverse ethnic elements, including Negroes. There are increasing signs of tension and ferment in both cities and suburbs, along with increasing vandalism and crimes against property. Evident, too, is the revolt of middle-class-reared youth against what they regard as the "phony" behavior of their elders and against the tendencies of the latter simultaneously to conform outwardly to public morality but privately to "compromise" this in many respects.[25]

Will the children of the suburbs be satisfied to return to the relative isolation and artificial comfort of their parents' communities, or will they choose something else? Will they, trying to solve the problems of the whole urban community, seek some new rapprochement with blacks and other less "developed" groups as their communities age? Suburbia itself may only be a stage or stopping-off place for those in the middle of the family cycle—for those with grade and high school children.

We are gradually seeing the emergence of the first television-reared generation. What are the implications for the parental role? For Christian nurture? for general education? Who will be prepared to interpret the many crosscurrents of life when the whole world streams into the living room? Television creates a new role for parents.

The suburban family is a great American experiment. Youths in the suburbs, while sometimes more organized than their parents, are less apt to form street gangs, as seems to be required for survival in inner-city areas. If anyone can bridge the generation gap, the suburban family ought to be able to do it. Yet this requires goodwill, a concern for persons, a resolve by parents not to exploit children and vice versa, and skills in maintaining good human relations. These goals are not too different from the agape ideal presented in the New Testament.

Organizational and Bureaucratic Transformation

Simultaneous with the rise of industrialization and urbanization is the phenomenon of "bureaucratization." Some have termed this an "increase in scale" or an increase in importance of the *vertical* relations of organizations to decision-making forces outside the local community, in contrast to horizontal relationships to competitive agencies on their own level.[26] In other words, bureaucratization means the removal of decisions from local agencies (and from families) to higher national headquarters, with a consequent lengthening of the chain of command with a greater depersonalization of communication and concern. This means a decline of local autonomy, also in the family, and the tying together of formerly independent local units into new kinds of giant networks or "systems" interrelated by means of technological, communicative, and economic factors. The demonstration of this new interconnectedness par excellence was the total electrical blackout of the northeastern sector of the U. S. one night in the mid-1960s as a result of someone's accidentally throwing the wrong switch in the Toronto, Canada, area.

While this new "totalism" rests on a technology-communications base, it is organizational in nature. It means that the individual and the family are locked into various "systems" or organizational networks. The individual today can hardly undertake any task except as a member of some organized group. There is no diabolical plot involved in this; it is only the quintessential application of rationality to the accomplishment of complex purposes within a highly complicated modern life. Computers have added a further dimension to the possibilities of "rational programming" and "systems engineering."

Currently there is considerable concern over the effects of bigness on the individual, on his personal life and choice. The evidence at present seems to be contradictory in nature. Some argue that fewer people today are self-employed and that more and more work for large corporations and the new supercorporations, the "conglomerates," formed out of the merger of one large-scale organization with another.[27] Some emphasize that individuals are forced to migrate and to move their families against their wishes in order to further corporation rationality. Some focus on the way in which modern organizations co-opt even the wives.[28]

Perhaps to counteract the danger of being locked into a system, some make a greater demand for freedom of individual choice and recognition of personal rights or group concerns. The increasing professionalization of worker levels, the growth in transferability of skills from one institutional sector to the other (for example, management in business to management in the church), the growing universalism of employment markets, the increase in self-organization among various levels of workers by means of their own occupational associations — all these things mean more freedom for the worker even when he is employed by a large corporation. For example, the recent movement toward unionization among public school teachers undoubtedly means a greater share of the national income as well as more freedom of determination for selves and families.

In general, also the growth of voluntary associations in modern American life means more sources of influence and more decision-making roles in the determination of national and local policies. Some modern corporations, it must be said, try to respect the private sector of their employees and try not to blanket the individual and his family with a kind of corporate paternalism. The emerging field of "industrial mental health," preceded by an earlier emphasis on "human relations," is allowing for a more humane treatment of the modern employee.[29]

Thus the influence of organizations on the individual and his family appears to be mixed. Organizations can provide social location for the family, be a source of a high standard of living, and stimulate new concerns and interests. Yet organizations can also interfere with family privacy and autonomy and disrupt family patterns and ties. Even voluntary associations can be tyrannical in the way they preempt the time of family members. The church should avoid playing the organizational game. It should not enmesh the family overly much in its *own* organizational system, allowing little time for family affairs or involvement in other systems. As a matter of fact, the local church perhaps ought to plead for some sort of overall coordination of leisure time within the community so as to avoid extreme competition for the individual and his family. Organization, to be compatible with divine creation, must allow individual choice, encourage personal and family identity and development, and escape from impersonal domination.

Changes in Ideology and Belief

Concomitant with the changes in technology and industrial life, in community structure, and in job organization are changes in ideology and belief. Changes in attitude and belief are of course prerequisites for outer organizational changes. Analytically, however, they can be discussed separately. Actually many of the changes in belief must have preceded the social changes. Some of these changes in values and beliefs relate directly to the family, more specifically to husband-wife roles, patterns of child-rearing, and forms of family interaction. Other changes — the trend to individualism, for example — affect the entire social order and, in turn, its parts, including the family. This section of the chapter will allude to some changes that have had a direct bearing on the family and its major societal tasks: the stress on achievement, the greater freedom for expressing natural feelings, the notions of historical and environmental conditioning via the behavioral sciences, and the new individualized morality.

Max Weber, in a landmark study of the emergence of the modern social order, called attention to the religious, specifically Calvinist, roots of modern individualist activism and achievement.[30] The "Protestant ethic" (as against Marx) believed in the power of the idea and saw the modern industrial order coming about, at least partially, as a by-product of man's search for assurance of his divine election. Weber held that Calvinism was influential in breaking the back of the medieval status quo and in putting the stamp of approval on achievement — all to the glory of God. On the other hand, Catholicism — and Lutheranism too — placed more emphasis on maintaining the status quo and on stressing that the world was evil and static. Even in Luther's view good children (and husbands and wives) took their places where they were. Luther stressed Christlike service to one another, but within a system of vocations which at that time was basically fixed. Calvinism, on the other hand, viewed all of life as expendable, as instrumental. Thus the very early Calvinist capitalists paved the way for a concept of instrumentalism, of seeking and achieving, of mastery over nature. They sought and they achieved, not for their own self-indulgence but to prove to themselves their worth before almighty God.

A product of all this was the rationalized modern industrial social order. It came about because the sons of the early Calvinist entrepreneurs continued the new emerging structure but did so for reasons other than those for which their ancestors began it; but the modern order was born. Some now allege that the "Protestant ethic" of self-discipline and delayed gratification is now alive most among the Jews, then the Catholics, and least the Protestants! [31] It may be that those who are most socially accepted no longer have to "prove" themselves.

Another landmark change directly related to the family is the greater freedom for the expression of natural feelings derived from the work of Sigmund Freud. We need not go into a full evaluation of Freudianism and psychoanalysis as an intellectual system to discount much of early Freudian teaching, for instance, his overemphasis on sexuality and his attempt to reduce all motivation to basically "sexual" origins. However, Freud's name is surely a household word, and everyone today accepts the fact that rationalism is inherently limited in social life by the protrusion of the "irrational" and "arational." Freud saw man as having physical urges or needs which had to be gratified and could not simply be suppressed. He protested against Victorianism and false modesty, which denied the goodness of creation and a proper appreciation of sexuality. His influence led to more permissive orientations to child-rearing. Together with developments in educational philosophy, it brought about a freer atmosphere for self-expression for the modern child, both in home and school. [32] Perhaps Freud had to overstate his point to make it at all.

Dr. Benjamin Spock's phenomenal best seller, *The Pocket Book of Baby Care,* first published at the end of World War II and in time for the postwar "baby boom," represents an interesting study in the implementation of Freudian permissiveness. [33] Millions of American children have been reared according to Dr. Spock's "common sense" point of view, and probably in a more permissive manner than their parents were reared in the period of environmental (Watsonian) "behaviorism" after World War I. Dr. Spock and his book were of course part of a new postwar wave, and he is probably as much "caused" as "causing." Nevertheless, it is interesting to note his own reactions to misinterpretations of his permissiveness. He is now less the apostle of an unbridled permissiveness and more the exemplar of the existentially aroused individual.

Other sets of influences (treated more fully in the next chapter), which hopefully have been beneficial for the welfare of the family, are the behavioral sciences. The most spectacular public demonstration of the utility of sociology, social psychology, and anthropology probably lies in the area of public-opinion polling, working with the operational assumption that human behavior is historically, socially, and culturally conditioned. Earlier theories were evolutionary and posited certain untenable cycles through which social institutions, including the family, were said to go. Later theory, influenced by the cross-cultural variations revealed in anthropology, was concerned with how individual behaviors contributed to the maintenance of other parts of the social structure. While the "functional" theory contributes to our understanding of how the family operates in the social order, it makes little room for social change or conflict and appears to be static in approach. Behavioral-science theory influences modern understanding of the family largely through the hundreds of courses taken by students while in college. It has increasing influence in the field of mental hygiene, delinquency control, and family education.

Many of the preceding influences have made an impact on moral, ethical, and theological thinking. Luther, in reacting against legalist theology, made much of the "freedom of the Christian man." Contemporary "situation ethics" would also make much of the freedom of modern man, but its understanding of the nature of social structure and human nature itself seems to be somewhat naive.[34] The revulsion against "moralism" and culture-bound ethics may be commendable; and it can be argued that many modern ethical decisions are not choices between black and white but various shades of gray. Yet the passionate attachment to Christ found in Luther's theology of ethics seems to be missing frequently from certain modern conceptions of the "new morality." The result is that many moderns grasp at "freedoms" without much in the way of a principle for self-discipline. The anonymity allowed by the modern automobile and the diversity of cultural traditions and rules subject many to more freedom than they can profitably stand. In the wake of this, much morality is likely to be simply the "fashion" followed within a particular peer group. The "new morality," then, may be a partial truth masquerading as the whole truth.

On the one hand, the New Testament ideal of love, of mutual respect, of concern for the other (as an end-in-himself and not a mere utility), and the equality of all in sin would seem to be compatible with some of the changes in family relationships, including some fluidity in male-female roles, child-rearing under less than totally restrictive conditions, the more pronounced stress on achievement (which puts a strain on family continuity), and strongly child-centered training (which strains parental patience). Christians can cope with the last two developments because they not only know their equality in sin but also practice the grace of mutual forgiveness.

On the other hand, a purely individualistic or hedonistic family ethic hardly seems to offer much for family stability at all. And a certain amount of such stability seems to be a *sine qua non* of effective child-rearing. In other words, love as a Christian principle can exist with varying kinds of family structures; but it cannot exist with total irresponsibility or anarchy.

Gibson Winter points out that the Russian experiment with the family in the first few years of the Revolution "made it obvious that a society without a strong, stable family life was doomed." Also made plain was the fact that such stability is necessary if society is "to accomplish its work and execute its political and scientific tasks"; that "a healthy family is not an option for a society. It is a life-and-death matter." There is no substitute for the home in providing fidelity, integrity, a sense of worth, personal dignity, self-confidence, encouragement, and love. More than ever modern man needs also the intimacy of the family relationships to overcome his loneliness and uprootedness, the near disappearance of intimate friendships, and the strains of life in a highly mechanized world. Winter asserts that "the resurgence of family life reaffirms certain personal values which our society has long neglected." [35]

CONCLUSIONS

This chapter has been concerned with the major social influences on the American family in the modern age. These are as follows:

1. After centuries in which both society and the family were closely related under the aegis of the church came the modern scientific age. Industrialization and technological development are

master factors in the creation of the modern order. The Industrial Revolution was an extension of man's brawn or muscle — by machines. Both the industrial and the technological revolution are a source of unease and of ease. They first removed the father from the family, and now are taking the mother, although on less than a total basis. On the other hand, industrial-technological developments provide a higher standard of living and increasing leisure time, which means more freedom for modern man. Concomitant effects are some modifications in the distinctions between the sexes, in the family and other relationships, and in increased and continuing interplay between familism and individualism.

2. The coming of the machine to the farm has pushed thousands of families toward the cities. Fewer farmers are needed, but needed are more and more machine operators in large industries and more clerical, sales, distribution, and management persons. Family mobility has increased greatly. As of 1968 two thirds of the United States population lived in 212 densely populated areas. The producing family has become the consumer family with larger buying power. This has both helped and hurt familism. Urbanization and suburbanization, especially the suburban development, provide the modern setting for family life. In many instances this involves further removal of the father and may result in the first wholly child-and-youth-centered world in history. While American affluence is most evident here, many of suburbia's children are alienated from their parents' values and search for a less proximate and more ultimate set of values, the mass media playing a decisive role.

3. The modern world also sees the family and its members enmeshed in various organizational networks, both voluntary and involuntary, which program their lives to the last minute and seem to allow little opportunity for idle choice or fancy. This can have a depersonalizing effect. On the other hand, with more leisure time available, individuals are increasingly organizing themselves through occupational associations and other voluntary agencies, which are having a counterinfluence on the demands of a highly organized economic and political system. The church should be concerned that there is a balance between organizational demands and the freedom of the individual and the family.

4. The problem of ideology is how to preserve faith in the old Christian absolutes and virtues, for instance, the Ten Commandments, and yet make them operational and relevant in the modern

world. The "Protestant ethic" made achievement and success part of one's religion. No doubt, it contributed to man's new achievements in our technological age. Psychoanalysis, the social sciences, and other new philosophies have destroyed some former illusions, the previous social distance, and the social rituals which kept one man from finding out about another with regard to sex, his social level, and so forth. It is hard for any man to "hide" from another man anymore. But there may be a value in exposing the "phony" side of life, for total honesty is also a godly virtue. But can honesty stand alone, without faith and hope and love? The individualism of new ethical and theological thinking has left modern youth with more freedom than they can profitably stand.

5. The American family has seen many of its "nonessential" functions stripped from it by modern life. But certain basic ones — childbearing and -rearing, personal maintenance, emotional and spiritual nurture, and the restoration of the individual — still remain. The American family, in particular, stresses achievement in its children and exists to see its children outdistance their parents. Such striving, however, may put undue strains on family structure. The family seems not only to be resilient and capable of fully surviving in the American environment but also to be one of the few remaining sanctuaries where people can simply be what they are and be accepted *as* they are. The family is needed to provide order and stability. In an individualistic or hedonistic society even love cannot exist with irresponsibility or anarchy. The family requires *some* sort of structure. The structures required by the family to fulfill its biological and social responsibilities toward modern society seem to allow for variety and some choice of emphases.

NOTES—CHAPTER 7.

1. Urbanization, industrialization, and bureaucratization are the themes chosen by Maurice Stein to tie together a number of independent studies of American communities done in the last four decades. See *The Eclipse of Community: An Interpretation of American Studies* (New York: Harper & Row, 1965).
2. Ernest W. Burgess, *The Family, From Institution to Companionship* (New York: American Book Co., 1945), pp. 26 — 29, 69, 527.
3. Daniel Bell, "Toward a Communal Society," *Life* (May 12, 1967), p. 112.
4. Kingsley Davis, *Human Society* (New York: Macmillan Co., 1949), pp. 394 — 396.
5. William A. Faunce, *Problems of an Industrial Society* (New York: McGraw-Hill, 1968), pp. 15 ff.
6. Harold L. Wilensky and Charles N. Lebeaux, *Industrial Society and Social Welfare* (New York: Collier-Macmillan-Free Press, 1958 and 1965), Ch. 3;

Willystine Goodsell, *A History of the Family as a Social and Educational Institution* (New York: Macmillan Co., 1930), pp. 424–25.

7. Harold L. Wilensky, "The Uneven Distribution of Leisure: The Impact of Economic Growth on 'Free Time,' " in *Work and Leisure,* ed. Erwin O. Smigel (New Haven, Conn.: College and University Press, 1963), pp. 107–11.

8. See Amitai Etzioni, *Modern Organizations* (Englewood Cliffs, N. J.: Prentice-Hall, 1964), Ch. 3; also Reinhard Bendix, *Work and Authority in Industry: Ideologies of Management in the Course of Industrialization* (New York: Harper & Brothers, 1956 and 1963), Ch. 5.

9. Faunce, Ch. 3, "Alienation in Industrial Society."

10. Ibid., Ch. 2; also Robert Blauner, *Alienation and Freedom* (Chicago: University of Chicago Press, 1964).

11. Forrest A. Bogan and Edward J. O'Boyle, "Work Experience of the Population," *Monthly Labor Review* (January 1968), p. 36.

12. See, for example, Abraham H. Maslow, *Toward a Psychology of Being* (Princeton, N. J.: D. Van Nostrand, 1962), pp. 91–92, 146–51, 177–200.

13. Peter H. Blau and Otis D. Duncan, *The American Occupational Structure* (New York: John Wiley & Co., 1967), Chs. 9 and 12.

14. See Marvin B. Sussman, "The Help Pattern in the Middle Class Family," pp. 380–85; and Eugene Litwak, "The Use of Extended Family Groups in the Achievement of Social Goals," pp. 477–84, in Marvin B. Sussman, ed., *Sourcebook in Marriage and the Family* (Boston: Houghton Mifflin, 1963).

15. Oscar Handlin, *Race and Nationality in American Life* (Garden City, N. Y.: Doubleday & Co., 1957); Charles E. Marden and Gladys Meyer, *Minorities in American Society* (New York: American Book Co., 1962).

16. See Thomas C. Fichandler, "The American Labor Force," in *Man, Work and Society,* ed. Sigmund Nosow and William H. Form (New York: Basic Books, 1962), pp. 106–107; Philip M. Hauser, "Labor Force," in *Handbook of Modern Sociology,* ed. Robert E. L. Faris (Chicago: Rand McNally, 1964), p. 183.

17. E. Gordon Ericksen, *Urban Behavior* (New York: Macmillan Co., 1954), p. 39.

18. See Noel P. Gist and Sylvia F. Fava, *Urban Society* (New York: Thomas Y. Crowell, 1964), Ch. 3, especially pp. 54, 71, 73.

19. Ibid., Ch. 9.

20. Charles P. Brinkman, "America on the Move," in *Christ for the Moving Millions: A Conference on Mobility,* ed. H. Conrad Hoyer (Chicago: Division of American Missions, National Lutheran Council, 1955), p. 7.

21. See Edgar M. Hoover and Raymond Vernon, *Anatomy of the Metropolis: the Changing Distribution of People and Jobs Within the New York Metropolitan Region* (Garden City, N. Y.: Doubleday, 1959 and 1962), Part 3; also *Report of the National Advisory Commission on Civil Disorders* (Kerner Report), (New York: Bantam Books, 1968), Chs. 6, 8, 16.

22. William H. Whyte Jr., *The Organization Man* (Garden City, N. Y.: Doubleday, 1956 and 1957), p. 378.

23. Herbert J. Gans, "Urbanism and Suburbanism as Ways of Life: A Reevaluation of Definitions" in *Human Behavior and Social Processes,* ed. Arnold M. Rose (Boston: Houghton Mifflin, 1962), pp. 625–48.

24. See note 14.

25. Richard E. Peterson, "The Student Left in American Higher Education," *Daedalus,* 97, 1 (Winter 1968), 304. He says: "Student leftists are upper-middle-class in their social origins. Their parents are politically liberal or radical."

26. Scott Greer, *The Emerging City* (New York: Collier-Macmillan-Free Press,

1965), pp. 33 – 66. See also Roland L. Warren, *The Community in America* (Chicago: Rand McNally, 1963).

27. It is true that fewer and fewer find it possible to work for themselves. See Fichandler in Nosow and Form, *Man, Work and Society;* also Lee Taylor, *Occupational Sociology* (New York: Oxford University Press, 1958), p. 31. Only 17 percent currently work for themselves.

28. Whyte, pp. 728 – 88; – Taylor, *Occupational Sociology,* pp. 458 – 63.

29. See Edgar H. Schein, *Organizational Psychology* (Englewood Cliffs, N. J.), Ch. 4.

30. Max Weber, *The Protestant Ethic and the Spirit of Capitalism* (New York: Charles Scribner's Sons, 1930 and 1958), pp. 95 – 128; 155 – 83.

31. Andrew M. Greeley, *Religion and Career* (New York: Sheed & Ward, 1963) is among those who make this point.

32. See Orville G. Brim Jr., *Education for Child-rearing* (New York: Russell Sage Foundation, 1959), pp. 29 – 52; also Daniel R. Miller and Guy E. Swanson, *The Changing American Parent: A Study in the Detroit Area* (New York: John Wiley & Sons, 1958), Ch. 8.

33. Dr. Benjamin Spock, *Baby and Child Care* (New York: Pocket Books, 1945 and 1957). In a new preface to the 1957 edition the author cautions against too much permissiveness and urges "a more balanced view."

34. This seems to be true, for example, for *Situation Ethics: The New Morality* by Joseph Fletcher (Philadelphia: Westminster, 1966).

35. See Gibson Winter, *Love and Conflict, New Patterns in Family Life* (Garden City, N. Y.: Doubleday and Co., 1958 and 1961), pp. 27, 190; Ch. 8.

CHAPTER 8

Family Relations and the Behavioral Sciences

PAUL G. HANSEN

It is often said that the family is the basic unit of society. If by this statement is meant the intimacy and closeness of interpersonal relations in the family group, or the universality of the family as a social institution, the popular statement conveys much truth. Yet it is important to remember that patterns of behavior and relationships within the family are also directly influenced by the society in which that family is a unit. The family thus is also a basic unit in the transmission of the culture and expectations of a particular society from one generation to another. No study of family relations can be complete without reference to studies of the cultural milieu as interpreted by the behavioral sciences.

Transition and Confusion

One of the major strains on family relations in 20th-century America is the changing pattern of roles and responsibilities in the home, especially as these alter traditional views of what is expected of husband and wife.

Ruth Cavan describes the comfortable past in these words:

The husband was the openly acknowledged head of the family, with well-defined duties; to earn or provide the living for his family, to provide the final but benevolent authority on matters of discipline and in decisions affecting the family as a whole, to maintain community and national elections. The wife was a junior partner, who contributed her opinions but accepted the decisions of her husband, who attended to the details of the household and the daily training of the young children, and who found her chief community outlets through the church and its attendant welfare activities. On the farm and in the village her time was well filled with the necessities of family life. In the cities some wives found it necessary to work to aid their husbands, but carried out this work in the same spirit that they did their housework, as a supplement to the husband's functions.[1]

Rapid and accelerating changes in American society have significantly affected the roles of the sexes, not only in the family but in all of society. Robert Blood and Donald Wolfe in their classic work on *Husbands and Wives* began with primitive societies to point out that by far the majority of past cultures have operated with a husband-dominant system. "Under pioneer conditions, rugged masculinity was at a premium . . . the more stark the conditions for survival, the more crucial the family decisions which must be made, the more unchallenged the authority-figure is likely to be." [2] However, as Americans moved from hunting to agriculture, or "from forest to farm," the dominance of the male was somewhat weakened by the importance of woman's contribution to the farm program. Then came the Industrial Revolution and the move from "farm to factory," with the corresponding absence of the male figure in the home. Still, marriage remained largely husband-dominated as women remained in the home. Even the gradual increase in professional occupations did not at first raise the status of women, since the professions required the type of education which was closed to women. Blood and Wolfe believe that the drastic changes in feminine roles which we see today did not really begin in American society until World War I.

The most drastic changes in feminine roles came with the entrance of women in appreciable numbers into the employment market during World War I. This movement continued into the booming 1920s. It helped families move beyond the necessities of life to economic, cultural, and recreational luxuries. The combination of greater education and employment of women produced a new generation of American wives.[3]

William Goode, who has written extensively on the changing patterns of our society, believes that more than mere technological changes are responsible for our changing values in regard to sex roles. Nor does he believe the change is entirely due to the economic profit motive. He writes:

I believe that the crucial, crystalizing variable — i. e., the necessary but not sufficient cause of the betterment of the Western woman's position was *ideological:* the gradual, logical, philosophical extension to women of the original Protestant notions about the rights and responsibilities of the *individual* undermined the traditional idea of "woman's proper place . . . ." [4]

Whatever the opinions may be as to the causes of confusion in sex roles, social scientists seem to be agreed on one thing: sex roles in the United States have been changing. "The effect of these changes has been to modify the old patriarchal pattern of masculine dominance in the direction of equalitarianism." [5]

Differing Viewpoints

What results the equalitarian movement will bring is yet a debatable point. There are those who believe that male and female roles are converging to the point where there is almost complete loss of masculine or feminine identity. Most of the writers who have adopted this position have also expressed concern over the so-called disorganizing effect on family and society when there is no clear-cut distinction in sex roles. For example, Margaret Mead, the noted anthropologist, wrote: "Girls have become more like boys and their goals as human beings have steadily approached each other." Helene Deutsch, a psychiatrist most noted for her work on the psychology of women, is known for her view that women are becoming disgustingly masculine through a neurotic striving after male roles. And Mirra Komarovsky, a family sociologist, described the role of modern woman as "no sex role at all, a role which demands of the woman much the same virtues, patterns of behavior, and attitude that it does of the men of a corresponding age." [6]

On the other hand, there are those who see male and female roles as even more distinct. Harvard sociologist Talcott Parsons states that "in certain respects the *differentiation* between the roles of the parents becomes more rather than less significant for the socialization process under modern American conditions" and that "the same is true of the roles of the spouses vis-à-vis each other." [7] Parsons holds that the male occupies an "instrumental" role concerned primarily with the manipulation of objects, while the female occupies an "expressive" role dealing largely with feelings and emotions. Morris Zedlitch Jr., a collaborator with Parsons in the family study, describes the American family of the 1950s as definitely oriented along instrumental-expressive lines.

"The American family," Zedlitch says, "maintains a more flexible pattern than most societies." Father helps mother with the dishes. Mother supplements the father's income by out-of-the-home work. "Nevertheless, the American male, by definition, *must* 'provide' for his family. He is *responsible* for the support of his wife and children. His primary area of performance is the occupational role, in which his status fundamentally inheres; and his *primary* function in the family is to supply an 'income,' to be the 'breadwinner.' There is simply something wrong with the American adult male who doesn't have a 'job.' American women, on the other hand, tend to hold jobs *before* they are married and to quit when 'the day' comes; or to continue in jobs of a lower status than their husbands. . . . And not only is the mother the focus of emotional support for the American middle-class child, but much more exclusively so than in most societies (as Margaret Mead has pointed out in her treatment of adolescent problems)." [8]

Clarification and Consistency

An attempt to bring order out of the chaos of conflicting opinions on changing sex roles has been made by sociologist J. Richard Udry. Following suggestions made by Betty Friedan in her popular book *The Feminine Mystique*,[9] Udry sees a gradual process toward equalization of roles being interrupted in the 1940s by the war years with their hero worship and exaltation of the traditionally "masculine" behavior. He notes that those voices deploring the convergence of roles were strongest in the forties or (as with Komarovsky) spoke from data collected in the forties. By 1950 (cf. Parsons) the war influence had almost restored the traditional family roles, and concern over the loss of male or female identity had greatly diminished. In the late 1950s and early 1960s the movement toward male-female equality has again become strong. Udry summarizes Betty Friedan's viewpoint and then cites other evidence in support of it:

> Until the last decade or so, Friedan claims, women were moving in the direction of recognizing themselves as entitled to other roles than the sex role of wife-mother. They had outgrown militant feminism, but educated women were carving out roles for themselves as human beings in addition to their sex role. However, a combination of social forces (including Freudian psychology, the American business and advertising community, organized religion, misguided

social science, and courses in marriage and family living) nipped the bud of feminine growth after World War II and persuaded American women to build their lives around a slightly modified traditional feminine sex role.[10]

Udry observes that this explanation is consistent with other studies and that the warnings against radical sex-role changing were also coming from other scientists. In the meantime the behavioral characteristics of different classes of women have been explored, for instance, the positive ratio between a happy marriage and the more educated woman.

The Current Scene

More recent writers in the field of the family have avoided the temptation to stereotype sex roles or to generalize about the functioning of those roles in the American home. These are wide differences to be found among families in the United States as to the authority exercised by various members. The so-called pioneer family, or extended-patriarchal family is still found, where the patriarch dominates his wife, his sons, their wives and children, and his unmarried daughters. Burgess and Locke state that "the matriarchal family" still exists, "particularly in Negro families," and in spite of rapid changes "the small patriarchal family, where the husband and father exercises control over his wife and children, is still found." They conclude, however, that "the trend of the family in the United States appears to be in the direction of the companionship family with control by consensus." [11]

The Negro Family

In their perceptive chapter on "The Negro Family," Burgess, Locke, and Thomes state that the American Negro family has been subjected to social change more than the family of any other racial or national group. Upon emancipation Negro families attained a fair degree of stability, but this depended somewhat on whether they had been house servants or field servants. Where the marriage attachments were loose during slavery, families broke up easily. The new freedom meant greater movement and, for men particularly, a loosening of familial attachments.

By 1910 one and two-thirds million Negroes had migrated from the state of their birth to other states, going mostly to the cities. In 1960, 72.4% of Negroes in the U. S. were living in cities, as compared to 61.7% in 1950. The urbanization of the Negro population since 1900 brought about the most momentous change in the family life of the Negro since emancipation. Family disorganization is shown by the fact that as of 1960, 5.6% of Negro husbands and 8.3% of Negro wives were separated, as compared to 1% of white men and 1.3% of white women.

The author says that historically the Negro family of the United States has been matricentric. Under slavery the mother remained the important figure in the family. The affectional relations of mother and child developed deep and permanent attachments. The father's family relationship was often casual and easily broken, one reason being that Negro husbands were sold more often. Thus the mother developed the role of mistress of the cabin. The slave mother and her younger children were treated as a group. This accounts for the matricentic family, especially in the lower class and in many middle-class Negro families today.

The 1960 census indicated that there is a larger proportion of Negro families with women heads than among whites, and more of these are found in the cities than in the rural areas. The matricentric structure is found most often in the lower and lower-middle classes, and the equalitarian structure more among the upper-middle and the upper classes. In fact, there are a number of different structures, including also the small-patriarchal family where the husband assumes the role of economic provider and exercises the chief authority. This, no doubt, comes from the fact that before emancipation house servants had assimilated the small-patriarchal form of the white family along with other white patterns of behavior.

Also, there is discernible the extended family, with grandparents, daughters, sons, grandchildren, nephews, adopted children, and others forming the family group, and the equalitarian structure, where there is greater economic independence and both husband and wife contribute to family income.

With regard to sexual and marital practices, again there is a wide difference. The temporary living together as man and wife without an official marriage is socially acceptable in the lower-lower class, is disapproved in the middle class, and is considered shocking in the upper class.

The authors point out that today children of Negro domestic servants lack the advantages which such children had under slavery, because now the mothers work away from home most of the time, and children are left with relatives or alone or under the care of the oldest child.

During slavery and in the uncertain period following emancipation, religion and the church gave Negro families a degree of security, a place for social activities, and an outlet for emotional expression.[12]

Family Authority Patterns and Social Class

There are numerous ways in which family sociologists have attempted to account for the varied pattern of family authority found in America today. Elizabeth Bott has shown differences due to occupation and area of residence, pointing out particularly the "connectedness of the family's social network," i.e., closeness to other relatives. Philip Slater has related parental roles to such factors as personality, mobility, and social isolation. Rose Coser has studied particularly the ambivalence found in the American middle-class families.[13]

Such detailed discussions are beyond the scope of this chapter. However, some reference should be made to the distinctions of social class, since these can have a very direct bearing on the church's work with families. Ruth Cavan has given us what is probably the best outline of social class differences in families, and her book will be relied on in this area.[14]

Cavan follows the description of social classes in America as given by W. Lloyd Warner and Paul S. Lunt in one of the first scientific studies of the American social-class system.[15] Here we have what is now almost a traditional division of classes into six levels: upper-upper and lower-upper, upper-middle and lower-middle, upper-lower and lower-lower. On the various levels there appears to be quite a distinct difference between the role expectations of families. Clifford Kirkpatrick has provided the terminology by which the different husband-wife roles in American society are currently described. Since it is generally conceded that it is the feminine role which has been subject to the most change, the terms are oriented toward the woman's point of view.

Kirkpatrick distinguishes the "wife-and-mother" role, the "companion" role, and the "partner" role, explaining them as follows:

> The *wife-and-mother role* is the traditional role of the married woman. It implies as privileges security, the right to support, ali-

mony in cases of divorce, respect as a wife and mother, a certain amount of domestic authority, loyalty of husband to the mother of his children, and sentimental gratitude from husband and children. Corresponding obligations include bearing and rearing children, making a home, rendering domestic service, loyal subordination of self to the economic interests of the husband, acceptance of a dependent social and economic status, and tolerance of a limited range of activity.

The *companion role* is essentially a leisure class phenomenon. The privileges pertaining to this role include pleasures shared with the husband, a more romantic emotional response, admiration, funds adequate for dress and recreation, leisure for social and educational activity, and chivalrous attentions. On the other hand, it implies as obligations the preservation of beauty under the penalty of marital insecurity, the rendering of ego and erotic satisfaction to the husband, the cultivation of social contacts advantageous to him, maintenance of intellectual alertness, and the responsibility for exorcising the demon of boredom.

Finally, the *partner role* corresponds to a new emergent definition of family relationships. The role entails the privilege of economic independence, equal authority in regard to family finances, acceptance as an equal, the exemption from one-sided personal domestic service to the husband, equal voice in determining the locality of residence, and equality in regard to social and moral freedom. The obligational side of the balance sheet would include renouncing of alimony save in the case of dependent children, an economic contribution in proportion to earning ability, acceptance of equal responsibility for the support of children, complete sharing of the legal responsibilities of the family, willingness to dispense with any appeal to chivalry, abrogation of special privileges in regard to children, and equal responsibility to maintain the family status by success in a career.[16]

It is quite obvious that the three roles as described by Kirkpatrick are never mutually exclusive, nor is the "ideal type" of any one role to be found in any one home. The descriptions do give a convenient terminology for pointing out the differences which exist in American culture.

Ruth Cavan observes that in the so-called upper-upper class the traditional "wife-and-mother" role is followed in all social contacts. The wife is expected to "minimize the traditions of her family and to extol those of her husband." Socially, however, they entertain and are entertained together, travel together, belong to social clubs together, and attend most functions in each other's company.[17]

In the lower-upper class (or *nouveau riche*) the roles are much the same as already described, except that the companion role is not as fully developed, and the social roles tend to be closer to those of the middle class from which the family has come.[18]

Differences between the upper-middle and lower-middle classes on the matter of husband-wife roles are so fine that they are unimportant here. Cavan says that the middle-class wife has a triple role "as wife and mother, as housekeeper, and as social arbiter." In a reversal of the situation in the upper-upper class, the *maternal* aspect tends to supersede the *wifely* aspect in the middle class. "Only during the first childless years of marriage do husband and wife place the sexual and social phases of their own relationship above the demands and welfare of their children."[19] The wife has the most prominent part in caring for the children, usually administering discipline except in extreme cases. As housekeeper, the wife also takes a personal interest in household chores, doing most of the work herself with the help of new home appliances. In the lower-middle class even part-time help is unknown. As "social arbiter," the wife keeps track of the social calendar, all social engagements being arranged through her. Should she happen to be the wife of a climbing executive, the middle-class wife also is expected to play a prominent part in community activities.[20] She forms what Cavan calls "the bulwark of the boards, committees, and volunteer groups that 'run' civic and community ventures."[21] In general it might be said that in the American middle class it is possible to see the most complete blending of the three distinct roles of "wife-and-mother, companion, and partner."

For the lower classes (particularly the lower-lower) Cavan has developed a picture of the family as not being "patriarchal" but "matrifocal." By this she means that the father, when present, exercises rather complete dominance over the home, but the stable and continuing family unit centers around the mother, both because of the higher death rate of lower-class males and the more frequent desertions ("poor man's divorce") and separations which occur. Summarizing the situation for *both lower classes,* Cavan writes:

In the normal family unit of husband, wife, and children, the father is the head of the family. Lower-class families are more nearly patriarchal than families in any other class. The husband asserts his authority more thoroughly and more harshly than in higher classes, keeping his wife and children in submission by physical force if necessary. He is the final authority and disciplinarian to whom the mother refers in her daily training of children; except in times of stress, he is the chief wage earner and controls the purse; he makes the final decisions for the family.

Nevertheless, it is the mother who rears the children, and it is with her that the children remain if the family disintegrates. The father, however, may make rules for the rearing of the children, which the mother enforces in his absence. The mother's role also is that of housekeeper, and the husband does not expect to participate in housekeeping tasks after he comes from work. The roles of husband and wife are more sharply drawn than in the middle-class where there is more sharing in planning and often in execution of the plans.

. . . Having fewer interests, husband and wife have less of a companionship and friendship relationship than the middle-class husband and wife achieve. . . . The roles of husband and wife are specific. The husband earns the living if he is able to do so, supports his family, is not cruel but may be strict, and is faithful to his wife (although discreet deviations are tolerated, especially in the lower-lower group). The wife bears and rears the children, keeps house, earns money if her husband is unable to earn all that is needed, and is faithful to her husband.[22]

The Balance of Power

Blood and Wolfe, in the study referred to previously, show that differences in husband-and-wife roles are due to what they call the "balance of power" in the respective marriage. The "sources of power," they say, are in the "comparative resources which the husband and wife bring to the marriage." And a "resource may be designated as anything that one partner may make available to the other, helping the other satisfy his needs or attain his goals." The balance of power, the authors state, "will be on the side of that partner who contributes the greater resources to the marriage."[23] Obviously there was a time when the "balance of power" lay with the greater physical strength. Today power in husband-wife relationships is based on a far greater variety of resources. J. Richard Udry lists seven "bases of family power": (1) personalities of spouses, (2) relative age of spouses, (3) relative education of spouses, (4) the employment status of the wife, (5) the occupational status of the husband, (6) the presence and number of children in the family, and (7) the stage in the family cycle.[24]

It might be assumed that in every case the more dominant personality would wield the greater power in a marriage. However, this expected result is altered somewhat by the interplay of cultural influences. For example, William F. Kenkel points out that while dominant males are more likely to get their own way, dominant women are less likely to influence decision making in the home.[25] In other words, the personal requirements for "family power" may be quite different for males and females.

Studies on the effect of relative ages of the spouses on the power structure in a marriage seem to bear out the fact that age is a very minor factor. While large differences in age seem to tip the scale in favor of the older spouse (usually the husband), the United States average of less than two years' difference in the age of spouses has made the age factor insignificant.

On the matter of education Blood and Wolfe have found that quite generally the spouse with the higher educational level has more influence in the marriage than he or she would otherwise have. The extra amount of influence seems particularly noticeable when one mate is college educated.[26] Udry comments: "Since men more often than women marry persons with less education than themselves, this alone might account for the slight influence edge most studies show for men."

Usually wives who are employed full time outside the home have more influence in family decisions than those who are employed part time, and the latter have more influence than those who remain at home. The power wielded by additional income is probably the decisive factor. However, one study reported by Udry "found that the housewives actually exerted *more* influence than their working counterparts." Apparently more research still needs to be done in this area.[27]

The occupational status of the husband has a great deal to do with his status in the home. This has been borne out by any number of independent studies. Udry writes: "The higher the social status of a family, the more the decision-making process is dominated by the husband, in spite of the fact that the wives in the high status families constitute most of the well educated women of America." [28] This is a clear example of the importance of "bargaining power" in terms of economic strength. Most women in the upper-middle and upper classes owe their status in the community to the occupation of their husbands and clearly recognize both the husband's greater prestige value and the wife's dependence on him. The opposite is, of course, the case with low-status husbands and wives who must work because of lack of income. The husband has so little to offer that his bargaining power is not great. He may even be tempted to "desert," convinced that his wife and children will be better off financially on "welfare" than if they tried to subsist on his meager earnings.

It has been demonstrated that childless couples tend to be more equalitarian than couples with children and that "the more children there are in the family the more influence the husband has." [29] This has been explained by the fact that a woman becomes more dependent the more children she has, so that her bargaining position becomes weaker with each addition to the family. She will have a much more difficult time finding another husband or even a job when she must be responsible for a number of children. It can be argued that perhaps the single most important factor bringing about the equalitarian relationship between the spouses has been the availability of reliable contraceptive techniques under woman's control.

Finally, the so-called stage in the family cycle has a bearing on the division of authority in the home. Early years of married life often show a more equalitarian pattern (perhaps due to the absence of children as noted above), and the middle years tend to be more completely husband-dominated. However, "very few wives over fifty are dominated by their husbands." [30] The confusing picture of family authority in America becomes even more bewildering when the fact is added that each family needs to be considered not only with respect to its situation but its situation at any given point in time.

Other Evidence from Studies

There have been a number of American research projects directed toward determining the relative "success" of marriages under different authority patterns. Unfortunately, there has been as little consistency in the results of these studies as in the patterns they attempted to study.

David Mace, a leading authority in the field of family counseling, writes:

> So long as extremes are avoided, there is evidence that departures from the "normal" pattern of personal interaction in marriage do not matter, if the partners contrive to satisfy each other's needs. The marriage of a strongly dominant person and an exceptionally submissive person may be successful where unions between two dominants or two submissives fail. We must be careful to leave room for these wide individual variations, and not to apply rigid criteria. Successful marriages display a remarkable variety of patterns.[31]

Atlee Stroup comments, however, that couples must still remember that "a reversal of traditional roles in a marriage may bring social pressure, especially on the husband. A man who allegedly is 'bossed' at home by his womenfolk is teased unmercifully by his male colleagues at work."

In an early study Paul Popenoe found that a democratic relationship in a family was rated happier than one in which either husband or wife dominated.[32] Many later studies have tended to confirm these findings.[33] Blood and Wolfe also confirm the point of view that wives are most satisfied in marriages with the least role differentiation and that the greatest overall marital satisfaction for both husband and wife is associated with equality in age, education, shared decision making, and shared household tasks.[34] Udry comments that some sociologists "maintain on theoretical grounds that role differentiation in the traditional direction is necessary for family functioning." He is referring to the comments by Parsons and Bales mentioned earlier in this chapter. He then states very dogmatically: "No evidence is available to support this position."[35] He concludes:

> The kind of decision-making structure a marriage develops is closely related to the satisfaction the couple finds in the marriage. Good marital adjustment and satisfaction with the marriage are found most often in couples with democratic-equalitarian patterns of behavior, and least frequently when one spouse dominates the scene.[36]

In his chapter on "Allocation of Resources" in marriage, Atlee Stroup succeeds in tying together the findings of the modern behavioral sciences on the subject of sex-role differentiation in the home:

> While further research is very much needed, it would appear that, other things being equal, the chances of marital success are greater if a given couple attempts to set up a democratic system of authority within the household, with the principle of mutual cooperation toward common goals dominating the relationship. This is especially true for educated couples in the United States.[37]

Sources of Sex-Role Differentiation

Whether the evident differences in sex roles throughout the many cultures under which man lives are largely biological and therefore relatively fixed, or are primarily learned and thus transmitted by the culture, is an issue under wide discussion. A look at both points of view can be helpful in the process of personal decision making.

Paul Landis has a good summary of the so-called biological emphasis in the whole matter of sex differentiation.[38] The concluding paragraphs are illustrative:

> *In conclusion,* male and female sex differences appear during embryonic development, insofar as certain anatomical differences are concerned. Glandular and hormone developments at puberty bring with them other marked sex-differentiating characteristics. These unique attributes of male and female, although often greatly modified by culture, still affect male and female emotional and social growth decisively.
>
> The softer flesh and more gentle disposition of the female, her different emotional and social reactions are, in part, attributable to the role for which nature has designed her—that of caring for and nursing the young. So also the aggressive, prowling disposition of the male, in part, is glandularly induced, although the culture may either thwart or encourage these tendencies. The differences in certain psychological and psycho-sexual responses of male and female also relate to the part each plays in nature. Man is gifted with sexual preparedness, in that he is always ready for the sex act. With the female, readiness usually involves some foresight and regard to the social consequences of the act.

Male and female are biological complements to each other, each being equally important to the process of reproduction and yet far different in specific capacities and functions. The female is handicapped by the menstrual cycle, by the burden of carrying the young, and by all the responsibilities which center around these functions. The male bears none of these burdens but in most cultures has to bear the economic burden of supporting the female and her helpless young.[39]

Very closely related to the discussion of biological differences between male and female are the conclusions in regard to what may be called innate psychological differences. Landis writes: "In the area of interests there are measurable evidences of significant psychological differences between male and female." He quotes Stanford University psychologists in support of this contention:

Women are consistently more intimate and personal than men. They are strongly interested in persons and spend more time and thought on people and personalities than men do. Excellent studies of young children show that girls very early are more interested in relationships with others, while boys are more interested in material things.[40]

Following the train of thought represented largely by the fields of genetics and psychiatry,[41] Landis uses such popular phrases as the following: "women's greater tendency to gossip and men's greater interest in material gain"; "woman will express herself in terms of how she felt . . . a man, in terms of what he said, did, or at least thought"; "women are more frequent readers of fiction"; "men are more inclined to be competitive, to outdo others . . . women are more interested in getting along with people"; "women are much more romantic in temperament and outlook than are men"; "women may be more intuitive"; "women are more temperamental"; and similar expressions which suggest that there are basic, inborn differences between the sexes in terms of psychology and temperament.[42] Despite the evidence he adduces, Landis cautions: "How much of this is conditioning by the culture and how much is innate difference is debatable." [43]

The viewpoint that differences in sex roles are largely culturally determined, or due to learning, is expressed most often by those who consider human behavior from a "cross-cultural perspective." [44] It is plain to everyone who travels or reads that every known society has some kind of sex role differentiation. Men and women are expected to behave differently. But the reason why there are these different expectations is still the subject of intensive study. Some opinions hold, for example, that personality difficulties which lead to homosexual or other deviant behavior, or the "Oedipus" and "Electra" complexes of Freudian psychology, may well be the result of a failure to appreciate that masculine and feminine behavior patterns can be inbred, and are not necessarily inborn.

Sex Roles as Values

Social scientists are quite generally reluctant to express what may be called "value judgments" in regard to any area of study. It is difficult, therefore, to develop any conclusion as to the direction American society should go in terms of sex-role differentiation. It would seem obvious from the total picture that, if nothing else, a greater amount of clarity is needed in defining modern sex roles. William Goode at least goes so far as to say that "much of the movement to give equality to the woman is interpreted as disorganizing." [45] Henry Bowman agrees that the home today is being threatened by the uncertainty and insecurity developed because of confusion in privileges and responsibilities accorded to husbands and wives. "A woman's choice of role is complicated today by the fact that she is caught between the pressures of three forces," he says. He then refers to the weight of "tradition," "biological nature," and "new found opportunity." Of the male he says, "One of the problems men face today is that . . . the individual man is expected to meet simultaneously both the traditional and the contemporary criteria of masculinity." [46]

It is generally conceded that the laws of a country reflect its value system, and if this is true, the trend in the United States is certainly in the direction of the equalitarian pattern in the home. From the activities of the Labor Department's Women's Bureau, which began in 1920, to the most recent legislation prohibiting discrimination in employment, even for reasons of sex (1964), the consistent direction of American law has been toward equal rights for women.

> In 1962 there were 35 jurisdictions which had minimum wage laws
> and in 19 of these jurisdictions the laws applied only to women
> or to women and minors. In 1962, 22 states had equal-pay laws

applicable to private employment which prohibited discrimination in rate of pay because of sex. They established the principle of payment of a wage rate based on the job and not on the sex of the worker. In regard to a day of rest, 22 states and the District of Columbia have established a maximum 6-day work week for women in some or all industries. In only six of the states is this standard applicable both to men and women. The implication of these laws is certainly "equivalent" rather than "identical" rights for women.[47]

While the census definition may still list the husband as the head of the family, the husband in most cases is still given the legal right to determine the place of residence for his family. In many states he may sue his wife for divorce on ground of desertion if she refuses to accompany him. The husband's occupation in many ways takes precedence over that of his wife. Changes in judicial interpretation and rapidly changing statutes may soon eliminate even these traces of the patriarchal society in our history.[48]

Toward a Complementarian Pattern

Ray E. Baber points out that today there is less likelihood of the authority of either husband or wife being *exclusive* and that evidence points toward greater happiness for the equalitarian or near-equalitarian marriages. Regarding full equality he asserts that it is doubtful "whether absolute equality, whatever the law, can be attained," and it is even more doubtful whether most women want it. Women "cannot be blamed for not wanting to be merely an 'auxiliary sex' with no real identity of their own, but neither can they achieve a workable philosophy of life simply by revolting against the past. They must give 'freedom' a social interpretation if it is to conform to their own ultimate welfare as well as that of their loved ones." [49]

American sociologists have chosen various terms to identify and describe the American family-relationship pattern: "colleague-family," with parents as leaders and children as junior partners; [50] "autonomous-nuclear," with freedom for personality development and a variety of activities; [51] and "semi-patriarchal," because "adaptation to modern equalitarian norms seems to be far from complete." [52]

Attention is called to the importance of the father for the emotional health of the children and the integration and strength of the family unit by sociologists and psychologists.[53] They are careful to point out that while women and men are increasingly equal, they are also separate and different (Miller, Swanson); that the traditional division of labor between husbands and wives is generally still in effect (Blitsten); that in many specific areas of conduct the husband is dominant in every family system of the West (Goode); [54] that a combination of factors leads to "a smaller, more mobile, and more equalitarian family and a more informal, intimate, and complex marital relation" with congeniality and compatability as a central criterion for a successful marriage; [55] that the family is in a transitional stage with an uneven movement toward the equalitarian pattern, becoming more and more a partnership.[56]

Family Roles in Other Cultures

No study of the human family can be confined either to the American culture or to the church in the West. The vast majority of families live under other cultures and have a different background. Ancient man before the discovery of the microscope knew nothing of the sperm and ovum and believed that the male planted the seminal fluid into the womb, and that the woman only harbored it and gave birth to the child. This left the impression that the man produces the child and the woman is the garden in which the child grows. This inferior concept of woman's part in conception and birth still prevails in parts of Africa.[57]

The tradition of the East was that a man wanted sons above all else, because of the headship of the male, but he wanted his own sons and not those of some other man; therefore he demanded chastity and exclusive rights over the sexuality of the woman he married. He himself, however, was not bound to sexual relations with her alone.[58]

In the traditional patrilineal family of China it is easy to see the value given to male children and the little attention given to female children. The extended family suited a country with a traditional type of agriculture and a traditional type of handicraft as the people's chief livelihood. While the father was dominant, the mother usually liked to serve (if possible) as interpreter of the father's orders.[59]

Changes in the structure of the Japanese family from lineal to nuclear have been proceeding rapidly in Japan since World War II.[60]

India also is experiencing a change in family-authority patterns. In a research study opinions were divided on the question of whether the husband should be dominating, or if control should be equally divided between the husband and wife. Formerly families were held together more by external pressures of law, religion, and society. Today these forces have begun to lose their effectiveness, and marital stability depends more on the cohesive power of an inner unity.[61]

Basing their opinions especially on the study of groups such as the Mundugumor and the Tchambuli in New Guinea, where the men are weak and submissive and fearful and the women aggressive, virile, and domineering,[62] writers in the fields of sociology and anthropology have concluded that "culture is the greatest single influence upon the family power structure." [63]

The emerging sense of world community is encouraging significant cross-cultural studies and comparisons of family relationships on all continents. International meetings bringing together educators and research personnel in family life, international circulation of ideas and research on family life, and expanded governmental, intergovernmental, and foundation projects affecting family life all contribute in some measure to an increased understanding of the basic similarities and the evident dissimilarities in family relationships throughout the world. Were this chapter written 10 years hence, it could reflect much of this emerging understanding.

Major Changes in Marriage and the Family

Keeping the theological perspective in mind, family-life sociologist David R. Mace at a conference on sexuality, marriage, and the family sketched the changing status of marriage and family living in today's world in terms of movement, which in most cases is still an ongoing process.

Dr. Mace identifies eight trends. These are stated and summarized in the following paragraphs.

1. *Marriage has changed from an institution to a companionship arrangement.* Formerly similar values and traditions held the larger family together. Interpersonal relations were considered of a secondary nature. Now the companionship aspect is first and the institutional aspect second. Christian writers are pointing to the positive theological dimensions of this companionship marriage.

Marriages cannot be held together today as formerly by external coercion. They must be held together by internal cohesion.

2. *Marriage has moved from partners with fixed roles to partners with fluid roles.* There has been much blurring of roles in recent decades with resultant confusion. Now many a wife has two or more roles, at least those of homemaker and wage earner. But the husband also has two or more roles. Today both husband and wife play many roles as they meet the demands of our changing culture.

3. *The extended family has been supplanted by the nuclear family.* The extended family fulfilled many family needs and supplied much assistance. We still have patterns of it in the Orient, in the African kraal, and even in North America. It still has important strengths. The nuclear family also has its strengths but often lacks restraints and persistence.

4. *Marriage has moved from being procreative-centered to being unitive-centered.* Both the unitive and procreative functions of sex in marriage are set forth in Scripture. History has emphasized the procreative. The population explosion deemphasizes it. The Hebrews permitted the man to put away a woman if children did not come of the union. Today the pressure is in the reverse.

5. *Marriage has changed from a short-span institution to a long-span institution.* The average wife is free of childbearing before 30 and as early as 26. By her early 40s she virtually has completed her major preoccupation as a mother. Medical science has added years to the average life-span, which now extends to the 70s. The parenthood task is completed earlier. The period when husband and wife are alone again has been extended. This has affected the nature of modern marriage.

6. *The family has moved from the one-vote system to the two-vote system.* Formerly obedience and subservience to the husband-father was emphasized. The two-vote system is much more complex and requires more by way of mature persons. Couples need to know how to manage good relationships. A successful marriage lies in the ability to resolve conflicts.

7. *We have moved from an ingroup type of marriage to an outgroup type of marriage.* In former years mating and marriage were mostly within the same nationality, social structure, religious belief. Now marriages are taking place across all national, racial,

and religious frontiers, partly as a result of a more democratic society and more ecumenical thinking in the field of religion.

8. *We are recovering in our time a more Biblical view of sex,* that is, one that is more positive. For some 1,500 years the church kept sex "in a tunnel" with a negative view. In the old days marriage itself was considered sinful when sex relations were enjoyed. Celibacy was elevated above marriage. There was a period of anti-sexual religion.

Man and wife are different. They serve each other in a complementary way. The concept of partnership is taking the place of arbitrary headship. While the father's role is somewhat blunted in modern society, he has not abdicated. The family is here to stay. As in the past, it will in the future adjust to cultural changes.[64]

Major Factors in Family Stability

Marriage is the socially approved and established arrangement for having children, whether the authority patterns be patriarchal, matriarchal, or equalitarian. Typically the family thus established provides not only for an orderly reproduction of the race but also for the economic support of its members, the channeling of sexual behavior, child-rearing, nurture in matters regarded as needful for the child's wholesome development, identification, and placement in the social structures of the community, and emotional supports and outlets. Patterns are established to help determine the behavior of persons related to one another—however closely or however distantly—through the ties of blood or of marriage.

Rules of behavior define deference among kinsfolk, eligibility for or exclusion from marriage, obligation for economic support or help in normal and crisis situations, and types of occasions for which ceremonial observances are appropriate. Children and adults alike experience the fact that the family and its members live under the authority of rules, customs, ceremonies, traditions, and expectations not only of the immediate family but also of the larger community. Every member of the family has roles and obligations which affect each other member and his own place in the community.

Parents and children have mutual roles and tasks based on full and honest communication and on mutual trust and confidence. The child needs opportunity to grow and develop according to his own potential and at his own pace. He needs to effect increasingly responsible relationships within his own family, with persons outside the family, and with institutions and agencies of the community. Thus he becomes imbued with character, conscience, impulse control, and consideration for others as guides to interrelational behavior.

The child's personality begins to develop as a result of his contacts with his mother and is significantly influenced by her encouragement to achievement, self-mastery, and socialization. Her attitude toward the child's father, whether present or absent in the home, her attitude toward men in general, and her own self-esteem as a woman have a marked influence on the child's personality development and reaffirmation.

For his part, the father's role of leadership, decision making, and limits-setting seem to be of critical significance for the child's effective socialization. At the same time paternal qualities of warmth, affection, support, strength, and firmness seem appropriate to the masculine model the child needs.

Each family member fulfills roles and functions according to his or her own competence or choice, according to familial or community expectations, and according to estimates of what is salutary in a specific situation. Each family needs to provide for adaptability, flexibility, and improvisation in roles and relationships as an effective preparation of its members for living in an era of rapid and accelerating change.

Where such relationships obtain, society gets stable, responsible family units which are totally consistent with the Biblical revelation of God's creative design for man's life in family and community. Cultural trappings and embellishments often obscure the basic functions and purposes. Sound family relationships can contribute to the basic civic righteousness so essential to any healthy society. Though forms and roles vary, marriage and the family fulfill God's creative and sustaining purposes for man's life in every era and habitat.

CONCLUSIONS

1. The family has been under close scrutiny in the last three decades by sociologists, psychologists, and anthropologists. The age-old family pattern in every known society and in most cultures has been chiefly patriarchal. Headship belonged to the husband-father, with his wife as the junior partner. This structure was well

suited to pioneer conditions and to an agricultural society. The extended family still has real strengths.

2. Changes in family relationships can be attributed to many factors, such as world wars, technological advances, economic conditions, feminism, woman suffrage, an ever larger percent of women in the labor force, the democratic state, and Protestant ideology. Sociologists think that the social situation is responsible for the confusion in the family and not the reverse.

3. The feminine role has been the subject of most changes. Modern woman is caught between three forces: her biological nature, social tradition, and new opportunities for self-expression and fulfillment in a technological society. Woman's role in our culture is threefold: as wife-mother-homemaker, as companion-social arbiter, and as partner in the household economy. Couples are doing more things together. After the children come, the mother becomes the central focus and provides continuity for family operations. Many factors in our society push the child toward the mother. Some observers are saying the American family is becoming more "matri-focal."

4. Surveys show that husband and wife roles vary according to social levels ranging from the lower to the upper classes. The large middle-class family tends to be most democratic or equalitarian. Generally, American families are becoming more flexible. The balance of power depends on the blend in each family. It accrues from the interaction of such factors as personalities, ages of mates, education, wife's employment, occupational status of the husband, presence and number of children, and the stage of the family cycle. Roles vary from family to family as the members fit themselves together in their proper place and order.

5. The marriage relationship helps to determine patterns. Partnership-type marriages tend to be most successful and happy. They include: mutual cooperation toward common goals, avoidance of extremes in asserting authority, husbands and wives satisfying each other's basic needs. Where these factors obtain, there can be success even with different patterns of family authority and control. The Negro family structure in America is varied, being deeply affected by many economic and sociological factors.

6. Social scientists have assessed the sources of sex differentiation. Culture in every age has played an important part in modifying

family behavior, as the preceding chapter has indicated. However, the biological differences of a heterosexual creation account for basic physical and psychological differences between man and woman. Man has a more "instrumental" and woman a more "expressive" role. This differentiation exists in every society. Man and woman are different, which suggests that their roles are intended to be complementarian.

7. In most of human history, as earlier chapters have pointed out, the monopoly of the male has prevailed in a patriarchal family structure and in a hierarchical society. In many lands this was partly due to the failure to understand that a fully bisexual activity was involved in the generation of the human offspring. A survey of family relationships in various cultures indicates that after many centuries of usefulness the patriarchal, extended-family pattern is giving way to the nuclear family structure. This is a varying, ongoing, still fluid process. Behavioral scientists debate whether male and female roles are converging or becoming more distinct. Rigid stereotyping of roles and radical sex-role changes are to be avoided. American law still holds the husband legally responsible for family income and place of residence.

8. There is no exclusive, absolute authority in either husband or wife in today's society. Absolute authority, in fact, is as unreal as it is doubtful. Woman is much more than an "auxiliary sex." A workable philosophy calls for interdependence as partners, with sufficient order and form for family unity and mutual service. It is apparent that in American society the pendulum is swinging definitely toward a more democratic form of family relationships, with parents responsible for their children.

9. The changes taking place are a composite of many movements related to marriage and family living. From the sociologist's view, certain shifts are noticeable in marriage: from institution to companionship, from the procreative to the unitive function, from the one-vote system to the two-vote system, from ingroup marriages to more outgroup marriages, from fixed roles to more fluid ones, from a short-span institution to a long-span institution, and from distorted views of sexuality to more Biblical views. These shifts from the extended (patriarchal) family to the nuclear (primary, restricted) family demand much more maturity on the part of husband and wife, father and mother, parents and children.

10. Marriage is the socially approved and established arrangement for reproduction, the rearing and socialization of children, character development, mutual support (physical, mental, spiritual), channeling sexual behavior, and for developing wholesome kinship patterns, customs, and ceremonies. It supplies the basic experiences for living. Each member of the family will continue to have diverse roles in and outside the family. These prepare him to make constructive contributions to a healthy society.

NOTES—CHAPTER 8.

1. Ruth Shonle Cavan, *The American Family* (New York: Thos. Crowell Co., 1963), p. 32.

2. Robert O. Blood Jr. and Donald M. Wolfe, *Husbands and Wives: The Dynamics of Married Living* (New York: Free Press of Glencoe, Inc., 1960), pp. 16 ff.

3. Ibid., pp. 22—23. See also Table 321, *Statistical Abstract of the United States, 1968:* U. S. Bureau of Census, Washington, D. C., 1968, p. 224; Forrest A. Bogan and Edward J. O'Boyle, "Work Experience of the Population," *Monthly Labor Review* (January 1968), p. 36.

4. William J. Goode, *World Revolution and Family Patterns* (New York: The Free Press of Glencoe, Inc., 1963), p. 56.

5. W. F. Ogburn and M. F. Nimkoff, *Technology and the Changing Family* (Boston and New York: Houghton Mifflin Co., 1955), p. 190.

6. Margaret Mead, "Introduction," in *Women: The Variety and Meaning of Their Sexual Experience*, ed. A. M. Krich (New York: Dell Publishing Co., 1953), pp. 9—24; Helene Deutsch, *The Psychology of Women* (New York: Grune and Stratton, Inc., 1944, 1945), Vol. I, 376; Mirra Komarovsky, "Functional Analysis of Sex Roles," in *Sourcebook in Marriage and the Family*, ed. Marvin B. Sussman (Boston: Houghton Mifflin Co., 1963), p. 127.

7. Talcott Parsons and Robert F. Bales, *Family, Socialization and Interaction Process* (Glencoe, Ill.: The Free Press, 1955), p. 24.

8. Morris Zedlitch Jr., "Role Differentiation in the Nuclear Family: A Comparative Study," in Parsons and Bales, p. 339.

9. Betty Friedan, *The Feminine Mystique* (New York: W. W. Norton & Company, Inc., 1963).

10. J. Richard Udry, *The Social Context of Marriage* (Philadelphia: J. B. Lippincott Co., 1966), pp. 48—51.

11. E. W. Burgess, Harvey J. Locke, and Mary Margaret Thomes, *The Family from Institution to Companionship* (New York: American Book Co., 1963), p. 19.

12. Ibid., pp. 77—98. Statistics for 1967 indicate that 23.7% of nonwhite families are headed by a woman, compared with 9.1% of white families. See *Table 42, Statistical Abstract of the United States*, 1968, p. 36. One must not read *racial* characteristics into these data. The matriarchal character allegedly characterizing the Negro family has historical and socioeconomic roots which are highly significant. The Negro man today is only beginning to find opportunities open to him to be truly "masculine" in the social-sexual connotation of that term in American society. The interested reader is referred especially to Jessie Bernard, *Marriage and Family Among Negroes* (Englewood Cliffs, N. J.: Prentice-Hall, Inc., 1966). In her well-documented work the author says: "One must dismiss, of course, any racial interpretation of the increase in female-headed families. This was neither the typical Negro family nor a characteristic Negro pattern even in 1960. Furthermore, the racial factor has remained constant and cannot,

therefore, be invoked to explain it" (p. 20). "Perhaps it is the incomplete structure of the female-headed family that explains its poverty, and perhaps, its poverty also explains its structure" (p. 23). True, 50.9% of all nonwhite families with incomes under $2,000 in central cities were headed by women (p. 41), and one in six Negro children does not live with his father (p. 124); yet, social scientists do not interpret this as corroborative of a matriarchal theory (pp. 91, 95 – 96, 120 – 21). Other studies include E. Franklin Frazier, *The Negro Family in the United States* (New York: Macmillan Co., 1957); Robert Blood and D. M. Wolfe, *Husbands and Wives* (New York: The Free Press of Glencoe, Inc., 1960), pp. 35, 99.

In the *Pastoral Psychology* (May 1968) article, "Sex Education and Life in the Negro Ghetto," Thomas Edwards Brown writes: "One impressive aspect of the lower class Negro family is the strength of the maternal role, especially in those families where there is no father in the home. In 1960, 47% of the Negro lower-class families in urban areas with children were headed by a female" (quoted by Brown from Lee Rainwater, "Crucible of Identity: The Negro Lower-Class Family," *Daedalus*, 95, 1 [Winter 1966], 181). "Even in the households where the father is present, the mother often carries the major share of responsibility for holding the family together, setting goals, and guiding the development of sons and daughters alike" (quoted by Brown from Kenneth B. Clark, *Dark Ghetto* [New York: Harper & Row, 1965], p. 70). This strong female role has provided remarkable resources for Negro families since the days of slavery when husband-wife relationships were virtually ignored and mother-child relationship provided the only real source of family continuity.

See also Arthur W. Calhoun, "Negro Sex and Family Relations," *The Annals of the American Academy of Political and Social Science,* II, 243 – 79. See also the chapters entitled "Racial Association in the Old South" and "The White Family in the Old South."

13. Elizabeth Bott, "Conjugal Roles and Social Networks"; Philip Slater, "Parental Role Differentiation"; Rose Laub Coser, "Authority and Structural Ambivalence in the Middle-Class Family" – all in Rose L. Coser, ed., *The Family, Its Structure and Functions* (New York: St. Martin's Press, Inc., 1966).

14. Cavan, pp. 97, 110, 122, 150.

15. W. Lloyd Warner and Paul S. Lunt, *The Social Life of a Modern Community* (New Haven, Conn.: Yale University Press, 1941), pp. 82 ff.

16. Clifford Kirkpatrick, *The Family as Process and Institution* (New York: The Ronald Press, 1963), p. 168.

17. Cavan, p. 97.

18. Ibid., p. 110.

19. Ibid., p. 122.

20. Wm. H. Whyte Jr., "The Wives of Management," *Fortune,* XLIV (October 1951), 86 – 88.

21. Cavan, p. 124.

22. Ibid., p. 150.

23. Blood and Wolfe, p. 12.

24. Udry, pp. 356 ff.

25. William F. Kenkel, "Sex of Observer and Spousal Roles in Decision Making," *Marriage and Family Living,* XXVI (1961), 185 – 86.

26. Blood and Wolfe, op. cit.; also Robert O. Blood Jr., *Marriage* (New York: Free Press of Glencoe, Inc., 1962). Both cited in Udry, p. 358.

27. Russell Middleton and Snell B. Putney, "Dominance in Decisions in the Family: Race and Class Differences," *American Journal of Sociology,* LXV (1960), 605 – 609; in Udry, p. 359.

28. Udry, p. 360.

29. David M. Heer, "Dominance and the Working Wife," *Social Forces,* XXXVI (1958), 341 – 47; quoted by Udry, p. 361.
30. Donald M. Wolfe, "Power and Authority in the Family," in Dorwin Cartwright, ed., *Studies in Social Power* (Institute for Social Research, University of Michigan, Ann Arbor, Mich., 1959), pp. 99 – 117; cited by Udry, p. 361.
31. David R. Mace, "Personality Expression and Subordination in Marriage," *Marriage and Family Living,* 15 (August 1953), 205 – 207; quoted by Atlee L. Stroup, *Marriage and Family* (New York: Appleton-Century-Crofts, 1966), p. 314.
32. Paul Popenoe, "Can the Family Have Two Heads?" *Sociology and Social Research* (September 1933), p. 13.
33. Allvar Jacobson, "Conflict of Attitudes Toward the Roles of Husband and Wife," *American Sociological Review,* 17 (April 1952), 146 – 50; Yi-Chuang Lu, "Marital Roles and Marriage Adjustment," *Sociology and Social Research,* 36 (August 1952), 365; Eleanore Braun Luckey, "Marital Satisfaction and Its Association with Congruence of Perception," *Marriage and Family Living,* 22 (February 1960), 49 – 54.
34. Blood and Wolfe, pp. 256 – 59.
35. Udry, p. 354.
36. Ibid., p. 361.
37. Stroup, p. 316.
38. Paul H. Landis, *Making the Most of Marriage* (New York: Appleton-Century-Crofts, Inc., 1960), Ch. 3.
39. Landis, p. 52.
40. Winifred Johnson and Lewis M. Terman, "Some Highlights in the Literature of Psychology of Sex Differences Published Since 1920," *Journal of Psychology* (1940), 9:327 ff.; – cited by Landis, p. 59.
41. For example, Helene Deutsch, *The Psychology of Women: Psycho-analytical Interpretation* (New York: Grune and Stratton, 1944), or Amram Scheinfeld, *Women and Men* (New York: Harcourt, Brace & Co., 1943).
42. Landis, pp. 59 – 65.
43. Ibid., p. 60.
44. William N. Stephens, *The Family in Cross-Cultural Perspective* (San Francisco: Holt, Rinehart, and Winston, 1963).
45. Goode, p. 57.
46. Henry A. Bowman, *Marriage for Moderns* (New York: McGraw-Hill, 1960), pp. 33 – 57.
47. Kirkpatrick, pp. 152 – 53.
48. It is significant that in many states and provinces of North America larger studies and conferences were taking place in the late 1960s on the place of woman in our society, i.e., The Third Wisconsin Governor's Conference on the Status of Women (March 1967).
49. Ray E. Baber, *Marriage and Family* (New York: McGraw-Hill, 1953), pp. 213 – 15, 377.
50. Daniel R. Miller and Guy E. Swanson, *The Changing American Parent* (New York: John Wiley and Sons, 1958), pp. 200 ff.
51. Dorothy R. Blitsten, *The World of the Family* (New York: Random House, 1963), pp. 34 – 37, 254 – 55.
52. E. E. LeMasters, *Modern Courtship and Marriage* (New York: Macmillan Co., 1963), pp. 29 – 32.
53. Nathan B. Epstein and William A. Westley, "Parental Interaction as Related to the Emotional Health of Children," *Social Problems,* VIII (Summer 1960).
54. Goode, pp. 54 – 73.

55. Leo Zakuta, "Equality in North American Marriages," *Social Research,* XXX (Summer 1963), 165.

56. Henry A. Bowman, *Marriage for Moderns* (New York: McGraw-Hill, 1960), pp. 25 – 58.

57. David and Vera Mace, *Marriage: East and West* (Garden City, N. Y.: Doubleday and Co., Inc., 1960), pp. 25 – 28, 40 – 42; Walter A. Trobisch, *Here Is My Problem,* No. 1 (Baden-Baden, Germany: Editions Trobisch, 1967), pp. 18 – 24.

58. Mace, pp. 40 – 41.

59. Martin M. C. Yang (of National Taiwan University), "Child Training and Child Behavior in Varying Family Patterns in a Changing Chinese Society," unpublished paper presented at the International Conference on the Family, New Delhi, India (December 1966).

60. See Shogo Kogano, "Changing Family Behavior in Four Japanese Communities," *Journal of Marriage and the Family* (Minneapolis: National Council on Family Relations), 26 (May 1964), 151.

61. Dr. Prema Ball (assistant professor of preventive and social medicine at New Delhi), "A Study of the Causes of Marital Maladjustment," an unpublished paper presented at the International Conference on the Family (December 1966).

62. Margaret Mead, *Sex and Temperament in Three Primitive Societies* (New York: McGraw-Hill Book Co., Inc., 1935), p. 119.

63. Dale L. Womble, *Foundations for Marriage and Family Relations* (New York: Macmillan, 1966), p. 341; also Gerald R. Leslie, *The Family in Social Context* (New York: Oxford University Press, 1967), Part 1, "Cross-Cultural Perspective."

64. A summary of an unpublished presentation by David Robert Mace, Ph.D., internationally recognized leader in the field of marriage and family counseling, for 14 years a Methodist minister in England, now professor of family sociology at Bowman-Gray School of Medicine, Winston-Salem, N. C., at the Intersynodical Consultation on Sexuality, Marriage, and Family, November 11 – 14, 1968, held under the auspices of The Lutheran Council in the U. S. A.

CHAPTER 9

The Churches' Response to Changing Family Structures

DAVID S. SCHULLER

To understand families, one must understand change. The last decades have witnessed a cultural shift in the Western world virtually unknown in history. Technological advances and, beneath them, shifts in ideas and concepts have accelerated the pace of change beginning mostly with the 20th century. A new civilization is emerging which is strikingly different from that of only a generation ago. Not only has the landscape changed; the behavior, expectations, and values of the world are in violent flux.

Combined with this, the United States faces the greatest "generation jump" in its history. In 1960, when President Kennedy was elected, over half of all Americans alive were over the age of 33. Their formative experiences had occurred during the twenties or earlier. By 1970 more than half of all Americans were under the age of 25. Over half the nation has been born after World War II. Thus in one decade the median of the United States will have dropped a full 8 years. This is the sharpest age drop in our history, possibly in all history.

Having described the sociological-technological changes earlier, our task now is to examine the churches' responses. What have the different branches of Christendom said to guide the structuring of families in this period of convulsive change? How have they described the masculine and feminine roles? How have they responded to the breakup of the patriarchal family and the development of new roles for husband and wife? What are churches teaching and counseling regarding parent-child relationships?

ROMAN CATHOLIC TEACHING

Casti Connubii, Pope Pius XI's encyclical letter of 1930, forms the inevitable beginning point for any discussion of contemporary Roman Catholic teaching regarding marriage and the family. A full 50 years had passed since Leo XIII had issued his encyclical *Arcanum Divinae Sapientiae* reasserting the divine institution, the sacramental dignity, and the perpetual stability of matrimony. Since God had instituted marriage and restored it and had "entrusted all its discipline and care to His spouse the church," [1] the 1930 letter was to guide the faithful in a new generation set into a world of increased dangers to family living. Although the question of family authority is not a key issue, the encyclical speaks with clarity regarding the position of the Roman Catholic Church.

The major discussion concerning the relationship of husband and wife is contained in a section entitled "Mutual Love":

> Domestic society, being confirmed, therefore, by this bond of love, there should flourish in it that order of love, as St. Augustine calls it. This order includes both the primacy of the husband with regard to the wife and children, the ready subjection of the wife and the willing obedience, which the Apostle commends in these words: "Let women be subject to their husbands as to the Lord, because the husband is the head of the wife, as Christ is the head of the church." [2]

Having reaffirmed the basic headship of the husband and the need for obedience on the part of the wife, the encyclical makes clear that the husband's authority is not to be despotic:

> This subjection, however, does not deny or take away the liberty which fully belongs to the woman both in view of her dignity as a human person, and in view of her most noble office as wife and mother and companion; nor does it bid her obey her husband's every request if not in harmony with right reason or with the dignity due to wife. . . . But it forbids that exaggerated liberty which cares not for the good of the family; it forbids that in this body which is the family, the heart be separated from the head to the great detriment of the whole body and the proximate danger of ruin. For if the man is the head, and as he occupies the chief place in ruling, so she may and ought to claim for herself the chief place in love.[3]

The 1930 letter is realistic. The wife's obedience is described as the subjection of a "companion," not that of a "servant." It recognizes the cases where exceptions will dictate another policy.

"This subjection of wife to husband in its degree and manner may vary according to the different conditions of persons, place, and time." [4] Where the husband neglects his duty, the wife must take over the direction of the family. "But the structure of the family and its fundamental law, established and confirmed by God, must always and everywhere be maintained intact." [5]

While the concept of family is dealt with briefly, and there is little instruction regarding the authority patterns between parents and children, parents are to receive children with joy and be concerned with their education. "For the most wise God would have failed to make sufficient provision for children that had been born, as so for the whole human race, if He had not given to those to whom He had entrusted the power and right to beget them, the power also and the right to educate them." [6] In summary, the words of St. Augustine are quoted: "As regards the offspring it is provided that they should be begotten lovingly and educated religiously." [7]

Authority Is Responsibility

This approach of the encyclical is developed in the instruction materials and popular writings of the Roman Catholic Church. The headship of the father is maintained. Every point of equality between man and woman is recognized; the complementary nature of their relationship is described, but the husband remains the "head" in marriage. The approach of Edward O'Rourke in his text *Marriage and Family Life* is typical. [8] Key sentences from the 1930 encyclical are quoted. The father's authority is defined as involving new burdens and responsibilities. Thus the husband and father becomes responsible for that which his charges do in response to his instructions. "The important point is that we must recognize a position of authority as an additional trust, not an opportunity to vent our spleen on our subordinates." [9]

The wife is to exhibit obedience. Since God ordains the headship of the male, the woman who obeys her husband as a duly constituted superior is ultimately obeying God. [10] Women are warned against the feminist notion that such obedience implies inferiority. The Virgin Mary is urged as a model, who while obviously superior to Joseph was nevertheless subordinate to her "less graced husband." [11] These discussions emphasize that the question is one of status, not of personal qualities. Therefore even women who are mentally or emotionally superior to their husbands are "obligated to a subordinate position." [12]

Accommodation to Modern Thinking

The writers seemingly are aware of a growing resistance to this doctrine of subordination-obedience regarding the role of women. They describe the impact of American culture on this concept of headship among Catholic people. Clemens, for example, quotes three studies which indicated strong equalitarian notions of family life among Roman Catholic couples. [13] Thus the main accent in a series of pamphlets on marriage and family living published by the Family Life Bureau of the National Catholic Welfare Conference is on the "complementarity" of the relationship. [14] The differences between male and female as they manifest themselves physically, mentally, and spiritually are described. Men and women are designed, then, to complement each other, to bring their own strengths to compensate for the weakness of the partner. Couples are warned not to expect the partners to have identical reactions, feelings, and experiences. They are further warned not to place their mate in a stereotyped category of supposed masculine or feminine characteristics. [15]

In dealing with the other aspect of the family authority question, the relationship of parents to children, Roman Catholic writers reflect the major emphasis of secular social scientists and family specialists. A strong bond of affection between parents and child is described. Overprotection and overaffection, however, are to be avoided. Discipline must be reasonable and must not involve the rejection of the child. Children are persons with human dignity; therefore they are not to be abused or treated in a despotic fashion. Mothers are to beware of finding emotional outlets in undue scolding or overly severe punishment. Fathers are to be more than family financiers or harsh disciplinarians; instead they are to be self-effacing. "Their whole life is lived to show love for their wives, to provide good things for their children, and to fulfill properly their obligations toward God." [16]

Clemens suggests that three divergent parental approaches to personality development stem from three basic philosophies. The first type applies a literal application of the principle that "children should be seen but not heard." He describes this as a form of domestic tyranny that distorts a child's personality and causes a severe lack of confidence. The second approach lies at the oppo-site end of the spectrum; it is "permissive" or "developmental." It is based on "the unbelievably fantastic theory that children should be left uninhibited by parental direction." [17] It assumes that "nature" will properly direct the growth and development of the child's personality. The third approach, which he approves, is one in which parents "employ reasonable direction and guidance" [18] for their children. His discussion of the use of parental intelligence and experience substituting for the lack of these qualities on the part of the child is a far cry from the absolutist position of demanding total obedience on the part of the child.

Decline of the Patriarch

Particularly Roman Catholic sociologists who have written in the area of marriage and family have increasingly recognized the changes taking place in the broader culture and the effect these are having on Catholic families. Kane's volume, *Marriage and the Family: A Catholic Approach,* is a good illustration.[19] He sees a fundamental problem, namely, "the necessity of adapting to social change without sloughing off those functions essential to adequate family living." [20] He describes the status men had in this country as the absolute heads of their families, supported by the most powerful sanctions the mores could provide. The mother's role was one of subordination; this position was supported even by the laws of the 19th century. The folk saying, "Husband and wife were one, but the husband was the one," was true of the traditional household.

Kane documents from practice the almost complete decline of the role of the patriarch in the contemporary family. The very term "father" has given way to "Dad" or "Pops." Children grow up not desiring to be like their father but expecting to surpass him; even the father expects this. The American father no longer exerts his authority by force but by knowledge, or often even by experience. The futility and helplessness of the father's role is reflected with some exaggeration in the comic strip "Blondie and Dagwood." Kane goes on to describe the "new mother role." [21] As the patri-archy has declined, the matriarchy has developed.

Knowing the clear position of the encyclicals, one expects a strong conclusion to the chapter in which a case is made for the headship of the father. However, the answers are not given. Very general reference is made to the nature of man, the teachings of the church, and the recent encyclicals of the Holy Fathers as being helpful. The main question Kane poses is whether Catholic families will attempt to insulate themselves from the general culture or perhaps enter it aggressively to attack the abuses and deficiencies of contemporary society. He suggests that in this task the social scientists will be of help.

Vatican II and Change

In the writings that have appeared since Vatican II (1962 – 1965) one senses a struggle in defining how much change of familial role will be necessary and desirable. A great deal of speculation prior to the sessions of the council anticipated more liberal solutions to some of the severe contemporary pressures on the family. What did Vatican II say? The *Constitution on the Sacred Liturgy* [22] provides for a revision of the marriage rite that will deepen the sacramental quality of marriage and clarify the duties of husbands and wives. In the significant *Constitution on the Church in the Modern World* married couples are considered in the discussion of the people of God: "Christian spouses, in virtue of the Sacrament of Matrimony, signify and partake of the mystery of that unity and fruitful love which exists between Christ and His church, and they help each other to attain to holiness in their married life and in the rearing and education of their children." [23] In later chapters marriage and family living are interpreted as a sharing in Christ's priestly function. The family is to be gradually transformed by the Christian faith in such a way that mutual love comes to permeate all the relationships of the family.

Marriage and family relationships find their fullest discussion in the first chapter of Part II, specifically addressed to "Fostering the Nobility of Marriage and the Family." [24] The concern of the whole document is to relate the Gospel to situations in contemporary life. Throughout the various sections man is viewed as one who was never intended to be a solitary creature, but one who in his innermost nature is a social being. The intimate partnership of married love is described as "rooted in the conjugal covenant of irrevocable personal consent," as established by the Creator and qualified by law and love.[25] The tension between conventional accents and newly emerging insights is apparent. Marriage is a "natural institution" ordained for the procreation and education of children. But a new emphasis is clear: "Marriage to be sure is not instituted solely for procreation; rather, its very nature as an unbreakable compact between persons and the welfare of the children both demand that the mutual love of the spouses be embodied in a rightly ordained manner, that it grow and ripen." [26] The constitution does speak of the equality of husband and wife. They are equal in dignity, in their rights and duties, in their authority and responsibility for their children, and in their mutual love.

Some comparatively new emphases in Roman Catholic writings sound a mystical note, as, for instance, when H. Caffarel asserts that "woman is subordinate to man because she is dedicated to his creative work and because in him and by him she fulfills her own personality and accomplishes her own mission." There is also a discussion of marriage and sex in a mystical-spiritualizing manner, which downgrades "preoccupation with the marriage bed" and upgrades internal feelings of husband and wife toward each other as more essential than coital intercourse.[27] The struggle to accommodate modern change in Roman Catholic moral theology is quite apparent. Thus Kane suggests that "the American father of today is closer to his family and closer to reality. His warmth, affection, and attention to his wife and children make the patriarch unnecessary and objectionable, and, if he had not already become so, obsolete." [28]

The Husband's Priority in a Marriage Partnership

John L. Thomas, S. J., research associate at Cambridge Center for Social Studies and a recognized authority in the field of family sociology, aware of the fact that the terms "authority" and "obedience" are unpopular in our democratic society, asserts that modern Americans obey more authorities than their ancestors once did and brings husband-oriented authority into proper perspective with the partnership concept of marriage.[29]

Authority is not a person's private preserve set forth in absolute human terms, but a "sacred trust," a "social function," a "service." "According to Catholic teaching only God has direct authority over the human person, all others have delegated authority; that is, their authority comes from God and they receive it because of their special position in relation to promoting the common good or the good of another." [30]

In anticipating the queries of all-out partnership advocates, Thomas asks: "But why must this authority be vested in the father? Granted that the family must have direction and a head, that somebody must work and plan for its future, why must it be the man?" His reply is: "Clearly both partners must contribute according to their ability; however, inasmuch as the mother is necessarily preoccupied with intimate household details and the immediate care of children, the father's overall leadership appears normal. Indeed, marriage counselors tell us it would be difficult to find the mother who isn't proud that she has married a man who will assume the responsibilities of leadership and authority in the home." [31]

Thomas recognizes that the function of authority in regard to children is quite different from that between husband and wife. With priority vested in the husband, it does not follow that he may exercise his authority arbitrarily or to fulfill selfish ends. The husband's authority is not based on a deficiency of the wife. Thomas bids him to remember that the purpose of his authority is to serve as protector, provider, and educator for the common good of the family. [32]

On the distaff side, the same consideration holds: Let both serve the common good in roles for which their natures equip them: "Husband and wife unite in marriage to form a unique partnership in which their distinctive qualities specify different roles . . . . Obedience also is a social function — a service which leads to God. To obey is an act that perfects a person just as does the act of commanding. In marriage both obedience and authority are required by the good of the family — they are also defined and limited by the demands of the good." The aims and objectives of Christian parenthood are determinative of the practice. [33]

Not only authority but also the love factor is derived from God, as Thomas points out: "Since all authority comes from God, and God is Love, all authority exercised in His name will be characterized by love. But love is the gift of self, so that in exercising authority in the family, the father is giving himself to the family according to the qualities which God has given him as a masculine person. Obedience is also an act of love, so that in obeying her husband in the legitimate exercise of his authority, the wife is giving herself to the family according to the qualities that God has given her as a feminine person."

When the authority-obedience functions of the husband and

wife partnership are viewed in the light of love-prompted service, capitalized "I's" quickly merge into a "we." And that is the change in pronouns Thomas envisions. He writes, "Experience shows that neither authority nor obedience is a source of tension among mature, happily married couples. Wholly dedicated to the happiness of their partners and the service of new life, each gives the best that he or she has as masculine and feminine persons." [34]

Document in Vatican Newspaper

In the pastoral document of the Italian episcopate entitled *Marriage and the Family Today* we have a recent and comprehensive statement of family relationships. This document in 21 sections states that marriage and the family are involved in the process of transformation going on in all society and that the new relationships are based to a greater extent on the free choice of the couple, with predominance of affective and voluntary aspects. On this the family stability depends more than on the social system. It recognizes the ascendancy of the principle of democracy, also in the home, and the psychological aspects in today's society, namely, a keener awareness of the need for identification and the defense of one's personality, the transformation of roles and parental tasks, the change in inner attitudes, and a widespread hedonism.

It quotes Pope John XXIII as saying: "Since women are becoming ever more conscious of their human dignity they will not tolerate being treated as mere material instruments, but demand rights befitting a human person, both in the domestic and the public life." This female emancipation, says the report, calls for a more solid moral formation in order to prevent woman from losing in society that freedom she intends to claim.

The document rejects, of course, the idea that sexual activity should be separated from any moral norm. It clearly enunciates the fact that married love is to be a perpetual gift of self to the other spouse, stressing that such love is expressed in the irrevocable personal consent with which the close community of life and love characteristic of marriage is established. It thus asserts again the indissolubility of marriage from the church's point of view.

The solidarity of the marriage, the report says, helps build up society. Marriage is rooted in the nature of love and of the conjugal community. Its solidarity is required for the education of children, and it is the primary factor in family stability. The educative function of the family is highlighted (in agreement with both psychology and pedagogy). The importance of properly supervised early childhood as determinative in the construction of personality is cited for the primacy of the family over other educational institutions.

The report speaks of the necessity of not renouncing the respectful, firm, and trusted exercise of authority. This is understood as a necessary service of love, to be practiced with the method of dialog and made credible by the testimony of example. Its purpose is to help the person of the child to acquire a progressive capacity of free and responsible orientation.

From this report we can draw the conclusion that in the basic pastoral action toward the family the church needs to work in close collaboration with all fields of human, economic, cultural, and social activity for a simultaneous improvement in all factors of parent-child relationships. Thus there is emerging a working relationship between theological concepts and sociological and psychological discoveries.[35]

MAINLINE PROTESTANTISM

Within the broad category of "Protestant" comment on family structure we are knowingly embracing a variety of opinions. On the one hand, mainline Protestantism speaks with a general voice; it is difficult to distinguish a Methodist and Presbyterian viewpoint in this area from a uniquely Baptist approach. On the other hand, there is a different accent, basically more conservative and traditional, among the more sectarian denominations. One might also distinguish at times a different position among Lutherans and Episcopalians. Relatively little has come to our attention from the Orthodox churches. In addition to the denominational divisions, one is also immediately conscious of cultural differences. Often the fact of a common American or European background overshadows denominational or confessional differences on this practical issue.

Some Emphases

Protestant churches are conscious of the fact that they possess no "Protestant theology" of the family in the sense that this has developed in the Roman Catholic Church. While certain accents, such as the sovereignty of God or the priesthood of all believers, may be used as the theological springboard for such discussion, no integrated system of belief and practice has been developed. Further, while a large number of Protestant works have dealt with the subject of love and sex within the last decade, relatively little attention has been given to family structures and roles.

Common emphases, alongside the priesthood of all believers, are the dignity and responsible independence of all members of the family. Applying this concept, Wallace Denton writes: "This means that, ultimately, each member has the right and responsibility for making his own decisions not only with regard to his relationship to God but also in other spheres of his life." [36] While other members of the family may counsel and guide, no one else "has the right to usurp this privilege and dictate to the individual." [37] Thus this Protestant principle has contributed to and has been supportive of what has been termed the democratic family.[38] Even where a more patriarchal form of family life has continued, an emphasis on the uniqueness of the individual and his God-given rights has prepared the soil for democratizing the family. As a result most Protestants were able to accept the gradual transformation from the patriarchal family to a democratic family without seeing it as a dire threat to the stability and order of the society.

SOCIOLOGICAL ORIENTATION

Furthermore, among mainline Protestants one finds a fair degree of sociological sophistication. Perhaps their critics would charge them with being more sensitive to the demands of the culture and the findings of the behavioral sciences than they are to a Biblical theology.[39] Keenly aware of the religious pluralism of the United States, Protestant leaders are reticent to make demands on their members in conflict with general standards supported by the broader culture.

In the background volume for the Home and Family Nurture of the Covenant Life Curriculum,[40] Roy Fairchild lists five different types of families in American life: (1) the rural family, found primarily in the Midwest, (2) the "old family" unit of New England and the South with its traditions and pride of social position, (3) the "old country" family with its Americanized children, (4) the Negro family, particularly among the lower socioeconomic level, and (5) the American middle-class family — the mobile, equalitarian, mother-organized, child-centered type that has become the "ideal" for all classes and groups.

Toward a Division of Responsibilities

These generalizations become more meaningful when we focus on specific questions. Consider first the idea of *headship*. From a former defense of the headship of the father in the family, Protestant treatises now sense headship as situational. To the question, "Who is to be the head of the family?" more literature will now ask, "Headship or leadership in what?" A division of leadership is envisioned wherein all the family tasks are accomplished without any great concern about who heads the entire endeavor. Economic needs, discipline of children, cleaning the house, preparing meals, organizing recreation, entertaining guests, keeping financial records, and fostering religious nurture will be overseen or performed by different individuals from one family to the next. Each family works out its own pattern, either by conscious decision or by default. The assignment of roles — and the patterns of authority implied — will vary with circumstances, such as the age of the children, the position of the family, and whether the mother is employed outside the home. Fairchild and Wynn, in their Protestant survey, summarize the situation quite well:

> To be sure, father is still regarded as "head" of the family; but headship has come to mean something quite unimposing in comparison with the views of both Protestant and Roman Catholic thinkers of a previous century. In that era, whether the differentiation of male and female found its basis in the Bible, in "natural law" or in functional necessity, the roles were kept quite distinct.[41]

This shift in headship is interpreted as the inevitable result of the growing acceptance of the full rights of women. The stereotype of women as being intellectually inferior, fragile, dependent, skilled only in the social graces, and generally weak has been exploded by research in the behavioral sciences and by the experience of emancipated women in the past generation. The concept of the headship of the male was automatically challenged when the subordinate role of women began to crack. Thus, while the headship idea still is found in Protestant literature, it is modified from its former absolute meaning.

Masculinity and Femininity

Another question which lies behind Protestant writings pertains to *masculinity* and the *male role*. Elton and Pauline Trueblood, among other observers, were disturbed by the "absurd belief" that men and women should play the same role.[42] They saw male and female roles as being different, complementary, and equally necessary. "The home, if rightly constituted," they wrote, "is a place in which the woman becomes more womanly and the man becomes more manly." [43] They suggest that a great deal of unhappiness has resulted from women trying to become pseudo-men and from the failure of men to assume the responsibilities which the headship of a home entails. Women and children are cheated if husbands and fathers do not take real leadership in the family.

A decade later Wallace Denton dealt with this theme in a chapter entitled "Demasculinized Men." [44] Questioning thoughts about masculinity are often expressed in both popular sociological works and in Protestant writings. There is a growing fear that men are no longer sure of their identity. The roles of men in the sphere of work are unclear, now that women work alongside men. The former patriarchal role is known but is not seriously considered a viable option. The uncertainty of men about their masculinity opens a host of problems in the husband-wife and father-child relationships. Confused and wanting to regain a sense of their masculinity, many men act out, in an exaggerated, childish fashion, roles that appear "very masculine" — excessive drinking, extramarital affairs, despotic family decisions.

Denton asserts that the patriarchal family began to decline as an aftermath of the Industrial Revolution. Quite simply, the patriarchal family was too inflexible to survive the transition into an industrial, technological age. Along with other Protestant writers, he sees the democratic type of family emerging from the ruins of the old patriarchal family.

Most recently the cries that warn us of the feminizing of men have been superseded by the suggestion that a new masculine role is emerging. Fairchild scoffs at the "alarmists" who warn about the reversal of traditional roles. He sees the modern male as so involved in his specialized occupation that he has either delegated family tasks to others or has abdicated them: "No longer sternly in command, nor apparently wanting to be, he sees himself as the 'head' of the family chiefly in his *providing task* and as an assistant to his wife in practically everything else." [45]

Vocation and Culture

Protestant writers recognize that man's vocational roles in his business, work, profession have eclipsed his familial roles. They leave open this final question of modern man's masculinity. No one knows what new shapes the emerging role of husband and father may assume in the next decades in Western cultures. By restricting the question to the level of the individual, many conclude it becomes less a question of whether a man is in charge of his family. They ask, rather, whether he is in charge of himself. If he is in charge of himself, he is more free to assume the position of responsible leadership in the setting of the family or in his job.

The other side of the coin, of course, is the related concern about the role of women and the question of femininity. Mainline Protestant writers today no longer see a single role for women that primarily involves being a wife, mother, and homemaker. Women now can legitimately fashion a variety of roles for themselves. Socially it has become impossible to establish one role for women; roles must change with the dynamics of society.

Church literature closely reflects the climate of the surrounding culture. During the late fifties and early sixties, when the question of "the unfulfilled woman" [46] was current in best sellers and women's magazines, this was reflected in popular church writings. The question was discussed from primarily psychological and sociological points of view. Most writers seem to be skeptical about how theology might honestly speak to such questions.

Key issues were and to some extent still are: (1) The very question of the role of women is dominated by concepts formulated by men; these need tempering with insight from a feminine viewpoint. Even what appear to be culture-free theological concepts often involve this same bias. (2) Since the time of the Industrial Revolution, women are being increasingly cut off from finding genuine fulfillment in their role as housewives, since the more highly valued tasks of society are those performed outside of the home for pay. (3) Women's behavior and values may be moving closer to those of men. Women may now hold jobs in virtually any area, drink, smoke, and wear clothing once mostly reserved for men. (4) Thus women confront serious value conflicts; the models from which they must select can be mutually self-excluding. (5) A new approach to fulfillment is advised—an approach which reassesses our attitudes toward work within the home and the role of women as molders of the next generation.

Parent-Child Relationships

Protestant writers see the fruition of family life in parenthood. Much has been written about the interrelationship of parents and children. Recent writings have moved away from the concept of rearing children as if it were a process of shaping and molding them as one would shape clay. The "subjecting of the will" remained a prime consideration; the child has to learn discipline early in life. Yet even this was not to be without love, as Horace Bushnell's *Christian Nurture* (1847) so well exhibits.[47]

We now recognize that the "hard-line" approach does not agree with what we know about child development and about the way one should educate a person to assume his role in an open society. The Biblical material was interpreted in terms of its time, namely, that people were being prepared to live in a closed, tightly constructed society. Each person had to assume a specific place; to question this or to attempt to move away from it was considered wrong. Thus children were taught obedience; their will had to be broken early; society could not tolerate rebels.

David Mace poses the problem clearly: We are attempting to rear children to live in a democratic society, with virtually unlimited freedom of choice and with the freedom of social mobility. If children are trained to be simply obedient and passive, they will be incapable of functioning in this society. Thus the difficult problem of the responsible use of freedom emerges, because a concommitant concern is the *abuse* of freedom. Some parents have become too permissive, and freedom has been thrust on children in given areas before they have developed the maturity to handle it. Disaster and broken lives follow. Thus one finds a renewed interest in the idea of discipline in the context of freedom. Most writers would agree with David Mace:

> Today, the one purpose of discipline is to establish clearly and plainly in the experience of the child that this is a world of law and order, even if it doesn't look like it. This means that discipline must be consistent. You fail terribly in discipline if parents don't share

the same principles and stand by one another and create a consistent world for the child so that he knows that this is wrong, not today, not yesterday, not tomorrow, but always. Thus he has a clear sense of values. It is through discipline that we give him values.[48]

BIBLICAL ORIENTATION

The preceding pages have recorded the departure from "fixed" interpretations and have noted the recourse to cultural and socio-logical norms and patterns as guides for "Christian" family struc-tures and roles. But these practices are not representative of all of Protestantism. In fact there is emerging a Biblical approach that is Gospel-oriented and yet keeps the sociological and cultural factors in view.

Father-Mother Role

Gibson Winter, who teaches ethics and sociology as a member of the Federated Theological Faculty at the University of Chicago, in his book *Love and Conflict: New Patterns in Family Life* describes the dilemma of the modern family. In the chapter on "Father in Fact" he deals with the father-mother role in present society.[49] He points to facts about men and women in our society which show that it is essential for the man to lead in the home—facts which sociologists are somewhat ignoring. Though a mother may work at another occupation, she rarely invests her deepest concerns in that occupation. She is almost always primarily concerned for the children. In this she needs the support and leadership of the man. Both husband and wife have concerns inside and outside the family, and so their leadership is a shared responsibility. This is not merely an accident. There is a natural basis for it in the physio-logical and temperamental differences between the sexes. This lies not so much in a natural superiority but in the complementary nature of their creation. Being a woman and bearing children leads naturally to child care, which in itself softens the temperament and disposes the person to provide a proper setting for nurture. In fact this sex differentiation is closely related to sexual intercourse.

The leading role of men is reinforced as women enter upon child-bearing. In fulfilling her sexual role by receiving her husband, she becomes even more dependent upon him in bearing his child. There is, of course, a mutual dependence in marriage or it would not be a relationship. But after childbirth a wife depends on her husband for her own survival and the life of her child.[50]

Even the fact of breast feeding and infant care demands affection, and the holding and fondling of her infant are just as important to growth as the food she supplies, and this too increases her dependence on man in her own demonstration of her womanhood.

Actually, the family is no longer the possession, even in the Christian household, of the husband. It is a place where his ministry of love is to be expressed. Winter indicates that this is quite in line with the New Testament modification of family relationships.

> Modern life has finally broken the arbitrary domination of men and freed women for a responsible role in society. Mutuality of love and responsibility is a practical possibility in the modern family. At present, however, we are seeking this freedom by throwing out all authority and subordination in the alliance. We are in no danger of restoring an arbitrary male domination. Our problem is quite the reverse. We are in danger of losing any male quality in our home life, with disastrous consequences for the whole family.[51]

Balanced discipline must involve the father, and that at the early ages of the child, because he is in a better position to dispense justice than the mother, that is, if he is properly informed and mother and father work together as a team in the discipline and guidance of the young. "Their children need a father who stands for something in the home. Women need a husband who will support and work in the home by being a real person when he is on the premises." [52]

Even the woman's discipline of the children should be exercised as an authority in alliance with her husband. This is one of the reasons why Winter speaks for the restoration of fatherhood in modern homes. The child should understand that his welfare depends both on his father and his mother. All the more is this necessary since modern society pushes the child to the mother. Winter emphasizes this alliance formed by father and mother:

> The man and the woman have to begin to think of themselves as male and female, trying to fulfill the responsibilities given to them by their own destiny in the family. This is not a gimmick. It is a new life. It is a new alliance.[53]

Women in our society, says Winter, create the fabric of communication and relationship in the community. More than ever, they are part of the living network of our society. A better community cannot be established by mere organization. It comes by good interpersonal relationships. But for good relationships you need something like a structure.

> We have been speaking thus far about the organization of the family; its system of discipline, division of authority, democratic leadership, and need for outlets. This is really the superstructure of the ship.[54]

Husband and Wife in the Bible

What makes Winter's book significant on this point is his separate discourse on "Husband and Wife in the Bible." [55] He traces all authority in heaven and on earth to Jesus Christ. There is no authority except from God (Rom. 13:1; Rom. 8:38). This includes the Great Commission (Matt. 28:18). This means: "The authority in work, government, family, and church is a relative authority, derived from God and held in answerability to God." [56] In fact he makes the point that authority as given by God is authority in community, in the togetherness of God's people in the power of the Spirit.

> This togetherness implies a mutual giving which pertains to all the orders of life and in a paramount sense to the family and the church. This focus on community does not mean that all hierarchy of power, all order of authority and subordination, is done away. Christ exercises His authority through love, but He remains Lord. The apostolic fellowship retains community in Christ and hierarchy of authority under Christ.

> The tension between these two elements is a commonplace of all life. The tension is never overcome but only deepened in the dissolution of one element or the other. In family life, love and discipline seem to be alternating attitudes of parents to children, whereas the two are really inseparable. Undisciplined love spoils and unloving discipline hardens. Were we not so afraid of authority, we could exercise it more often in love as an expression of love. In Christ we see perfect authority and perfect love united.[57]

Authority in Mutual Love

Interestingly Winter shows that the father in the Old Testament had a dominating position because he was viewed as a source of strength for the whole family and all the blood children. The New Testament does introduce a new element; but this is not in contradiction as much as in real continuity with the Old Testament. The New Testament restores the dignity and status of woman as a child of God (Gal. 3:26-28).

> The New Testament views marriage in terms of a mutuality of love in Christ in which the man and woman stand together. This is expressed for husbands and wives in Ephesians 5:21: "Be subject to one another out of reverence for Christ." There is, in other words, a recognition that the man and woman stand answerable to the Lord for the life in love to which they have been called. The link between husband and wife is Christ and the form of this link is the relationship of mutual love.[58]

Winter proceeds to Acts and to the letters of St. Paul, which show an appreciation for women's gifts. These letters show women being entrusted with responsibility. They uphold the authority of the father in the family, but as authority transferred by Christ into a sacrificial type of care. "The domination and arbitrary action of husbands have been done away by Christ. They are to act toward their families as Christ acts for the church." [59] Winter then develops the analogy of husband and wife on earth to Christ's lordship over the church in Eph. 5:21-33. Even here the man's authority is answerable to God, and the wife's submission is "as to the Lord." Even the wife's obedience to the husband should not lead her in any way to transgress her obedience to the Lord, for the Christian husband is to be protector and sacrificer for the life of the family. So, according to Paul, human fatherhood finds its pattern in conformity to Christ's authority and self-giving. This is a far cry from any legalistic teaching of imposed parental authority.

The New Testament pattern of male authority is not simply patriarchal, nor is it an arbitrary authority pattern, but it is authority set in a context of mutual love, which gives dignity to the woman's role. Husband and wife are treated as a unity, especially also when the New Testament speaks of their authority over the children. Then Winter adds these trenchant words:

Our tendency today is to assume that we can eliminate the authority of the husband over the wife and yet retain the authority of husband-wife over the children. The Bible is more realistic about marriage than modern man, for the truth is that in dissolving the one hierarchy we destroy the other.[60]

The love of the father for the family cannot be separated from his authority over the family or his love to Christ.

And yet, having said so, Winter declares: "This pattern is not a blueprint or set of formulae. The pattern is actually the expression of the person of Christ which will find its realization in the concrete fatherhood of our own families." This means then that

The natural subordination (not inferiority) of wife to husband is transformed and fulfilled in Christ. The husband continues as answerable to God for the order and welfare of his family, but the family is no longer his possession to use and enjoy. The family is the place where his ministry of love is to be expressed.[61]

Survey Findings

One should expect then that both the New Testament teaching and the cultural aspects of family living in our society would be reflected in the thinking and functioning of church-related families. A number of surveys bear out this observation. Roy W. Fairchild reports:

Because of the Biblical picture of clear male dominance in the family, one might expect *devout religious people* to be less *equalitarian in the home*. On the contrary, some research studies indicate that the more devout the family, whether Roman Catholic or Protestant, the more young people report a fifty-fifty pattern of dominance in their homes.

The *particular assignment of roles* to be taken by husband and wife depends upon many factors: (1) the age of the children, (2) the aptitude of the individual for certain work, and (3) the organization of the spouse's own childhood home, as well as (4) where father works and (5) whether mother holds a paying job outside the home. It is not enough for the Christian family to hark back to a clearly male-centered, rural society and say that its pattern is the will of God for today. All of the factors mentioned above have a bearing on the problem. God's history is real; life moves on. And He nowhere promises to keep this a simple, rural world.[62]

Fairchild's studies indicate that many Christian parents seem to be more concerned about developing happy relationships in the family than about conveying the essential meaning of the Christian faith, which must first be a strong reality in the minds of the parents before it can be caught by the children.

He indicates that forced obedience boomerangs because self-control and self-discipline is not the goal. He goes on to say that "it is only when discipline is *internalized* that children become disciples," [63] and that "humorless moralism is the antithesis for the freedom which we have under the Gospel." Today's parents must be a team, with fathers and mothers bringing different gifts to the arduous task of raising their offspring.[64]

Fairchild points out that the Bible never speaks of the "Christian family"; rather it speaks of the "church in your house" when a household comes under the sway of the good news of Jesus Christ and intends to live for Him. The relationship of church and home, then, is not the relationship of two separate things to each other. The church is in the home and the family is in the church when Christian nurture occurs in families and the families are fulfilling their mission in society.[65]

Perhaps this will serve as an indication of the major lines of thought found in Protestant writing on our question. One must add that many churches are seeking specific means of ministering to families that are attempting to adjust to sociological changes. Although the quality of theology may have been weak in analyzing the problem, churches are asking how they can use the Gospel in working with today's family. As the secularization of American family life proceeds, the churches are reemphasizing the family's need for the fellowship of the church and the church's need to work with families.

In a Lutheran survey made by Paul G. Hansen in 1952 the majority of married and single laity favored "shared authority" in the home, except the pastors, of whom 60 percent indicated this was "not their teaching." The laity also affirmed that their practice in the family generally conformed to their expressed views.[66]

EVANGELICAL-CONSERVATIVE PROTESTANTISM

Churches which have a more "fundamentalist" theological orientation represent another category. Their material is characterized by a somewhat literalistic use of the Bible, by a tendency to simplify material into lists and rules, by greater sympathy for older, established forms and practices of family life, by great accent on personal piety, and by less openness toward evolving patterns of personal and family living.

In the question of headship, for example, most discussions build directly on Eph. 5:23: "The husband is the head of the wife as Christ is the Head of the church." Women are advised to be grateful for being relieved of some responsibilities. Men are not to take advantage of their position but are to use it responsibly. One author, for example, in a popular treatment entitles a chapter "The Christian Wife's Responsibility of Subjection." He claims that the apostle Paul defines the nature, ground, and extent of the obedience that a wife owes her husband. His argument is that the wife's obedience is part of her obedience to the Lord. "Thus the obedience is spiritual in motive and religious in objective." [67] But the man's superiority is rooted also in nature: "He is larger, stronger, bolder; has more of those mental and moral qualities which are required in a leader." [68] Finally, regarding the question of the extent of subjection, he answers that the wife is to be subject to her husband "in everything." While this extends to every department of life, it is limited where it may conflict with one's allegiance to God.[69]

THE LUTHERAN POSITION

In his chapter on "The Christian Faith and Family Life" Harold Haas presents what might be called representative American Lutheran thinking on family structures, authority, and roles. He refers to marriage and the family as structures of creation that arise out of man's interior and exterior necessities, created neither by a fiat of the church nor of the state nor by some kind of social agreement. Given man as he is, marriage and the family in some form will inevitably arise out of his heterosexuality. The Creator provided for companionship in depth (Gen. 1:27). It is God's intention that man and woman are to live in complementary harmony, mutually serving each other's need in a fusion of their very beings. (Gen. 2:23-24)

But marriage and family are to be seen also as included in God's work of redemption through God's grace in Christ. The restoration of relationships of man and woman to each other is possible and, in fact, a part of God's divine purpose. Though hostility is never foreign to our natures, those who are in Christ express love, forgiveness, peace, joy, and service also in the marriage and family structure. It is this recovery of a Biblical orientation that the Lutheran Reformation emphasized.

"Structure and function," says Haas, "are so integrally related that we must hold them together in our thinking." They belong to the total configuration in familial and extrafamilial relations.[70]

Modern life as never before exerts a centrifugal force drawing members from one another and from the family center. Individualism and hedonism have penetrated marriage and the family as dominant philosophies in many cases, and personal happiness has been substituted for mutual service and family solidarity. Also secularism has had a corrosive effect on family stability, and sex has developed into almost an idolatrous relationship. Only as faith in God is awakened can this idolatry be abandoned.[71]

Gen. 2:18 reveals that sex differentiation makes possible a unique type of community in which man and woman have a profound need for each other. They are drawn together to discover something of the meaning of maleness and femaleness as part of the mystery of creation. Thus, while man and woman are different, they are also complementary and each supplies to the other something that he cannot find within himself. This difference is more than biological; it affects the nature of the relationship, the outlook on life, and the role to be played. The fact that woman is more intimately involved in childbearing and child-rearing than man is neither the result of historical accident nor cultural conditioning but is a matter of a basic fulfillment that has its roots in creation.

> The biblical record indicates in various places the subordination of the woman to the man. While it seems obvious that some of the more sweeping statements will be mainly a contemporary androcentric point of view, there is also something more fundamental involved. It is a realistic appraisal and acceptance of certain facts of creation . . . at basic levels of life, in marriage, to the world at large. "The head of the woman is the man" (1 Cor. 11:3). Even this is conditioned however by the headship of Christ in self-giving love of a man to his wife and a recognition of their oneness.[72]

"This is, of course, no argument for the inferiority or superiority of man or woman to each other, but neither is it a suggestion of egalitarianism." Gen. 1:27 and Gal. 3:28 are cited in recognition of "the spiritual dignity which God has given alike to both man and woman." But this does not mean that they are to strive to be alike. Man and woman are created to be complementary to each other, in their togetherness to constitute a created whole. In such a conception neither ideas of egality nor of superiority nor inferiority have any place.[73]

> The home becomes a Christian *calling* and the nucleus of Christian community. In understanding marriage in terms of faith and in making the countless ethical decisions necessary in family life in accordance with commitment to Christ, these structures of creation become at the same time vehicles of God's blessings and a witness to His purpose in Christ. Thus they have an evangelistic function. It is faith, therefore, that is determinative of Christian marriage and family life.[74]

This position is corroborated by Carl F. Reuss:

> What distinguishes the Christian from the non-Christian family in modern America is not so much a difference in outward form as a vital difference in inner spirit. It is the difference which total commitment to the living Christ makes in His disciples. It is a difference which does not just happen, but one which is caused.
>
> The two-sex world is of God's creation. Sex differences are not only for reproductive purposes but also for the enrichment of the whole of human life. Male and female complete and complement one another in the fullness which difference brings. Of the two sexes, man is the head, woman the helper, in God's design. (See Gen. 1:27; Gen. 2:18-24; Gen. 5:1-2; Mark 10:6)[75]

EUROPEAN VIEWS

In his book on the ethics of family living L. Brøndum indicates that the breakdown of the patriarchal system in the home has resulted from the enfranchisement of women in society which had to result in her enfranchisement at home. This Scandinavian author finds the basis for this in the Biblical, Christian, and human view of man. Woman's subordination (just like slavery) was not directly removed by a decree in the New Testament, but was basically removed nevertheless by the spirit in its Word.

Nevertheless he indicates that problems have arisen. Who makes the decisions? One parent or both parents? Or the child? Both parents may decide at the same time but not decide the same thing. And so the child lacks the decisive word that it needs to hear and is confused besides. This leaves the choice that the stronger of the two parents determines the decision, or that the decision is made by talking over the problem in a loving spirit.

So the family is not to be compared in this regard to a school or the management of a corporation. In the Christian home the supreme element is that the child be loved; love should have the last word. Usually the person who deals most of the time with the children naturally gives the decisive word in matters concerning the children's conduct.[76]

An extensive German study speaks to the modern family under the "worldly" and "spiritual" regimen of God as an encounter between sociology and theology and their relation to each other. Under this broader aspect Helmut Begemann explores the relationship between the Christian church and the new "partnership family" as the "church in miniature," since the family is both "prototype" and "copy" of the church structure. He further examines the "partnership family" in regard to authority, orderings of God, and community relations. He sees these as parts of "the order of creation." [77]

In a later treatise Begemann, while still critical of modern society and while not seeking an easy accommodation, nevertheless suggests that the old ordinances of another time no longer fit the present situation. Christian ethics, he asserts, proceeds from the Gospel and is an expression of agape, but within the framework of God's creation order.[78]

CONCLUSIONS

1. Major cultural shifts have produced a crisis in marriage and family relations. This change has manifested itself also in the structures of family life and authority patterns. The younger generation in most cultures is questioning inherited patterns and is attempting to devise new forms that are more equalitarian.

2. Earlier Roman Catholic writings tended to support a patriarchal type of family structure. Such writings customarily utilized arguments from natural law to provide a foundation for Biblical statements regarding the life of husband and wife and of parents and children. The man was seen as being naturally superior; thus he was to be the head of the family, with his wife subjected to him. Subjection was not to diminish the dignity of the woman; the husband was to exercise control in love.

3. A change in Roman Catholic writings on family structure began to occur during the 1950s. Men with sociological or psychological training attempted to integrate insights from these disciplines with the church's teaching about the family. The major shift was signaled by Vatican II. In the documents of the council a conscious attempt was made to avoid the pitfalls created by the terminology of the past. There are more references to "conjugal love" and to "mutual help and service." Authority and obedience in the husband-wife *partnership* and in the parent-child relationship are seen as an expression of love to God in harmony with the Gospel.

4. Mainline Protestant writings within recent decades tend to see patterns of family living as dynamic and as changing to meet emerging needs. The technological revolution and the enfranchisement of women are given as major causes of change. Christ's call to discipleship is seen as freeing men from old legalisms, including that of patriarchal patterns of family relationships. The concept of the priesthood of all believers and life under the Gospel are seen as the theological foundations for Christian thinking about the family.

5. As church bodies attempt to speak to the modern situation, they must beware of the subtle danger of permitting sociology to write ethics. While sociology discloses extant patterns of family living, there is a temptation for many people that "what is happening" becomes the norm of "what should happen." Sociology has attempted to avoid the role of establishing norms; it is curious, therefore, that social practices become more and more the establisher of norms and mores.

6. Church leaders are recognizing the changes modern society has brought in the family. They recognize the shifts in the vocational roles of men and women. They note the fact that some men are becoming "feminine" and some women "masculine," that there is a greater division of responsibilities in the family, and that headship in certain areas is given sometimes to men, sometimes to women, depending on their capabilities. The headship of the father is not forfeited but modified to fit present situations. The complementary roles of man and wife are seen as rooted in God's order of heterosexual creation. Male "authority" is seen in the context of a mutual love which gives dignity to the role of the woman. Structure and function are seen as interrelated. The headship of Christ in the church is suggested as the pattern.

7. After passing through a period when much Protestant writing on the family encouraged a permissive relationship between parents and children, once again a concern is evident for discipline and the formation of adults who will be able to assume responsibility. As a consumer society, which is abstract and anonymous, becomes more pervasive, an indispensable function of the family will be to build and preserve personal values. Thus a family must give its growing children their freedom neither too early nor too late.

8. While attempting to remain faithful to the Bible, the writings of those representing evangelical-conservative Protestantism tend to oversimplify modern problems, to show greater sympathy for family patterns of the rural past, to utilize lists of rules and codes, and to place a greater accent on personal piety than on concern for societal institutions.

9. Most Lutheran writings fall into the category of "structural ethics." Marriage and the family are seen as structures of creation that arise by the will of God and provide for the interior and exterior necessities of man. Thus the "subordination" of woman to man is a realistic appraisal and acceptance of certain facts of creation. We are not dealing with a question of equalitarianism, but of a complementary relationship between husband and wife. Life under the Gospel is faith working by love rather than conformity to a system of rules.

10. There is a notable difference in current religious literature on family structures, roles, and relationships. Some writings are almost exclusively sociological in orientation. Other studies are mainly Biblical and theological in orientation. In both Roman Catholic and Protestant studies a Biblical, creation-based approach is emerging which is also Gospel-oriented. While it regards Christian family relations as an expression of love to Christ, it is realistic enough to keep the cultural and sociological factors in a rapidly changing society in clear view.

NOTES—CHAPTER 9

1. *Casti Connubii,* published by the Missionary Society of St. Paul the Apostle, 401 West 59th Street, New York, N. Y. 10019, copyright 1941, p. 1.
2. Ibid., pp. 7—8.
3. Ibid., p. 9.
4. Ibid., p. 9.

5. Ibid., p. 9.
6. Ibid., p. 6.
7. Ibid., p. 6.
8. Edward W. O'Rourke, *Marriage and Family Life* (Champaign, Ill.: The Newman Foundation at the University of Illinois, 1956).
9. Ibid., p. 112.
10. Ibid., p. 112.
11. Alphonse H. Clemens, *Marriage and the Family: An Integrated Approach for Catholics* (Englewood Cliffs, N. J.: Prentice-Hall, 1957), p. 87.
12. Ibid., p. 87.
13. Ibid., p. 87.
14. *Together in Christ: A Preparation for Marriage,* National Catholic Welfare Conference pamphlet, 1312 Massachusetts Ave., N. W., Washington, D. C. 20005, no date.
15. Ibid., under "Man and Wife," pp. 10 – 13.
16. O'Rourke, p. 159.
17. Clemens, p. 261.
18. Ibid., p. 261.
19. John J. Kane, *Marriage and the Family: A Catholic Approach* (New York: The Dryden Press, 1952); see Ch. 4.
20. Ibid., p. 60.
21. Ibid., pp. 67 – 69.
22. Walter M. Abbott, ed., "Constitution on the Sacred Liturgy," *The Documents of Vatican II,* tran., ed. Joseph Gallagher (New York: Guild Press, 1966), pp. 137 – 78.
23. Ibid., "Pastoral Constitution on the Church in the Modern World," Ch. 2, pp. 222 – 31.
24. Ibid., pp. 249 – 58.
25. Ibid., p. 250.
26. Ibid., see Section 50, pp. 253 – 55. This quotation occurs in the final paragraph.
27. H. Caffarel, *Marriage Is Holy,* tran. Bernard Murchland (Chicago: Fides Publishers, 1957), pp. 71 – 73; Leon Joseph Suenens, *Love and Control: The Contemporary Problem* (Westminster, Md.: The Newman Press, 1961). See the magazine *Marriage* published by the Benedictines at St. Meinrad's Archabbey in Indiana; Mary Rosera Joyce, "The Meaning of Man and Woman in Marriage," *Marriage,* XLVIII, 10 (October 1966), 14 – 19.
28. John J. Kane, "The New Look in American Fathers," *Marriage,* XLV, 8 (August 1963), 24; Monica Breault, "Why Is a Mother?" *Marriage,* XLIII, 9 (September 1961), 45 – 48.
29. John L. Thomas, *Looking Toward Marriage* (Notre Dame, Ind.: Fides), 1964.
30. Ibid., p. 263.
31. Ibid., pp. 265 – 66.
32. Ibid., pp. 264 – 65.
33. Ibid., pp. 266, 268.
34. Ibid., pp. 266 – 267.
35. *Pastoral Document of the Italian Episcopate,* "Marriage and the Family Today," in 21 sections, appearing in the Dec. 4 (pp. 7 – 8) and Dec. 11, 1969 (pp. 6 – 7) English edition of *L'Osservatore Romano,* the official Vatican newspaper. In addition to Roman Catholic works cited in this chapter, the student will get valuable insights from F. X. Arnold, *Woman and Man: Their Nature and Mission* (New York: Herder and Herder, 1963), especially Chs. 2 to 5.

36. Wallace Denton, *What's Happening to Our Families?* (Philadelphia: The Westminster Press, 1963), p. 42.

37. Ibid., p. 42.

38. While some churchmen have objected to the use of the term "democratic" as being neither sociologically correct nor theologically sound, it has been commonly used since World War II to describe the new family type which was seen emerging in America in contrast to the patriarchal patterns of an earlier period. See Ernest W. Burgess and Harvey J. Locke, *The Family: From Institution to Companionship* (New York: American Book Co., 1945). This is one of the classical works interpreting this motif.

39. "It is a fact that sociology involuntarily serves this kind of ethics, the so-called new morality, by disclosing what actually exists and is being practiced. Sociology uncovers human behavior, and both writer and reader, who accept the sociological results and consider them representative, are liable to think that democratic majority decisions are right and will conform to them. By representing its results, sociology furthers the tendency in people to adapt their behavior and to consider and declare as ethically right what the majority does. In this way, sociology may, almost unnoticed, change into ethics." Helmut Begemann, "Christian Ethics in the Face of the Changes in Marriage and Sexual Behavior," *Lutheran World,* XIII, 4 (1966), 396–411.

40. This is the authorized curriculum for the Presbyterian Churches, the Moravian Church, and the Reformed Church in America. See Roy Fairchild, *Christians in Families: An Inquiry into the Nature and Mission of the Christian Family* (Richmond, Va.: The Covenant Life Curriculum, 1964), pp. 27–28.

41. Roy W. Fairchild and J. C. Wynn, *Families in the Church: A Protestant Survey* (New York: Association Press, 1961), p. 28.

42. Elton and Pauline Trueblood, *The Recovery of Family Life* (New York: Harper & Brothers, 1953), pp. 88–90.

43. Ibid., pp. 88, 90.

44. Denton, pp. 55-73.

45. Fairchild, *Christians in Families,* p. 32.

46. See especially Betty Friedan, *The Feminine Mystique* (New York: Dell Publishing Co., 1963).

47. Horace Bushnell, *Christian Nurture* (New Haven: Yale University Press, 1947), pp. 50–51; 72, 76, 204, 212, 275. Modern writers appear often to see only the extremes of the more authoritarian patterns of the past. Their statements should be tempered with what Horace Bushnell taught in his significant book, which first appeared in 1847. He laid great stress on teaching children by the character, faith, love, spirit, and example of parents. Note Ch. 5.

48. Evelyn M. Duvall, David R. Mace, and Paul Popenoe, *The Church Looks at Family Life* (Nashville: Broadman Press, 1964), pp. 94–95, 155–67.

49. Gibson Winter, *Love and Conflict: New Patterns in Family Life* (Garden City, N. Y.: Doubleday and Company, Inc., 1958).

50. Ibid., p. 52.

51. Ibid., p. 54.

52. Ibid., p. 56.

53. Ibid., p. 58.

54. Ibid., p. 64.

55. Ibid., pp. 65–68.

56. Ibid., p. 65.

57. Ibid., p. 66.

58. Ibid., p. 66.

59. Ibid., p. 67.

60. Ibid., p. 68.

61. Ibid., p. 68.
62. Fairchild, pp. 30−31.
63. Ibid., p. 11.
64. Ibid., p. 135.
65. Ibid., p. 50.
66. This 1952 Lutheran survey included 3,400 couples, 750 unmarried young people, and 1,000 pastors in three synods: The Lutheran Church−Missouri Synod (German background), The Evangelical Lutheran Church (Norwegian background), The Augustana Evangelical Lutheran Church (Swedish background), residing in all parts of the United States and chosen by an approved, objective method (random sampling). The following data deal with family authority and responsibility. The responses of the laity are indicated by M (married) and S (single, not yet married); and the pastors' responses by P. The answers to three questions are given in percentages under four classifications. The third question was not asked of the pastors.

		Right/Yes	Not Sure	Never Mention	Wrong/No	No Answer
Do you believe it	M	11%	3%		84%	2%
is right for the	S	10%	5%		84%	1%
husband to have	P	37%		1%	60%	2%
final authority						
in the home?						
Do you believe it	M	96%	1%		2%	1%
is right for both	S	96%	1%		2%	1%
husband and wife	P	83%		2%	14%	1%
to share						
authority by						
common agreement?						
Does the practice	M	91%			5%	4%
in your home	S	78%			12%	10%
agree with your						
belief expressed						
in above questions?						

67. Norman V. Williams, *The Christian Home* (Chicago: Moody Press, 1952), p. 32.
68. Ibid., p. 32.
69. Ibid., p. 36.
70. Harold Haas, "Christian Faith and Family Life," Ch. 5 in *Christian Social Responsibility*, Vol. 3 of *Life in Community*, ed. Harold C. Letts (Philadelphia: Muhlenberg Press, 1957), pp. 148−51.
71. Ibid., pp. 154−57.
72. Ibid., p. 161.
73. Ibid., pp. 160−62.
74. Ibid., pp. 173−74.
75. Carl F. Reuss, *The New Shape of the American Family* (Minneapolis: Commission on Research and Social Action, The American Lutheran Church, 422 S. 5th Street, Minneapolis, Minn. 55415, 1963).
76. L. Brøndum, *Familielivets Etik* (Copenhagen: Nyt Norsdisk Forlag Arnold Busck, 1963), pp. 46−48.
77. Helmut Begemann, *Strukturwandel der Familie* (Hamburg: Furche-Verlag, 1960), Chs. 9−12.
78. Begemann, "Christian Ethics in the Face of Changes in Marriage and Sexual Behavior," *Lutheran World*, XIII, 4 (1966), 396−411.

CHAPTER 10

The Family Under God

OSCAR E. FEUCHT

Given the Old and New Testaments, which are the inspired record of selected dealings of God with man and which have the special purpose of revealing His saving grace in His words and actions, we must recognize that the Scriptures contain both descriptive and prescriptive elements. Among the descriptive elements are many things purely historical, cultural, and political, as well as the sins, weaknesses, and shortcomings of people as they reacted to God and to their environment. Many of these are recorded to show man's rebellion against the revealed will of God. The Scripture lists these incidents for our warning (1 Cor. 10:11). We should not, however, raise these descriptive statements, nor the ceremonial and political laws of Israel now superseded by the Gospel, to the level of "universal law," that is, make them prescriptive for all time.

Our search is for those teachings of the Bible which record, illustrate, and interpret God's great plan for man's salvation and for man's relationship to Him and his fellowman. Christians have always regarded these teachings as the prescriptive elements of the Scriptures. Some schools of theology "equalize" and "literalize" all of Scripture without due regard for the distinction between sin and grace, between Law and Gospel, and without due regard for the New Testament's interpretation of the Old Testament under the full orb of the Gospel of Jesus Christ.

We come now to a summarization of the explorations made in the preceding chapters. We have surveyed several millennia of time, various currents of thought, and different cultures, philosophies, and theological orientations. We ask: Have moderns something to learn from history? More particularly, what does this review of family-authority patterns and structures have to say to Christians in the late 20th century as they look on the family under the spotlight of the Gospel?

In the first chapter key questions were proposed, which get at some of the particulars of our quest. In this chapter we give a summary response on the basis of our findings. We did not find an authoritative answer for all of these questions; nor was that our objective. We did hope to see each question in the light of many disciplines, yet always from the viewpoint of evangelical Christianity, that is, Christianity rooted in the Gospel.

1. *What are the chief family structures and patterns in changing American society today, and how do they compare with those of other cultures?*

There have been more changes in American society in recent decades than in preceding centuries. These changes are more apparent in Western than in Eastern cultures. Yet even in the latter cultures there are tendencies toward a less patriarchal and more democratic pattern as almost all societies yield to Western folkways and absorb industrialization and urbanization, sociological and technological changes. The trend in the West is strongly individualistic and culture-oriented. The extended, paternalistic family pattern suited agricultural, tribal, and feudal societies. As societies become more industrial and urbanized, more diversified and professionalized, the extended family pattern is being widely replaced by the small, more flexible, nuclear family of today. The authoritarian family is declining. Yet in one and the same community one finds various patterns existing side by side in varying degrees — the patriarchal alongside the democratic, the former chiefly in the lower income, less educated types of families. The more general emphasis is on the individual's dignity, rights, and responsibility. This has affected American society even more than European and Asiatic societies. While the direction is toward more equalitarian forms, the need for some form of "headship" which does not destroy the uniqueness of male and female roles is recognized. The unconditional obedience demanded by parental discipline in the past has given way to more considerate dealing with the problems of children and youth.

2. *What does the Old Testament teach or imply regarding family-life patterns with particular reference to husband-wife and parent-child relationships?*

The Old Testament and New Testament form a continuity, an unfolding revelation, also with regard to husband-wife and parent-child relationships. Though the Scriptures do not as a rule give us dogmatic, scholastic answers, they do provide the basis for a Christian view of the universe, of the family of man, of man's relationship to God, and of familial and interpersonal relationships.

The Old Testament establishes monogamy as the basic pattern for marriage. Marriage and the family are presented as divine institutions. Christ confirmed this creation-pattern of marriage (Matt. 19:3-9). Old Testament scholars differ on the creation accounts as to whether they give a complementarian and partnership view of husband-wife relations or a male-domination account. (Gen. 2:18 seems to reflect a companionship pattern.) They differ over the question whether the words "rule over" and "desire for" represent a primeval ordinance or a description of the results of the first (original) sin. Neither of the creation accounts (Genesis 1 and 2), however, asserts that a domineering role was assigned to the husband.

Though there are many examples of bigamy, polygamy, concubinage, harlotry, and divorce in the Old Testament record, these are exceptions rather than the rule. They are expressions of man in his fallen state, or they are intrusions from other cultures. Divorce was regularized (for certain causes and because of the "hardness of the heart") by Deuteronomic law. However, it was rejected by the latter prophets. The basic teaching is that marriage is to be patterned after God's covenant relation to His people. This was the model (Mal. 2:14-16; Is. 54:1-11; etc.). The steadfast love *(chesed)* of God for His people is taught as the pattern for husband-wife and parent-child relationships.

The family ethos throughout the Old Testament is patriarchal and patrilineal. Male authority and responsibility prevailed, both outside and inside Israel. It was a man's world. Headship belonged to him. On the other hand, no antifeminism is taught. The Old Testament has scenes of the tenderest nature regarding husband-wife relations. The Song of Solomon, however it may be interpreted, and other statements and examples call for companionship and for what we would call romantic love and marital fidelity.

As for parent-child relationships, alongside the harsh words on the discipline of unruly children are the tender, considerate words of love and filial care. The significant directives of the Decalog and of the passages on the spiritual and social nurture of children are to be a reflection of God's covenant with Israel (Deut. 6:1-9; 7:6-9; Ps. 78:1-8; Book of Proverbs). Marriage and the rearing of a family are not optional. They are basic for society. Nor are they merely "secular" or "natural." They are part of the life of faith and the means for perpetuating the *zera* (seed) and with it carrying forward salvation history. Marriage and family have a theological significance!

3. *What does the New Testament teach or imply regarding these family relationships, and how are we to interpret the passages dealing with the submission of the woman (hypotassein)?*

Faith working by love is a germinal New Testament teaching. It applies not only to justification before God by grace through faith but also to marital and familial relationships. Jesus and the apostles emphasize the forgiveness and love taught by the Gospel. This radical newness was to penetrate every social structure.

The subordination of the woman to the man, as established in the Old Testament, was not revoked in the New Testament; rather it was substantiated by the Holy Spirit through the pronouncements of the apostles. Jesus accepted Jewish family patterns and advocated no change in structure (appealing to Genesis 1 and 2). But He emphasized the dignity and value of every person, showing high regard for women and giving special attention to children. Agape — self-giving love and service, as demonstrated by Christ's love for the church — is the new model for husband-wife and parent-child relationships.

By the employment of the Greek word *hypotassein* the New Testament retains superordination and subordination also, in a wide sense, as part of the family structure. It uses this word to describe the relation of the Father to Christ, of Christ to the church, of husband to wife, of parents to children, but never as abject subjection or as degrading inferiority. Many teachers in the church have failed to see the difference between subordination (as used in 1. Cor. 11:3; 15:28) and slavish subjection. Children are to be subordinate to their parents, whose experience and leadership God uses.

Love, not law and duty, is to be the motivation. Service to others is the objective. We are to fit ourselves together in our proper place and order! The New Testament sees no contradiction between freedom in Christ and subordination in many roles and places in society (Romans 13; 1 Peter 2 and 3). This order antedates the fall into sin. It is sin that has turned authority into tyranny and liberty into license.

Ephesians 5 emphasizes the service of the husband to the wife (more so than the reverse). Living under grace and in the Lord leads to a kind of partnership without the autocratic and legalistic male dominance often attributed to Biblical passages.

The word "obey" is dropping out of many marriage ceremonies. It may be used if understood in the light of a beneficent order of creation. The tone of the New Testament would be better reechoed if for "obey" we substituted Eph. 5:21: "Be subject to one another out of reverence for Christ."

A Gospel-oriented family pattern helps to make the Christian family "a church in your house," where all members contribute to each other's spiritual growth and build each other up in love. (Eph. 4:12-16; Col. 3:12-25; Romans 12; 1 Corinthians 13)

4. *Is a single, universally normative family structure and operational pattern ordained by God, or are family patterns and forms usually established by culture?*

Anthropologists, sociologists, and psychologists tend to say that family patterns are largely of cultural origin and are determined by the family's environment and the needs of every age. The historian sees family structures as related to civilization; he sees family government as the prototype of political government. The pragmatist says that whatever works most effectively usually determines family regulations; functions determine forms.

Culture and folkways do influence religious practices. In our more mobile and intimate society they can be strongly influential in setting up new models and forming customs, conventions, and manners which are imbued with ethical significance. We are never divorced from current social and cultural changes. Families are affected by our rapidly developing technology, industrial civilization, modern mobility, and new insights from the behavioral sciences. All of these assert their influence on the family and contribute to modifications and changes.

As we look around in our world—shrinking in size and coming into every domicile via the mass media—we are confronted with European, Asiatic, African, as well as American family structures and folkways. In fact, we see in our own society various family patterns from the patriarchal to the most equalitarian, in varying degrees but with a strong trend toward partnership. Man usually adjusts to his environment and its varying factors.

Christian theologians see in the very order of creation—the "givenness" of man and woman, heterosexuality, biological differences, certain feminine and masculine endowments—the divinely established base for marriage structures and family relationships. The Scriptures give us their consistent teaching on one mankind (Acts 17:26), one lordship of the Creator-God, one order in nature, one basic, normative family structure. This is affirmed by Jesus in Matthew 19 and by Paul's argumentations in Romans 1 and 2.

Lutheran theologians have seen in the term "structure" a large-scale relationship which defines people's responsibilities to each other in the familial, governmental, commercial, and social worlds. These are seen as moral in nature, more or less durable in time, and as the doings of God for the welfare of man. These structures form the criteria by which God constantly evaluates man's performance. Thus God has provided a basic order within which a particular society will be able to work out suitable forms and make wise modifications for beneficent family government and administration. A single, universally normative family structure is ordained by God.

5. *In what sense and in which spheres does the Bible teach the equal personhood of man and woman and of husband and wife?*

Much of tradition has been prejudiced by the "male-dominance theory." A careful exegetical study of the creation account does not yield a doctrine of male "superiority" and female "inferiority." Man and woman are alike as human beings, but they are also different. Husbands and wives are not equals in all things. In addition to their biological differences, they have psychological differences, are born with different endowments and potentials, grow up under different circumstances or environments, have varying experiences in life, and variously develop their gifts and abilities.

Male and female however are created by the same God with dignity, rights, and beneficent purposes intended. God wants these endowments to be sustained and protected and to fulfill a common purpose: service to God and man as set forth in the creation account and in the Decalog. As with God there is no distinction of persons, so let there be none in our social realm (James 2). But God alone is impartial!

Male and female are embraced in God's plan of redemption. In this sense the Bible teaches the equal personhood of man and woman. In the realm of the kingdom of God there is no male or female — both are of equal value in the sight of God (Gal. 3:28). In marriage man and wife have the same conjugal rights (1 Cor. 7:3-5). Their equality in the sight of God is clear, and it should be reflected in husband-wife relationships. Husband and wife, parents and children need each other for mutual growth and happiness. To this we must add their equal status in the priesthood of all believers. (1 Peter 2:5, 9-10)

A higher status of woman is recognized today in other aspects of life: in social, business, civic, and political realms. Women have now entered almost all professions and vocations in our rapidly developing producer and consumer world. There has been and still is a tremendous shift of women to new and different careers as the result of suffrage, higher education, and an expanding world economy. The women's rights movement has had much to do with expanding the world of women.

In the whole realm of nature there are nevertheless differences. These differences are part of God's creative design and are intended for distinctive purposes and the general welfare of mankind. Both the Old and the New Testament teach the equality of man and woman before God as well as their differentiation as inherent in our heterosexual creation. Man and woman complement each other in many ways and in many spheres of service. This wider field of service is well reflected already in the Old Testament Book of Proverbs, especially in chapter 31.

6. *To what extent is Christ's relationship to His church as Servant, Savior, and Head to be the pattern for Christian family structure and interaction?*

The germinal teaching of the Old Testament is God's covenant relation to His chosen people. This relationship of benevolent concern is to be reflected between husband and wife. The ideal of partnership is more implied than specifically taught. The New Testament gives an extension of Old Testament teaching. It is most explicitly set forth in Eph. 5:21 to 6:4. As Christ loved the church, so the husband is to love his wife. No higher model could have been given. As Christ served, unto death on the cross, so husband and wife are to serve each other for their mutual well-being and happiness and in the fulfillment of their specific roles and functions. They are in a sense "servants" to each other.

The headship of the husband as taught in the New Testament is not one of autocratic, overbearing superiority. That image is derived from fallen mankind and is obnoxious to God. Headship serves the purpose of good order, but only when it is benevolent and helpful and when it ministers to the spouse and serves the best interests of the family. The New Testament emphasis on marriage "in the Lord" makes Christ's love and servanthood the model. It never stands for autocratic demand and servile obedience, but for sympathetic love and self-giving service "as Christ loved and served the church."

Thus both Old Testament and New Testament contain in essence the same pattern, which is "Christian" only as the love of Christ is the *modus vivendi* of individual members of a family. When Christ's beneficent rule is in the heart, it will manifest itself in the total family operation and the interaction of its members. Naturally this love is reflected in the wider realms of Christian social action. The uniquely Christian ethos of salvation by God's grace, accepted by Spirit-given confession-repentance-faith and actualized in a faith that works by love, permeates the New Testament and governs all human relationships, also those of the family.

7. *How are order, responsibility, and authority related to love, nurture, and service in the Christian family?*

Order and responsibility are necessary for man's welfare. From Scripture we have seen that order, responsibility, and authority are found even in the relationships between Father, Son, and Holy Spirit. They have been found helpful and necessary in family, tribe, nation, and business. Sound structure is basic to any corporation and institution. Superordination and subordination can exist without dominance and without loss of personal dignity. The difficulty arises from improper, degrading, depersonalizing, and unethical (sinful) use of authority. Sin makes tyrants of people.

Family headship is not cancelled out, but it is given a new dimension and potential by the Gospel. The Christian faith's chief fruit is love. Agape elevates all relationships, especially those in marriage and in child guidance. Our union with Christ by a common faith lifts all our relationships, both inside and outside the family, to a new level. Where the Gospel is comprehended, there respect, consideration, love, and service grow.

By our very creatureliness we belong to God's order or structure. The Decalog presupposes authority and responsibility. We cannot emancipate ourselves from this order and from these norms. They belong to life. They form God's design for all mankind. Under the Gospel they take on higher meaning.

In Luther's theology of the two kingdoms (Chapter 6) "law and order," "obedience and submission" are not equated with "legislation" but with God's orderings in creation. Christians accept this ethos. It is God's ordering that a man can't bear a child, but a woman can. There is really no escape from this; one only accepts it as a fact. The Christians' response of love and service in all areas of life is a demonstration of faith. Only at the end of the age (the *eschaton*) will all differences and failures be wiped out. Husband and wife, parents and children are to live under God's creative order and His benevolent authority.

The New Testament does not annul the creative order nor remove the headship *(kephale)* structure. This structure in fact relates to the whole theological universe (1 Cor. 11:3; Eph. 5:21 to 6:4; Deuteronomy 6 and 7; Colossians 3; etc.). The key is supplied by Eph. 5:21, "Be subject to one another out of reverence for Christ."

What Christian theology affirms, psychology confirms, namely, that every member of the family needs affection, nurture, and service — in varying degrees and at the various stages of life — to become well-balanced persons able to live responsibly in our world.

8. *How should the Christian family of today regard the many modifications that are taking place in our changing culture?*

The catastrophies of war, changes in political systems, the almost cataclysmic changes in culture and technology, industrial and sociological changes, and especially urbanized living and the new totalism (being tied into the machine age and locked into a business or labor system) have greatly influenced family living. Business is computerized. Industry is automated. These are described in some detail in Chapters 7 and 8. In many instances these have contributed to family disorganization.

On the farm and in the factory machines are doing most of the work. The inner city has turned into a ghetto. The city has expanded into suburbia with its family-related advantages and disadvantages.

Regarding the family itself David Mace has put his finger on the major changes: (1) Marriage has changed (for many Americans) from institution to companionship; (2) partners with fixed roles find themselves partners with fluid roles; (3) the family is changing from the extended family to the nuclear family; (4) marriage is more unitive-centered than procreative-centered; (5) childbearing is restricted to a shorter time span; (6) at the polls and in many homes there are two votes; (7) marriages cross national, social, religious, and even racial barriers; (8) we are perhaps recovering a more positive and Biblical view of sexuality.

Modern appliances have freed men and women from hard labor and drudgery. The number of women students in college is rapidly approaching the number of male students. Woman's roles are widening in the industrial and business worlds. She has three major roles in the home: (1) as wife, mother, homemaker, teacher; (2) as companion to her husband and social leader; and (3) as partner and business associate — especially in her consumer role. This is a far cry from the producer-homemaker role of colonial days. Due to the greater absence of the father, the family is becoming more matrifocal.

As a consequence of our new technology, no child will any longer live in the world of his parents. Nevertheless the childbearing, feeding, clothing, sheltering, equipping, restoring, and supporting functions of the family will remain. So will socialization, personal maintenance, preparing for old age, and the transmission of a heritage. In all of these the family plays the basic role.

Although many functions have moved out of the home, the family plays a vital role for the development of personality, for mutual acceptance, better communication, and understanding. The affectional and nurturing roles can still be best supplied by the home. At this point the behavioral sciences and family-life education sponsored by the church are needed more and are making more contributions. Parents, by their attitudes, values, verbal and nonverbal "teaching," help most with the physical, social, psychological, emotional, and religious growth of the child. There is no substitute for the family in supplying personal identity, affection, a value system, a philosophy of life, and appreciation of creation and culture. And all of these need the cement of the Gospel if the family is to be God-directed and life-oriented. These functions need to be fulfilled positively over against a growing individualism that can be disorganizing and destructive. The home in most instances can best supply good work-philosophy and vocational guidance. Every person needs a sense of service and a satisfying place in the world. Both the instrumental role of the father (husband) and the expressive role of the mother (wife) are needed in our society. A common faith and the recreative power of the Gospel are needed as integrative forces uniting the family, equipping it with a Christian family ethos, and preparing it to make intelligent, God-pleasing adjustments and significant contributions in a changing culture.

Under the subtitle "A Long Way from Extinction" John Charles Wynn writes: "Indeed, many of the values of the family of yester-year not only are with us yet; some of them have even been reinforced. A greater proportion of the total population now lives in family groups than a century ago. More of the population marries now than then. More married couples live together into their retirement years than ever before." [1]

9. *On the basis of Biblical theology, what position should the church take in regard to woman's role outside the home?*

The confinement of women to the narrow roles of a preindustrial society, as sometimes advocated in the church, is not supported by this study. The Bible records examples that go far beyond the German oversimplification that restricts woman's domain to *Kinder, Küche, Kirche* (children, kitchen, church). There is an illustrious list of "famous women" in both the Old and the New Testament record.

Emancipated by modern technology from many tedious chores, women are being given their God-intended status as persons. By inclination they are richly endowed for many callings. Higher education prepares them for thousands of positions, from heads of state to domestic servants. They are making significant contributions in social, medical, and educational fields.

Also in the church, where their work has seldom been adequately recognized, women serve as directors of education, in evangelism, and in multiple social service roles. The volunteer woman worker is making church and civic projects possible.

The roles of women outside the home are widening. Their individual freedom needs to be respected and the expression of their many talents encouraged. The role of wife and mother must be given priority. Changes in society, as they affect marriage and the family, ought to be constantly evaluated on the basis of Biblical norms and the needs of the individual family. They need to be seen in the light of the Christian mission and Christian experience. The church should speak a word of prophetic judgment as cultures, structures, and special problems (e.g., abortion) endanger the basic functions of the family. The church needs to develop a far more effective ministry to families to nurture them in the faith and to utilize families in the extension of mission and ministry, never forgetting the Spirit-blessed work of so many Christian fathers and mothers in equipping their children for the discipleship life.

10. *What are the theological and educational implications of this study for the church today?*

Our extensive review of family structures, roles, and relationships from three perspectives: historical, sociological, and theological, has widened our focus and helped us identify varying factors that affect family living. We have distinguished between the normal and abnormal, between prescriptive and descriptive examples and assertions of Scripture and the surrounding cultures. They have helped us get at basic theological concepts.

The family is not an accident. It is a God-ordained structure based on a heterosexual creation with built-in drives and norms. Monogamy is the norm. Fidelity is the key. Love is the integrating force. Sexual intercourse in marriage is both unitive and procreative. The superordination and subordination taught in both Old and New Testaments is intended for the sake of good order and is needed for the responsible upbringing of the child. Especially in the Old Testament the model for marriage is the covenant relationship between God and His chosen people. The family is designated as the carrier of God's plan of redemption through the Messiah. The Gospel of forgiveness in Christ, with agape (self-giving love) as its chief fruit, is fully unfolded in the New Testament and is the key to Christian family relationships.

With the fall into sin came man's distortion of the creation design. Estrangement, disorganization, infidelity, and divorce are intruders disturbing the God-intended harmony. The mores of other cultures and of the surrounding nations influenced Israel's life and brought with them wrong models and inequities. Yet the basic pattern was never lost. Sin always brings inequalities, injustices, and tyranny, then as now.

Every society has some kind of sex-role differentiation. Historians, sociologists, and psychologists have helped us see such variations. The balance of power in any given family depends on the resources of the individuals. Personalities, relative age and education, employment status of the wife, occupation of the husband, presence of children, and the stage of the family cycle help assess the balance of power in each family. By God's intention male and female complement each other. Leadership in every family varies with the gifts, talents, and vision of the husband-wife partnership and the tasks to be accomplished.

Success in a family depends strongly on its inner unity and cohesive power. Stability is dependent on many factors, such as order, norms, roles, mutual trust, confidence in each other, attitudes, and sense of responsibility. Functional religion is related to all of these factors. God alone has ultimate authority in the marriage covenant. Good family operations also call for open communication, effective methods of dialog, a trustworthy example, and genuine love and service. All of these are necessary for the adults as well as the children of the family.

Many terms are currently used to describe family structures and relationships. They are borrowed from various disciplines. The term "democratic" has political overtones. It may be used to imply the equality of all members irrespective of age or experience. It may also deny the need of a head or president. The term "equalitarian" may reflect good understanding and relationships, but when overemphasized it may prematurely raise children to the status of adults. The term "patriarchal" has implications of sovereignty vested in the father-head and thus has autocratic overtones. The term "authoritarian" befits a dictator but not the head of a closely knit, friendly household where every person, from newborn infant to senior citizen, has his personhood respected and his life enriched by mutual services.[2]

The term that sociologists and theologians are beginning to use more often is "partnership." All members of the family have needs to be served. Each member has services to give to other members. Family members are unequal in their gifts and maturity, but they are to be equal recipients of love and service. For the Christian family that wants to develop as a fellowship, "partnership in Christ" has much in its favor. It makes the Gospel the prime unifying force; it helps develop a style of life which demonstrates God's love. The Scriptures give us no dogmatic formulas or specific definitions.

"Complementarian" is another favored term. It suggests a shared leadership, each member supplying particular skills. The mother usually has the deeper concern for children; but she must be supported by a father who stands for something, otherwise we are in danger of losing the male quality in the home. Father and mother form a coalition. In Christ perfect love and authority are united. Where the operation of the home becomes a Christian calling, there is an inner spirit, given us by Christ, by which structure and function are held together. The chief task of the church, then, is to help each couple and every set of parents to discover this unity and to practice it as part of being subject to one another out of reverence for Christ. (Eph. 5:21)

Superordination and subordination are in God's plan. Sin and grace, judgment with love, confession and forgiveness permeate God's revelation in Christ. The implications of our study suggest that we avoid authoritarian terms and overgeneralizations. The Bible does not give us a picture of the father ruling his household as an autocrat. Instead it suggests that the father serves as a shepherd and nurturer in the spirit of the Gospel, respecting the individual dignity and worth of every member of the family. In a Christian family all members are partners as they teach and admonish, encourage and assist, speak and live their newness in Christ. (2 Cor. 5:17-21; Col. 3:12-17)

Many changes have affected marriage and family living. It is often feared that these will destroy the basic foundations of family, state, and church. History provides some interesting illustrations. The Soviet Union under the first flashes of communistic philosophy attempted to set aside family structures, only to find negative results and the necessity to revert back to basic, time-tested family structures and norms.

No school or church can fully substitute for the Christian family in transmitting Christian discipleship as a way of life. The family has tremendous influence in giving a sense of values, in setting life goals, in developing basic knowledge and functions by which both church and society are reshaped in every generation. The behavioral scientists assert that the family is not only here to stay but is a basic building block for modern society. One sociologist calls the family "the major transmission belt for the diffusion of cultural standards to the oncoming generation."

The educational implications of this study are most significant. The church of today is worship- and organization-centered. We have institutionalized worship and education both in the public and private domain. This despite the best insights of Christian and secular education which tell us that a family is needed to nurture the whole person. Total growth cannot be achieved by segregating the home from the school. It is hoped that nurture in its broader sense will be accepted by all church leaders and that churches and schools will equip parents for their tasks of giving each generation a Christian understanding of the universe. Nurture includes the physical, mental, emotional, social, and spiritual growth of the child. If the Christian tradition is to be handed on, the family will have to play a decisive role. Home, church, and school need to work together. And in the American system of education the home must be the integrating agency.

"The importance of the family as a fundamental social unit and the role of the family in determining the character and structure of society are fully accepted by all men and women of insight and reason," says Ruth Nanda Anshen.[3] She asserts that there is no need to abandon the basic family structure, as some pragmatists suggest, because sound moral and religious codes lie behind the basic family pattern.

The Bible is not a book of sociology or psychology. It gives us basic structures and bases for a Christian ethic. Chiefly it is a book of salvation history, giving us its unique, life-changing Gospel of God's grace in Christ. This Gospel affects our way of life, our whole ethos. It effects a spirit which actuates manners, customs, moral attitudes, practices, and ideals. It does not always give specific directions in minute details. But it does supply the spirit of the Christian family on the basis of faith, hope, and love.

More than four centuries ago Martin Luther taught:

The family occupies a fundamental relation to both civil and divine government, since it has the training of the future citizen and servant of God. By natural and divine right, authority is lodged in the parents, who occupy at once the threefold office of prophet, priest, and king. It is their function to instruct, to train, and to govern. The immediate end to be attained is the welfare and happiness of the family itself; and more remotely, the preparation of the young for useful and righteous living after their departure from the paternal roof.[4]

NOTES—CHAPTER 10

1. John Charles Wynn, "The American Family—Surviving Through Change," *Presbyterian Life,* 23, 5 (March 1, 1970), 29.
2. For further discussion and evaluation of these terms see David and Vera Mace, *Marriage: East and West* (New York: Doubleday & Co., Inc., 1960), pp. 297, 299.
3. Ruth Nanda Anshen, ed., "The Family in Transition," Ch. 1, *The Family: Its Function and Destiny* (New York: Harper & Brothers, 1949), p. 3; see also pp. 226, 255.
4. From F. V. N. Painter, *Luther on Education,* Concordia Publishing House, paperback, 1965 reprint.

Indexes

Index of Topics

Abortion 228
Afer, Victorinus 83
Agape; see also Love; 20, 61
Annulment, grounds for 87—88
Apocrypha of Old Testament, Sirach
　35; Tobias 47
Apostolic Constitutions 80—81
Aquinas, Thomas 93, 95
Augustine of Hippo 82—83, 189
Authority, parental 112, 145; shift in
　182; vested in father 194

Ba'al (husband), meaning of 31, 53 fn
Baber, Ray E. 175
"Balance of power" in marriage 168
Bales, Robert F. 171, 183 fn
Baptist position 196
Basar; see also Flesh; meaning of in
　O.T. 28
Bayith (house), meaning of 32, 53 fn
Begemann, Helmut 28, 35, 48, 59, 60,
　61, 62, 63, 211
Behavior, patterns of 161
Behavioral sciences 159 ff, 197, 198
Behaviorism 152
Bell, Daniel 138
Bertinetti, Ilse 26
Beweddung (betrothal) 89
Bigamy 35, 49
Biological factors in marriage 100, 173
Birth rate, rising 187
Blitsten, Dorothy R. 176, 185 fn
Blood, Robert 160, 168, 169, 171
Bott, Elizabeth 165
Bowman, Henry 174
Brown, Thomas Edwards 184 fn
Bultmann, Rudolf 69
Brøndum, L. 210
Brunner, Peter 19
Burgess, E. W. 163
Bushnell, Horace 126—127

Caffarel, H. 193
Calhoun, Arthur W. 125, 134 fn
Calvinism; *see also* Protestant position;
　128, 151

Casti Connubii; see Papal encyclical
Cato the Censor on changed status of
　women 76
Cavan, Ruth Shonle 159, 165, 166, 167
Change in marriage and family life 23,
　177—179; organizational and
　bureaucratic 139, 149; technologi-
　cal and industrial 140
Chesed (steadfast love); *see also Agape*
　and Love; 40, 47, 50, 51, 219
Child sacrifices 33
Childbearing 139, 202, 209
Child care 139, 145, 203, 209
Childless marriages 170
Chivalry and women 92
Christ, new life in 58, 63, 68, 71
Christ, role of Lord and Servant 63
"Christian" family 114
Christian family, roles in 206; *see also*
　Roles
Christian Fathers on marriage 78 ff
Chrysostom 81—84
Church and family life 93, 150
"Church in your house" 207
Church, women in 68, 93
Civil law in Old Testament 47
Clan as larger grouping 32
Classes, social 166—168
Clemens, Alphonse H. 189, 190
Clement of Alexandria 78, 79, 96 fn
"Colleague family" 175
Community work, women in 167
Companion role 166, 188; *see also*
　Roles
Complementarian pattern 175
Complementary role 189, 199; *see*
　also Roles
Concubinage 35, 38, 219
Consensus, family control by 163
Cooley, C. E. 17
Coser, Rose 165
Covenant love; see also *Chesed* and
　Love; 39 ff
Covenant and creation interlinked 43 ff
Covenant Life Curriculum 197
Covenant promise 45

Covenant theology 50, 197
Creation, ongoing in marriage 43
Creation, order of 69, 100, 211
Cultural change, effects of 12; *see also* Change
Cultures, family roles in other 94, 177, 218
Culver, Elsie Thomas 37

Daniel-Rops, Henri 94, 97 fn
Decision-making in family 169, 171
De Grazia, Sebastian 14, 24 fn
"Demasculinized men" 199
Democratic family patterns 16, 18, 193, 210
Denton, Wallace 197, 199
Desertion, "poor man's divorce" 167
Despotism 18
De Tocqueville, Alexis 126
Deutsch, Helene 161
De Vaux, Roland 34
Differences, men and women 172
Dike, Samuel W. 126
Discipline 17, 203, 210
Divorce, Jesus' teaching on 60; in pagan society 77; Old Testament on 42, 47, 50; New Testament on 58
Domination, male 38
Duties, table of 63, 71

Education, effect on marriage 163
Elert, Werner 102, 117 fn
Elmer, Manuel C. 131
Emotional differences, men and women 172
Employment; *see also* Working women; discrimination in 174; effect on women's decision-making 169
Ephesians 5:25-30, explanation of 62 f
Episcopal position 196
Equalitarianism 161, 170, 175, 198, 206, 209
Eschatology 64, 108
Estate, family as 101
Etzem (bone), meaning of in O.T. 28
Evangelical-Conservative position 129, 207
"Expressive" role of wife 182
Ezekiel the Prophet 41
Ezer (helper), use of term 26

Fairchild, Roy 116 fn, 197, 199, 206
Fakkema, Mark 129
"Familism" 138, 144
Family, Christian 114, 206; control by consensus 163; divine institution 28; "extended" 17, 84, 163, 178,

182; kinds of function in 13; life cycle 143; Luther on 99 ff; rural 197; stability 179 f
Family and church 17, 150
Family life; *see also* Change and Family; change in 23; patterns of according to Genesis 1–2, 25–29; democratic patterns 16, 18, 193, 201
Family Life Bureau of National Catholic Welfare Conference 190
Father, absence from family 14, 42; authority vested in 194; *paterfamilias* 85, 129; priest and educator 34
Fatherhood, need of restoration 203
Federal Council of Churches 128
Femininity 199
Festivals, Old Testament 34
Feudal system, marriage in 86–88
"Filiarchy" 147
Flesh; *see also Basar;* use of term in O.T.; "one flesh" 63–65
Forgiveness in marriage and family life 109, 115
Fourth Commandment, Luther on 110 ff
Frankish Law 86
Freedom for children 17, 152; for women 31, 162; Luther on Christian freedom 153
Freudianism 152
Frontier, women on 124
Fulfillment, woman's sense of 200 f

Genesis 3:15, various translations 29 f; interpretation 55 fn
Gifta, meaning of 85
Gnosticism 78
God as Father 35, 109
God's order, family as 101 ff
Goode, William 160, 174, 176
Goodsell, Willystine 121, 135 fn
Gospel, life under 22, 57, 61, 63, 68, 72, 107, 217, 221
Grace, women's equality in 60
Grelot, Pierre 27, 46–48

Haas, Harold 208–210
Hagar, Frank N. 126
Headship of household; see also *Kephale* structure; husband as head 18, 188, 208, 209; situational headship 198
Hellenism 58–60
Heterosexuality 208, 210, 228
Horkheimer, Max 133
Hosea the Prophet 39
Husband; *see* Headship, *Kephale*

structure, and Roles
Hypotassein, meaning of 65 – 67, 220; *see also* Subordination

Ignatius of Antioch 68, 96 fn
Immigration 127, 145
Individualism 138, 140, 144, 156
Industrial Revolution 140 f, 146, 199
"Instrumental" role of husband 182
Isaiah the Prophet 40

Jaeger, Werner 59
Jentsch, Werner 59
Jeremiah the Prophet 41
Jesus, salvation history fulfilled in 45; teaching on marriage 57 – 61; *see also* Christ
Johnsen, Gisle Christian 130
Judaism 51, 58, 59, 73 fn, 220
Julian Laws 77
Justin Martyr 79

Kaehler, Else 62, 74 fn
Kane, John J. 191, 193
Kenkel, William F. 169
Kennett, R. H. 39
Kephale (head) structure 19, 225
Kirkpatrick, Clifford 165
Köhler, Ludwig 37
Komarovsky, Mirra 161, 162

Landis, Paul 172 – 173
Leisure; *see* "New leisure"
Levirate marriage 32, 50
Locke, Harvey J. 163
Love; *see also Chesed* and *Agape;* mutual 188; place in O.T. marriage concept 46 – 48; self-sacrificing 63; stress on in Judaism 51; with use of authority 194
Luchaire, Achille 88
Lunt, Paul S. 165
Luther, Martin, on family 99 f, 151, 153; on freedom 153; two-kingdom theology 105 ff; *see also* Reformation
Lutheran position 68, 129 – 131, 151, 208 – 210; *see also* Reformation
Lutheran survey 207, 216 fn

Mace, David 171, 177, 185 fn, 186 fn, 201, 226
Malachi the Prophet 42
Male domination 38
Manorial home life 90
Marriage, childless 170; Christian Fathers on 78 ff; codes in O.T. 33; democratic idea of 70; divine origin 28; era of Judges 35; era of Kings 36 – 37; era of Patriarchs

32, 44; era of Prophets 38 – 42; exilic and postexilic 43 ff; European views 210; Jesus teaching on 57 – 61; forbidden degrees 33; mutuality in 62 – 65; ongoing creation in 43; as partnership 194; spiritual-mystical nature 193; Reformation teaching 99 ff; Saint Paul's teaching 61 – 65
Masculinity 199
Matriarchy 11, 109, 198
"Matrifocal" families 167
Mead, Margaret 161, 162, 183 fn
Methodist position 196
Micah the Prophet 39
Miller, Daniel R. 176
Minimum wage laws 174
Mixed marriages 79 f
Mohar (marriage present) 38
Monogamy 29, 34, 35, 49, 143, 219; Hosea's witness for 39
Morality 152; *see also* "New morality"
Mosaic laws on marriage 33, 121
Multiple marriages; *see* Polygamy
Mundium, meaning of 85
Mutual love 188; *see also Agape, Chesed,* and Love
Mutual roles in family 179
Mutuality in marriage 62 – 65, 203, 208
Mystery of marriage union 64
Mystical-spiritual nature of marriage 193

National Catholic Welfare Conference, Family Life Bureau 190
Negro families 148, 163 – 164, 181, 183 – 184, 197
"New leisure" 14, 144, 150, 155
"New morality" 153
Nuclear family 53 fn, 175, 178

Obedience 194, 218
Ockham, William of 93, 95
Oikos (house), meaning of 59
Order, family as God's 101 ff
Ordination of women 74 fn
Ordnung und Stand, Luther on 101
Origen 80
O'Rourke, Edward 189
Orthodox (Church) position 196

Paideia (nurture of children) 59 – 68
Papal encyclical 187 ff
Parental office, authority of 112, 145
Parsons, Talcott 161, 171
Partner role 27, 165, 194
Paterfamilias 85, 129; *see also* Father
Patriarchialism 11, 16, 31, 125, 167, 175, 180, 193, 211

Patriarchs, marriage under 29 ff
Patterns of marriage and family life; *see also* Roles; complementarian 175; democratic 16, 18, 193, 201
Permissiveness 201
Physical differences, men and women 172
"Placement" in family 101
Polygamy 35, 36 – 37, 38, 47, 49
Polygyny 29
Pope John XXIII 195
Pope Leo XIII 188
Pope Pius XI 187
Popenoe, Paul 171
Population density 155; mobility 146
Presbyterian position 128
"Protestant ethic" 156
Protestant position, mainline 196 ff; *see also* under various denominations
Puritanism 120 – 122
Psychological differences, men and women 172 – 173

Redemption, order of 69
Reformation teaching on marriage 99 ff
Relationships, husband-wife 62, 169; in family 207; parents-children 70 – 71, 201
Reuss, Carl F. 136 fn, 210
Rights, women's 125
Roles, marriage and family 151, 154, 161, 172, 182, 202, 206; changes in 159, 161, 165 – 166; vocational 200; *see also* Patterns, Relationships and Structures
Roman Catholic position 27, 127 – 128, 151, 187 – 196
Rural families 160, 197

Saint Paul on marriage 61 – 65
Salvation history, family in 42 – 48
Schillebeeckx, Fr. Edward C. 42
Schlier, Heinrich 68
Schmiedeler, Edgar 128
Seed (*zera*), use of term in Bible 44 – 45, 220
Sex, differentiation 161, 172; effects of 209; in family-life functions 172; values in sex roles 174
Sexuality, divine origin 25; Freudian teaching 49, 152
Slater, Philip 165
Sociology, influence of 13, 131, 153, 197, 221
Song of Solomon, allegory 46, 55 fn
Spock, Dr. Benjamin 152
Stand und Ordnung, Luther on 101
Stauffer, Ethelbert 61

Stroup, Atlee 171, 172
Structures in marriage and family 19, 29, 51, 59, 128, 150
Subordination of woman 17, 21, 23, 31, 65 – 67, 69, 71, 193, 206, 210; not the same as "subjection" 67
Suburban families 13, 17, 146 – 148
"Success" in marriage 170
Survey, Bureau of Census 146; Lutheran 207, 216 fn
Swanson, Guy E. 176

Table of duties, 63, 71
Tacitus 84 – 85
Talmud 59
Television, effects of 14, 148
Tertullian 79
Thielicke, Helmut 35, 69
Toledoth (generation, family history) 44
Thomas, John L., S. J. 193 – 195
Thomes, Mary Margaret 163
Trever, Albert A. 77 – 78
Tribe as larger grouping 32
Trueblood, Elton and Pauline 199

Udry, J. Richard 162, 169, 171
Unity in marriage, physical and spiritual 64
Urbanization 13, 137, 145, 156 fn

Values in sex roles 174
Vatican II documents 192
Vatican newspaper 195
Virginity compared to matrimony 93
Virtues of woman in Proverbs 46
Vocational roles of husband and wife 151, 200, 210
Von Rad, Gerhard 52 fn
Von Skal, George 126

Wallace-Hadrill, J.M. 85
Warner, W. Lloyd 165
Weber, Max 151
White House Conferences 131
Whyte, William 147
Widows, provision for 87
Wife, equality "in Christ" 63; in church 68, 93; as "junior partner" 159; *see also* Subordination
Wife-and-mother role 165
Williams, Jay 90, 97 fn
Winter, Gibson 202, 207
Wolfe, Donald 160, 168, 169, 171
Woman; *see also* Relationships, Roles, Subordination, Wife; frontier life 124; as "helper" (*ezer*) 26; in labor force 15, 143, 174 f, 200

Women's Bureau of Labor Department 174

Wood, Leland Foster 128

Wynn, John Charles 116 fn, 198, 227

Zedlitch, Morris Jr. 161, 162

Zera (seed), use of term 44—45, 220

Index of Scripture Passages

Old Testament

Genesis
1:26-28 — 25, 27, 28, 43, 61, 64, 208, 209, 210
2:4-25 — 26, 27, 47, 61, 63, 64, 208, 210, 219
3:15 — 44
3:16 — 29, 30, 49
3:20 — 26, 27
4:1, 19-25 — 31, 44
6:9 — 44
9:11, 21-28 — 44
10:32 — 44
11:1, 7-9 — 44
12:1-3 — 45
15:5 — 45
16:6 — 32
17:7 — 45
21:9 — 32
26:24 — 48
28:13 — 48
29:17-20, 29-32 — 47
31:53 — 48
32:10 — 48
34:21 — 38
37:27 — 28
38:15-19, 24 — 47

Exodus
12:21-27 — 34
13:14 — 34
20:12, 17 — 33, 34, 40, 48
21:15, 17 — 33, 40
22:16 — 38
34:15-16 — 33

Leviticus
18:6 — 28, 48
19:3 — 40
20:9 — 33, 40

Deuteronomy
4:9 — 34
5:16, 18 — 33, 44
6:1-9 — 34, 220, 225
7:6-11 — 33, 35, 220
11:18-21 — 34
17:14-17 — 37
21:14, 18-21 — 33, 34, 40

22:13-30 — 33
24:1-4 — 33, 40, 50, 51
25:5-10 — 50
27:16, 46 — 33, 34, 40, 48

Joshua
7:14-18 — 32
9:3 — 35

Judges
1:21, 27-35 — 35
2:23 — 35
3:5-6 — 35
4:5 — 36
5:30 — 35
8:29-30 — 35
9:2 — 28
11:30-40 — 35
21:12 — 35

1 Samuel
15:50 — 36
18:25, 27 — 36, 38
25:42-44 — 36, 38

2 Samuel
2:2 — 36
3:2-5, 14-16 — 36, 38
5:1, 13 — 28, 36
11:27 — 36
15:16 — 36
19:12-13 — 28
20:3, 8 — 36

1 Kings
11:1-20 — 36, 38
16:31 — 38
17:8 — 38

2 Kings
4:8 — 38
5:1 — 38
9:37 — 38
11:1-21 — 38
16:3 — 33
21:6 — 33
22:14-20 — 38
23:10 — 33

1 Chronicles
  3:1-8 — 36
  11:1 — 28
  14:3-7 — 36

2 Chronicles
  11:21 — 37
  13:21 — 37
  22:2 — 38
  23:21 — 38

Nehemiah
  5:5 — 28

Job
  31:15 — 43

Psalms
  22:9-11 — 43
  33:20 — 26
  45 — 47, 51
  70:6 — 26
  78:1-8 — 33, 34, 220
  104:27 — 43
  105:9-45 — 45
  136:25 — 43
  139:13 — 43
  145:15-16 — 43
  147:8-9 — 43

Proverbs
  5:15-23 — 46
  6:20 — 46
  10:1 — 46
  15:20 — 46
  25:14 — 80
  29:17 — 80
  30:11, 17 — 46, 223

Song of Solomon
  1:1-3, 16 — 46
  2:6 — 46
  4:16 — 46
  7:8-9 — 46
  13:14 — 46

Isaiah
  50:1-3 — 40
  54:1-11 — 40, 219
  58:7 — 28
  62:1-5 — 40, 41

Jeremiah
  2:23 — 33
  3:18 — 40
  7:31 — 33

Lamentations
  1:1-20 — 41

Ezekiel
  16:1-6, 20-21, 31, 32, 38, 60 — 33, 40,
    47

Hosea
  2:2, 15, 19-20 — 39, 40, 45
  3:3 — 39
  4:12 — 39

Micah
  2:9 — 40
  6:8 — 40
  7:2, 5-6 — 39, 40

Malachi
  2:14-16 — 42, 51, 219

New Testament

Matthew
  1:1 — 45
  1:2-17 — 45
  12:46-50 — 107
  19:1 ff — 29, 50, 61, 64, 69, 219
  20:26 — 63
  22:37-39 — 63
  23:11 — 63
  28:18 — 204

Mark
  1:15 — 57
  9:35 — 63
  10:2-12, 43 — 61, 63

Luke
  1:54-55, 67 — 45
  2:51 — 67
  3:23 — 45
  10:17-20 — 66

John
  4:53 — 60
  5:39 — 46
  8:56 — 46

Acts
  3:25-26 — 46
  10:24, 48 — 60

11:14-15 — 60
16:15, 31-33 — 60
17:26 — 222
18:8 — 60

Romans
4:13-25 — 46
8:7 ff — 61, 67, 204
10:3 — 67
11:32-33 — 106
13:1, 5 — 67, 204, 221

1 Corinthians
7:3-5, 17-24 — 65, 69, 223
10:11 — 217
11:3 ff — 18, 19, 65, 69, 70, 209,
    220, 225
13:8-13 — 58, 70, 221
14:15, 33-36 — 67, 68
15:27-28 — 67, 70, 220
16:16 — 67

2 Corinthians
5:17-21 — 61, 63, 230
9:13 — 230

Galatians
3:6-29 — 46, 58, 60
3:26-28 — 205
3:28 — 64, 69, 107, 209, 223
5:6 — 9
5:13-14 — 61

Ephesians
1:22 — 67
2:10 — 9
4:12-16 — 58, 221
5:17-20 — 67
5:21 ff — 33, 60, 63, 67-70, 205, 223,
    225, 230
6:1-9 — 71

Philippians
2:5, 8-9, 13 — 9, 47, 63
3:21 — 67

Colossians
1:9-14 — 57
2:1-23 — 57, 61
3:1 ff — 57, 67, 71, 225, 230
4:1 — 57

1 Timothy
1:11-12 — 70
2:11-14 — 67, 69
3:3-4 — 67, 69, 70

Titus
2:5-8 — 67
3:1 — 67

Hebrews
2:5-8 — 67
12:9 — 67
13:21 — 9

James
2 — 223
4:7 — 66

1 Peter
2:5-18 — 67, 70, 223
3:1, 5, 10, 22 — 67, 69, 70

1 John
3:1-14 — 58

Revelation
21 — 63